Where
Love
and
Imagination
Colour
the
Dark

WAKE
FOREST
UNIVERSITY
PRESS

Edited by Adrienne Leavy

Where Love and Imagination Colour the Dark

Essays on Thomas Kinsella

First edition

For permission, write to
Wake Forest University Press
Post Office Box 7333
Winston-Salem, NC 27109
wfupress.wfu.edu
ISBN 978-1-943667-10-9 (paperback)
LCCN 2024937317
Designed and typeset by Crisis
Cover photograph by John Minihan
Printed in Canada
Publication of this book was made possible
by generous support from the Boyle Family Fund

CONTENTS

Drifting on the quick void
Where love and imagination
Colour the dark
Which is the nearest we might get to Truth.

THOMAS KINSELLA,
"Christmas Eve 1950"

Dedicated to Eoin and Phil Leavy

ACKNOWLEDGMENTS

I would like to thank the following people for their advice, assistance, and support in the making of this book: First, I would like to thank the late Thomas Kinsella and the Estate of Thomas Kinsella for permission to quote from his work. More broadly, I would like to thank Tom and the entire Kinsella family for their assistance and encouragement throughout this project, and the late Eleanor Kinsella, who facilitated my first meeting with Tom back in 2010 when I was a doctoral student. Both Mary O'Malley and Gerard Smyth convinced me to push forward with this study, and their wise council is much appreciated. I would also like to thank my former dissertation adviser, Professor Gregory Castle of Arizona State University, who read a draft of the introductory chapter, and Professor Emeritus Jonathan Post of UCLA, who read a draft of chapter 12. John Minihan generously granted permission to use his photograph of Thomas Kinsella on the cover of this book. Thanks are also due to Wake Forest University Press for making this publication a reality, to Alex Muller and Jefferson Holdridge for their consistent support and enthusiasm, and to interns Madison Casey, Natalie Bradford, Holly Thompson, and Anna Gramling for their assistance in copy-editing drafts of this manuscript.

I gratefully acknowledge permission to reprint copyrighted material in this book as follows: the epigraph included is taken from "Christmas Eve 1950," published in *Last Poems* by Thomas Kinsella (2023). My thanks to Carcanet Press and the Estate of Thomas Kinsella for permission to reproduce these lines. All excerpts from *Thomas Kinsella: Collected Poems* (2006) have been made available through Wake Forest University Press. All excerpts from *Thomas Kinsella: Collected Poems* (2002) have been made available through Carcanet Press. A debt of gratitude is also owed to Michael Schmidt and John McAuliffe at Carcanet Press for permission to quote from *Late Poems* and *The Dual Tradition*, and to The O'Brien Press for permission to quote from the poetry and prose in *A Dublin Documentary*. A version of Thomas Dillon Redshaw's chapter, "Making the Great *Tain*, 1951–70: Thomas Kinsella, Louis le Brocquy, and Liam Miller," first appeared in *New Hibernia Review*. I am grateful to both Thomas Dillon Redshaw and David Gardiner at *New Hibernia Review* for permission to include his essay in this book.

The librarians at the Stuart A. Rose Manuscript, Archives, and Rare Book Library (MARL) in the Robert W. Woodruff Library at Emory University have been very generous with their time and support to both myself and other Kinsella scholars over the years, and I thank them for their professionalism and assistance, specifically Carrie Hintz, Gabrielle Dudley, and Rachel Detzler. Thank you to Megan Mulder and the Dolmen Archive in the Z. Smith Reynolds Library at Wake Forest University for help with additional archival images as we completed this manuscript. I would also like to thank the librarians in the UCD Special Collections Library, which holds "The Thomas Kinsella Collection, of his Published Works."

I am indebted to all of the contributors to this volume for the quality of their scholarly work and their commitment to this project despite the timing, which saw the bulk of the work in this book completed during the Covid-19 pandemic and thus under extremely trying circumstance for all of the writers involved. Their dedication to this book becoming a reality notwithstanding the restrictions they all faced, both professionally and personally, is evidence of the high regard in which Thomas Kinsella is held. Finally, I would like to thank my family, Bryan Murphy, Connor Murphy, and Niamh Yue, for their steadfast support.

With this collection of essays, we hope to introduce new readers to the unique voice that is Thomas Kinsella.

A NOTE ON ABBREVIATED CITATIONS

Many of the chapters in this book make use of the following abbreviated citations for certain works by Thomas Kinsella. These abbreviations appear either as parenthetical in-text citations or in the endnotes of each chapter, depending on the preference of the author for the ease of reading. A full list of works by Thomas Kinsella, in chronological order, is included in the Bibliography.

CP *Collected Poems 1956–2001* (Winston-Salem, NC: Wake Forest University Press, 2007; Manchester: Carcanet Press, 2002)

DD *Thomas Kinsella: A Dublin Documentary* (Dublin: O'Brien Press, 2006)

DT *The Dual Tradition. An Essay on Poetry and Politics in Ireland*, Peppercanister 18 (Manchester: Carcanet Press: 1995)

LP *Late Poems* (Manchester: Carcanet Press, 2013)

RP *Thomas Kinsella: Readings in Poetry*, Peppercanister 25 (Dublin: Dedalus Press, 2006; Manchester: Carcanet Press, 2006)

PO *Prose Occasions 1951–2006*, ed. Andrew Fitzsimons (Manchester: Carcanet Press, 2009)

T *The Tain* (Dublin: Dolmen Press, 1969; London: Oxford University Press, 1970)

Where Love and Imagination Colour the Dark

INTRODUCTION

I

This collection of essays on Thomas Kinsella aims to provide an accessible companion for readers of Kinsella which illuminates his remarkable poetic corpus and also highlights his critical writings and achievements as a translator, editor, and anthologizer of Gaelic literature. Writing about Kinsella in his essay "The Place of Writing," Seamus Heaney characterized his work thus: "Since the later sixties, this deeply responsible poet has been absorbed in a slowly purposeful, heroically undeflected work of personal and national inquisition."[1] The material in this volume affirms Heaney's observation, as poets and critics pay tribute to the importance and centrality of Kinsella both to the Irish poetic canon and to modern poetry in general.

Born into the working-class neighborhood of Inchicore, Dublin, in 1928, just six years after the founding of the Irish Free State, Kinsella was one of the most distinctive living Irish poets until his recent passing in December 2021, with a body of work unlike that of any other contemporary Irish writer. Kinsella, who came of age in the post-World War II era, began his long and distinguished career in the 1950s, and he continued to publish new work regularly in the early decades of this century, along with working on a series of poems that was published posthumously in 2023.[2] His early work, which includes *Another September* (1958) and *Downstream* (1962), was characterized by an elegant formalism and a lyrical style deeply influenced by W. H. Auden. Both collections garnered substantial critical praise in Ireland and England and were endorsed by the Poetry Book Society in Britain, and early awards included the Guinness Poetry Award and the Denis Devlin Memorial Award. In 1965 Kinsella resigned from a promising civil service career in the Department of Finance and moved to the United States, where he was writer-in-residence at Southern Illinois University, Carbondale, for three years.[3] He subsequently accepted an invitation from Temple University in Philadelphia to join the faculty as Professor of English and began his tenure at Temple in 1970. Embarking on a bifurcated academic career, he taught poetry for an academic semester in Philadelphia and brought American students to Dublin the following semester for instruction and immersion in Irish literature, culture, archaeology, and history, a practice that continued for twenty years until his retirement from Temple in 1990.

The intellectual force and historical range of Kinsella's poetry reflects his lifelong search for understanding and meaning amid the chaos of lived experience. His poems are characterized by a symbiotic relationship between autobiography and the aesthetic rendering of reality. In his view, "poetry is an accurate medium for the expression in permanent form of any kind of significant reality,"[4] and the poet's task as an artist is to find an adequate response to such significant experience which is then communicated to the reader. His work engages with profound questions central to the human condition: ideas of the self and its attempts to accommodate the contemporary world; the relationship between life and art and love and art; the inevitability of erosion, suffering, and decay with the ever-present recognition of individual mortality. These concerns are often mediated through the prism of Kinsella's familial history and the "*established personal places*" of his childhood.[5] His journey as a writer and the impulses that drive his work are themes that resurface time and again throughout his poetry. As he writes in "Worker in Mirror, at his Bench," "I am simply trying to understand something / – states of peace nursed out of wreckage."[6] This emphasis on a search for meaning has continued unabated, with the most recent articulation occurring in "Anatomy," from the 2011 sequence, *Love Joy Peace*, where the poet confesses that he "presumes from inadequate data / to understand the whole."[7]

Kinsella's work does not fit conveniently within the conventions of Irish lyric poetry. While acknowledging Yeats as "a great artist," the elder poet's work could not serve as a model since Kinsella viewed Yeats as isolated in the tradition of Irish literature, arguing in his critical work, *The Dual Tradition*, that although Yeats "values what he can in Gaelic literature, and uses it . . . his living tradition is solely in English." Thus for Kinsella, "Yeats stands for the Irish tradition as broken."[8] Notwithstanding this assessment, Kinsella absorbed Yeats and wrote at length on his poetry, most notably his close reading of "The Tower" in *Readings in Poetry*. More recently, Kinsella published close readings of two early Yeats poems from *The Rose*, "To the Rose Upon the Rood of Time" and "To Ireland in the Coming Times." Characterizing these poems as "poems of distinction," which absorbed "the colonial predicament into the subject of the career," Kinsella has argued that "these two poems at the beginning of his career established between them a statement of policy and an agenda that take account of the difficulties and opportunities of the colonial position."[9] Rejecting Yeatsian heroic ideals and received forms as his work matured, Kinsella turned instead to the modernism of James Joyce, William Carlos Williams, and Ezra Pound. Arguably, his poetry shares an affinity with the modernist aesthetic of the 1930s Irish poets, Thomas McGreevy, Brian Coffey, Denis Devlin, Samuel Beckett, and Louis MacNeice, rather than with the subsequent generation of Austin Clarke and Patrick Kavanagh, who in their own very different ways also sought to circumvent the all-encompassing shadow of Yeats. Clarke and Kavanagh's individual poetic struggles offered no consolation to the younger Kinsella, who dismissed their unique poetic strategies as they failed to offer a way forward for his own development as a poet. As Kinsella rather bleakly acknowledged, "the poetry of Clarke and Kavanagh in the 1930s is written in an enclosed Ireland, a religious and post-colonial dead end."[10]

Kinsella's abandonment of traditional forms of rhyme and meter coincided loosely with his move to the United States and the publication of *Nightwalker and Other Poems* by the Dolmen Press in 1967 (a slightly revised American edition was published by Alfred A. Knopf in 1968). In this key collection, Kinsella's poetry began to turn away from his early formalism toward a more open-ended, fluid aesthetic, which was simultaneously characterized by a more introspective focus. The long title poem "Nightwalker," set in the Lemass-era Irish Free State, features a nocturnal nightwalker through whom public and private experience crystallize in a Joycean stream of consciousness. A biting satire on the political and economic realities of Ireland in the early 1960s, the poem was a stark departure formally and thematically from Kinsella's previous work. Kinsella has spoken admiringly about the colloquial vigor of American modernism evident in the work of Williams, and he has credited the American poet for demonstrating "creative relaxation in the face of complex reality."[11] Similarly, his respect for Pound's "commitment to the craft of poetry, and his precision in language" is something on which he has frequently commented.[12] Certainly, the open-ended, meditative sequential poetics of Kinsella's mature work, with its frequent cross-referencing and allusions to earlier poems, bears structural comparison with Pound's *Cantos*, while the working-class Dublin syntax that is audible in his city-centered poetry is testament to the plain speaking diction favored by Williams in works such as *Paterson*. Eamon Grennan comments perceptively on this exposure to American poetry:

> I might even hazard that it is the American revolution in his own verse that enables Kinsella to get beyond the poetic influences of Yeats and Auden to the prose virtues of articulated consciousness that Joyce offers in *Ulysses*. If for Stephen Dedalus the shortest way to Tara is via Holyhead, the shortest way to a native Irish consciousness in modern poetry may be via Paterson, New Jersey, and Hailey, Idaho.[13]

Nightwalker was followed with an even more unconventional collection, *Notes from the Land of the Dead* (1972), published in *New Poems* in the US in 1973. Kinsella's evolving view of life as an ordeal surfaced clearly in this volume with poems that focus on personal and cultural history through psychological explorations of the self and the subconscious. In celebrated poems such as "Hen Woman," "A Hand of Solo," "Ancestor," and "Tear," Kinsella confronts the female anima and the Great Mother as well as the Irish *Cuilleach*. These deeply autobiographical poems drew their inspiration from the theories of the Swiss psychologist and psychiatrist Carl Gustave Jung (1875–1961), in particular Jung's theory of mythic archetypes and his concepts of "the collective unconscious" and "individuation," which are imaginatively interpreted by Kinsella in the form of a journey inward and a descent into personal and historical unconsciousness. Aside from Yeats's aesthetic interest in occultism and spiritualism, Kinsella's creative interest in dreams and psychoanalysis has no other counterpart in modern Irish poetry. Indeed, one would have to look to the American writer Charles Olson to find another example of a poet who has successfully absorbed Jungian psychology into their poetics.[14] In addition to *Notes from the Land of the Dead* and *New Poems*, sequences including *One* (1974), *Song of the Night and Other Poems* (1978), and *Songs of the Psyche* (1985) continue the poet's psychic explorations into his own past and that of his ancestors and further extend his shift in form, tone, and allegorical speculation. In these poems, numerous encounters with male and female ancestors along with archetypal figures enable the poet to recover childhood memories and attain a form of aesthetic self-awareness through confrontation with the ghosts from his past.

This inward direction in Kinsella's poetics was not confined to the poet's own ancestry, as he also began to draw on the quasi-mythical stories of the first peoples of Ireland contained in *Labor Gabála Érenn* (*The Book of Invasions*), to aesthetically explore the Irish past. As Dillon Johnston reminds us, in a Jungian context *Labor Gabála Érenn* "serves as a metaphor for the collective unconscious; specifically, it represents the Irish nation's collective memory of successive invasions and of the necessity for repossession as this memory manifests itself in dreamlike images within one individual's consciousness."[15] Kinsella drew upon this material to weave the myths of primal creation into the psychological repossession of his own personal origins. Poems such as "Touching the River," "Nuchal (a fragment)," and "Survivor" in *New Poems* recount stories of the first invasions and settlement of Ireland. Personal psychic excavations facilitated by mythological memories of pre-Christian Ireland continue in a subsequent volume, *One* (1974). For example, the narrator in "Finistère" is Amergin, the legendary first poet and Druid for the Milesians in the Irish Mythological Cycle. This poem recounts the original journey to the uninhabited land of Ireland, yet it is also a journey of self-discovery for the poet who confesses, in a parallel aside to this tale, that "A maggot of the possible / wriggled out of the spine / into the brain."[16]

With the establishment of the Peppercanister Press in 1972, Kinsella further distinguished himself from his peers in that he now had an unprecedented ability to control how he published his work. Peppercanister was conceived as a form of draft pamphlet publication, which allowed the poet considerable freedom to revise and edit his work before issuing it in trade publications. The first publication from Peppercanister was *Butcher's Dozen: A Lesson from the Octave of Widgery*, an impassioned response to the findings of the Widgery Tribunal Report on the killing of thirteen civil rights demonstrators in Derry on Bloody Sunday.[17] Commenting on the seriousness of the poetic project commenced in *Notes from the Land of the Dead*, Heaney noted "the fact that the first poem to appear from the press was his fierce, head-on assault on the British cover-up of what actually happened on Bloody Sunday only underlined the independence and resolution of what he had undertaken."[18] The poem, which is unique in Kinsella's oeuvre and was described by the poet as "an immediate doggerel, in a borrowed Irish form,"[19] was written and published within a week of the release of the Widgery Report. Undeniably, this publication had damaging consequences for Kinsella's reputation in Britain, and arguably also in Ireland and the US, as the poet's aesthetic response to this blatant injustice was often simplistically conflated with a hard-line nationalistic stance which he never espoused.

The decline in Kinsella's audience was compounded by the fact that the Peppercanister method of publication removed his work from mainstream publication channels. The Peppercanister pamphlets were usually published in limited editions and were later collected and released in book form in groups of four or five. *Butcher's Dozen* was quickly followed by two elegiac sequences for his friend, the composer Sean Ó Riada (1943–71), and a sequence to commemorate the tenth anniversary of the assassination of President John F. Kennedy. Together, these four Peppercanisters were subsequently released under the title *Fifteen Dead* (1978). In general, Peppercanister Press continued to first publish all of Kinsella's subsequent work, most recently *Fat Master* (2011) and *Love Joy Peace* (2011).[20] It was not until

Carcanet Press published *Thomas Kinsella: Collected Poems* (2001) in England and Ireland, and Wake Forest University Press published *Thomas Kinsella: Collected Poems* (2006) in the US, that the full range and scope of Kinsella's work was readily accessible.[21] Compounding the poet's low visibility is the fact that Kinsella was a very private person, and he rarely engaged in public readings. Moreover, the interviews he granted over the years were typically published in academic journals and therefore not readily accessible to the general reader.

Criticism of Kinsella's poetry often described his work in generalities as being difficult or obscure. The question of difficulty has a bearing on Kinsella's critical reception, for as David Lynch points out, "he is a writer regarded as central and at the same time marginal, his poetry both canonical and existing on the fringe."[22] The poet's refusal to conform to conservative expectations of the well-made lyric, his rejection of rhetoric and stylistic excess, coupled with his practice of textually cross-referencing earlier work and significant experiences, have arguably alienated some readers; however, for the committed reader, attuned to the themes and concerns of his work, Kinsella's technical experimentation and unique aesthetic vision offer a rich and exciting interaction with poetry. In the poet's own estimation, he was an artist who was always striving to communicate "with the reader who is ready to meet a poem's necessary demands," thus completing "the act of communication."[23] Commenting on the poems in *Wormwood* (1966) and *Nightwalker and Other Poems* (1968), Seamus Deane observed that "no image in these poems leads a casual life,"[24] and his assessment is equally applicable to all of the poet's subsequent collections, as Kinsella's precision and exacting way with language is crucial to his aesthetic and foundational to much of his work. This aesthetic rigor is justly perceived as a strength by Johnston who points out that, "[A]lthough Kinsella has written as lyrically as any Irish poet in poems such as 'The Shoals Returning,' he can relinquish graceful phrasing to manifest the truth of the turbulent world and its shadow psyche."[25]

II

Notwithstanding that Kinsella is generally recognized as one of Ireland's foremost poets, his mature work has not received the sustained critical attention it deserves in book-length form. However, there have been several valuable studies undertaken which have productively considered different aspects of the poet's career. Maurice Harmon's 1974 volume, *The Poetry of Thomas Kinsella*, was the first book-length study of Kinsella's poetry. Harmon provides a thorough critical introduction to Kinsella's early work until 1973. Thereafter, with the exception of a number of scholarly essays, the critical attention paid to Kinsella was negligible until the early 1990s.[26] Thomas Jackson's study, *The Whole Matter: The Poetic Evolution of Thomas Kinsella* (1995), was the first comprehensive study on Kinsella's poetry to be published in North America. Jackson concentrates on the influence of Jung, Joyce, and the Anglo-American Modernism of Pound and Williams on Kinsella's work up through the publication of *Open Court* in 1991. Donatella Abbate Badin's *Thomas Kinsella* (1996), offers a critical introduction to Kinsella's life and work which emphasizes the continuity in Kinsella's early and later poetry, focusing on the interdependence of his works. Badin, who has translated most of Kinsella's work into Italian, argues that when Kinsella's themes and images are explored carefully they constitute an organic whole. Divided into three periods, her study looks first at Kinsella's early work up through *Nightwalker and Other Poems*, focusing next on the Jungian-inspired poetry of the 1970s and early 80s, and ending with the Peppercanister volumes collected in *Blood and Family* in 1988 and *From Centre City* in 1994. Badin's book also includes an early interview with the poet and a detailed chronology of his life and work. Also appearing in 1996, Brian John's monograph, *Reading the Ground: The Poetry of Thomas Kinsella*, provides another account of Kinsella's Jungian-influenced poetry and the importance of early Irish literature and mythology for his work. John pays particular attention to *Notes from the Land of the Dead* and Kinsella's use of material drawn from *The Book of Invasions* to support the psychological quest detailed in poems such as "Finistère," "Nuchal," "Survivor," and "The Oldest Place." As with Badin's book, his study traces the poet's development up to the publication of *From Centre City*.

Derval Tubridy's study, *Thomas Kinsella: The Peppercanister Poems* (2001), takes as its starting point the view that "[P]eppercanister is not simply a press: it is a series of distinctive and interconnected poetic sequences that build together to form a loosely structured whole."[27] Divided into five chapters, Tubridy's discussion starts with the initial Peppercanister, *Butcher's Dozen*, and concludes with Peppercanister 19, *The Pen Shop* (1997). Throughout the book, key images of the cover art and illustrations are reproduced in order to show their visual importance to the text of each Peppercanister sequence. In *The Sea of Disappointment: Thomas Kinsella's Pursuit of the Real* (2008), another perceptive Kinsella critic, Andrew Fitzsimons, provides a chronological journey through the structural and thematic development of Kinsella's writing, analyzing the underlying impulses "behind Kinsella's re-evaluation of poetic procedure." By examining Kinsella's early work, particularly the unpublished work, Fitzsimons locates the reasons for Kinsella's aesthetic realignment as one orientated on ideas of disappointment and dissolution, arguing that even at an "early stage of his writing, disappointment motivates desire for aesthetic development."[28]

Maurice Harmon revisited his work on Kinsella with a comprehensive study published in 2008 to coincide with Kinsella's 80th birthday. Harmon charts Kinsella's progress from lyric poems and meditations about fragility and impermanence to complex modernist assessments of individual isolation and helplessness in the modern world. Harmon, who has the benefit of being fluent in Gaelic, brings depth to his analysis of Kinsella's translations from Gaelic literature. More recently, in *Confronting Shadows: An Introduction to the Poetry of Thomas Kinsella* (2015), David Lynch provides an accessible introduction to Kinsella's poetry from different eras of his career, revealing the ways in which his work is a response to the ordeal of modern life.

For the present volume, I have intentionally invited contributions from a variety of perspectives in order to present an interdisciplinary and comprehensive range of responses to Kinsella's lengthy career. Many of the contributors are poets themselves; some have written monographs or edited collections of essays on Kinsella and other Irish poets. Not every individual collection is treated in detail, as this would have necessitated a two- or three-volume edition. However, all of the significant developments of Kinsella's career are discussed in the chapters that follow, and I am confident that, collectively, they present a thorough analysis of his entire poetic arc and reinforce the fundamental importance of Kinsella's extensive translations from Gaelic literature.

III

James McCabe has argued that "Kinsella may be said to represent the last in the Big Four authors from Dublin, following Yeats, Joyce, and Beckett," and this study begins with several chapters devoted to assessing the aesthetic importance of the city for Kinsella, both as a site of intimate, personal memories and as a site of his own development and maturity as a poet.[29] In the opening chapter, Gerald Dawe contextualizes the period when Kinsella came to intellectual maturity in the 1950s and 60s. With good reason Kinsella has been called "the pre-eminent poet of modern Dublin,"[30] and Dawe argues that Kinsella is also the pre-eminent poet of colonial, pre-independence Dublin because much of his poetry deals with or alludes to the urban villages which sprang up around Dublin's inner city during the nineteenth and early twentieth centuries. In addition to outlining the particular social and cultural environment which shaped Kinsella's development, Dawe draws attention to what he perceives as an under-examined aspect of Kinsella's poetry, namely, the poet's "shifting fascination over many decades" with the mystical, magical past, and his discussion of the often ignored Peppercanister volume *Littlebody* (2000) illustrates this point. In a telling comparison that calls out for further study, the final section of Dawe's chapter looks at the radically different critical reception afforded to Kinsella's work and that of his Belfast-born contemporary Padraic Fiacc (1924–2019).[31]

In Chapter Two, Hugh Haughton focuses on *A Dublin Documentary* (2006), which gathers together Dublin memories of Kinsella's childhood composed across his career, and intersperses them with autobiographical commentary, photographs, and reproductions of family manuscripts. In this work, which confirms the city's importance to the poet's development, Kinsella carefully rearranged a number of important autobiographical poems from how they appear in the individual Peppercanisters and in his *Collected Poems*. Through a detailed consideration of the verbal commentary and visual context in which each poem is placed, Haughton reads *A Dublin Documentary* as "an elaborately created work in its own right, offering a radical reconstruction of the dispersed poems of childhood scattered in other collections, embodying his chronic quest for origins and destinations in a topology of its own." Haughton's chapter demonstrates how Kinsella re-reads and re-treads the ground in Dublin, and also the ground of his identity, "as the poet reconstructs his doctored recollections of places, and anchors his ambitious over-arching poetic project in this geographically objective but also fiercely subjective Dublin."

Kinsella has written of his admiration for Joyce on several occasions, praising him as "the first major Irish voice to speak for Irish reality since the death-blow to the Irish language."[32] Indeed, the shadow of Joyce looms large over Kinsella's work, and as Gerard Smyth argues in Chapter Three, "the poet's urban imagination matches and mirrors Joyce's in many ways, and for both writers, it was the city that sparked their artistic consciousness." Moreover, the "gravelly but sonorous" poetic voice in poems such as "Dick King" is one that Smyth says was instantly recognizable to him as the "natural register of the Dublin dialect," and the remembered childhood voices he "heard on the street corners of my own Dublin in the 1950s and 60s." In a wide-ranging discussion of Kinsella's major Dublin poems and sequences, Smyth maps the inner-city topography that entered the particulars of these poems—Inchicore, Kilmainham, Bow Lane, Phoenix Street, James's Street, and the nearby River Liffey. Smyth writes that it was in these streets and urban villages that Kinsella found his first bearings, remembering "many things of importance happening to me for the first time." In recording so much of the Dublin life of his family, "as well as recognizing his roots and the laboring classes of his old neighborhood," Smyth reads Kinsella as the natural inheritor of the Joycean mantle in Irish poetry.

Mary O'Malley shifts the focus away from Dublin in the first part of Chapter Four, discussing several other key Kinsella poems of place, specifically his poems of landscape and the western seaboard. Reading "The Shoals Returning," a poem in memory of the Sean-nós singer Gerry Flaherty, and "The Poet Egan O' Rahilly, Homesick in Old Age," O'Malley observes that "Kinsella leaves nature and landscape alone. He lets it speak for itself." Comparing the Connemara-based "Carraroe" with Richard Murphy's "The Cleggan Disaster," O'Malley identifies a poetic authority in Kinsella's treatment of the West of Ireland, noting that "Carraroe was placed up against Philadelphia, logically and without strain." Commenting on Kinsella's bilocation between Philadelphia and Ireland for much of his writing life, O'Malley sums up this influence on Kinsella's poetry: "Always a foot here, and one there, as the best place poets have, the eye clarified and refined by the view from the far shore." Returning to Kinsella's Dublin poems, O'Malley argues that from her vantage point in the West of Ireland, these poems allowed her to see the capital city as "a real place, inhabited by people and creatures I could believe in." O'Malley also discusses the importance of *An Duanaire 1600–1900: Poems of the Dispossessed* (1981) to her own development as a poet and argues that Kinsella and Ó Tuama's anthology "is one of the essential books for any Irish poet with an eye to the origins and trajectory of our poetic heritage." She closes her discussion with commentary on one of the few poems Kinsella has written about America, "Wyncote, Pennsylvania: a gloss." As Wyncote was the birthplace of Pound, it is telling that Kinsella chose to set his American place poem in this locale, and O'Malley reads a subtle reference to "Pound's insistence on the need for a rigorous aesthetic," an aesthetic which Kinsella emulates throughout his body of work.

In Chapter Five, Andrew Fitzsimons takes as his starting point Kinsella's *ars poetica* from the 1950s, the early artistic manifesto, "Baggot Street Deserta." A poem which anticipates Kinsella's later work, it is also as Fitzsimons argues, "a poem that in its own moment is concerned with looking back, with the past a living pressure, with 'Unfinished Business' (the original title of the poem), poetic, personal and political." Fitzsimons examines the "moment" of "Baggot Street Deserta," meaning the poem's relationship with its historical moment, the mid-to-late-1950s; its literary moment, in Ireland and internationally; and its moment within Kinsella's work in the light of his subsequent achievements. Crucially, Fitzsimons situates Kinsella's work in a broader international context by taking a comparative approach, with discussion of how Kinsella's work parallels and contrasts with his contemporaries in the English language. Fitzsimons also draws instructive aesthetic parallels with poets of the period writing in languages other than English.

Kinsella has devoted a considerable portion of his career to translating Gaelic literature, with the most celebrated endeavor being his influential 1969 translation of the ancient Irish epic, *Táin Bó Cúailnge*, which he worked on over a period of fifteen years. Thomas Dillon Redshaw argues in Chapter Six that had *The Tain* not been published at that precise historical moment, and not by Liam Miller's Dolmen Press, and not with Louis le Brocquy's illustrations, "the epic's status may well have remained entirely a local, narrowly Irish matter." With the establishment of Miller's Dolmen Press in 1951, emerging poets such as Kinsella, John Montague, and Richard Murphy had an Irish publisher who could support their work. Dolmen Press was the first poetry press in Ireland since the Yeats sisters' Cuala Press, and Miller's involvement was of critical importance to Kinsella's early career. Drawing extensively on the archival material in the Dolmen Press's Special Collections at Wake Forest University, and the Kinsella Papers in Emory University, Redshaw's chapter details the background and publishing history of Kinsella's monumental translation, and the crucial role that both Miller's design and le Brocquy's striking black and white brush drawings contributed to the success of this canonical work. Situating the importance of this work historically, Redshaw further demonstrates that as a result of their unique artistic collaboration, "the book went immediately to the very center of Irish literary, artistic, and cultural life in the early 1970s."

In his discussion of Kinsella's *Tain* Redshaw notes "the role that translating the *Táin Bó Cúailnge* played in the evolution of Kinsella's poetry has yet to receive sufficient commentary," and one hopes that the present volume will encourage further study in this area. However, one obvious example of such influence is found in Kinsella's poem, "The Route of *The Táin*," from *New Poems*. The poem describes a walk that Kinsella undertook with his wife, along with Miller, le Brocquy, and Harvard scholar Gene Haley (who assisted with the place names of the *Táin*), in the County Louth area where Queen Medb's army marched on the Cattle Raid of Cooley. In Chapter Seven, archaeologist Paul Gosling, who has written extensively on the route of the *Táin*, subjects the poem to a close reading. Gosling analyzes the circumstances which prompted Kinsella to write the poem and the rich topographical content underpinning the work. As in other Kinsella journey poems, the journey always involves an inner, psychological journey as well as a physical one, and Gosling argues that "The Route of *The Táin*" is best understood as a meditation on the project to translate and publish the stories in *Táin Bó Cúailnge*.

The erosion of the Irish language in the eighteenth century resulted in a profound cultural transformation and disinheritance in Ireland, which Kinsella characterized as a "calamity."[33] In his influential talk on "The Irish Writer" at the 1966 MLA Conference in New York, Kinsella powerfully articulated the dual tradition of Irish poetry as one marked by division and loss. Recognizing that the line of descent from Irish language poetry for the modern writer is mutilated, Brian Caraher discusses in Chapter Eight how Kinsella compensated for this void by devoting a considerable part of his career to recovering, documenting, and rendering accessible the dual tradition of Irish writing—Gaelic and Anglophile. Caraher argues that Kinsella's long-standing and heroically sustained work as an anthologist, conservator of other poets' work, editor of neglected poetry, and translator and renewer of distinctly Irish poetic traditions is announced in Kinsella's signature critical work, *The Dual Tradition: An Essay on Poetry and Politics in Ireland* (1995). Subjecting this essay to a close reading, Caraher argues that the text underscores the editorial rationale and cultural mission of Ó Tuama and Kinsella's 1981 anthology of neglected Irish poetry, *An Duanaire*, and the strategies he followed when documenting the dual tradition in his landmark edition of *The New Oxford Book of Irish Verse* (1986).

In Chapter Nine, Lucy Collins focuses on *A Technical Supplement* (Peppercanister 6, 1976), a sequence comprised of 24 poems with illustrations taken from Diderot's *Encyclopédie*, which she argues, "exemplifies Kinsella's use of the physical self to interrogate the act of writing itself, and one that displays the complexity of his approach to the subject position in his poetry." Drawing on manuscripts and draft materials at Emory University, Collins illustrates the poet's elaborate process of writing, revising, and publication, which demonstrates "the long reach of Kinsella's creative process." Her analysis of the theme of violence in this work confirms Deane's assertion that "Kinsella has absorbed the shock of mass atrocity into his poetry so deeply that the issues he raises have very little of the local or peripheral about them."[34] Several of the poems in this sequence focus on the slaughter of animals in an abattoir, while in other poems of self-investigation images of violence also predominate. Commenting on the search for self-knowledge in *A Technical Supplement*, Collins concludes, "the recreation of the visceral is embedded so deeply in this philosophical process that it becomes inseparable from inquiries made about and through language."

In Chapter Ten, Alex Davis focuses on the five most recent Peppercanister sequences collected in *Late Poems: Marginal Economy* (2006), *Man of War* (2007), *Belief and Unbelief* (2007), *Fat Master* (2011), and *Love Joy Peace* (2011). Davis also analyzes Peppercanister 25, *Readings in Poetry* (2006), in which Kinsella offers critical readings of Shakespeare's Sonnets 29 and 30, along with Yeats's "The Tower" and T. S. Eliot's "The Love Song of J. Alfred Prufrock." Kinsella's *Late Poems*, this chapter claims, follows Yeats's example, as articulated in *Readings in Poetry*, in its risks and extremity. Davis argues that stylistically these later poems are "very much part of the evolution of Kinsella's work since the late 1960s," and that collectively, the volume "represents continuation and self-reflection upon earlier preoccupations." The Shakespearean sonnets examined in *Readings in Poetry* serve as touchstones for commentary on Kinsella's own solitary writing, while in *Man of War*, mankind's capacity for self-destruction is explored through the diaries of the Roman Emperor Marcus Aurelius. In *Fat Master* and *Love Joy Peace*, Kinsella celebrates the beauty and grace of art, epitomized by artists such as Bach and Michelangelo. In a close reading of this important collection, Davis expands upon Harry Clifton's review of *Late Poems* which characterized Kinsella's poetry as "stripped to its essence."[35]

This volume also foregrounds the importance of visual art in Kinsella's work, which was evident from the inception of his career with early works such as the 1954 translation *The Sons of Usneach* (published in two editions, one with Celtic illustrations by Mia Cranwell, the other with line drawings by Bridget Swinton) and Kinsella's first collection, *Poems* (1956), with illustrations by Elizabeth Rivers. In Chapter Eleven, Derval Tubridy looks at the significance of art for the development of Kinsella's poetic career and argues that Kinsella's relationship with art is fundamental to his aim of "eliciting order from significant experience." Building on her earlier monograph, this chapter also examines the source and aesthetic relevance of the diverse range of imagery used in the books published by the Peppercanister Press, arguing that these images are integral and necessary for a full reading of Kinsella's mature work.[36] She concludes her chapter by arguing that it is only with a deeper understanding of the ways in which Kinsella has deployed art in his poetry we can complete the "dynamic" act of reading about which Kinsella has spoken, and fully understand his response to the "significant experience" of Modern Ireland.

Throughout Kinsella's career, the female figure, whether real, archetypal, or aesthetic, has been evoked as central to the poet's process of understanding the ordeal of existence and his continuing aesthetic project of self-interrogation. Although Kinsella's critics have long recognized the poet's tendency to problematize the tensions between the demands of romantic love and art, there has to date been minimal detailed commentary on the aesthetic importance of Kinsella's wife, Eleanor Kinsella (often referred to as "the Beloved"), to his body of work. In Chapter Twelve, I seek to redress this omission by tracing how Eleanor's presence in Kinsella's poetry as lover, wife, companion, and Muse has developed from his first lyric love poems to the creatively important long meditative poem "Phoenix Park," which was followed by the dissonant marriage sequence *Wormwood* (1966) and by the Peppercanister sequences *Out of Ireland* (1987), *Madonna and Other Poems* (1991), *The Familiar* (1999), and *Love Joy Peace* (2011). I argue that, collectively, these poems and sequences "affirm Eleanor as a dynamic enabling force whose presence is central to Kinsella's poetic project of personal understanding."

IV

Commenting again on Kinsella, Heaney astutely observed, "From his early, formal and syntactically compact poems of the 1950s, when he defined his purpose as the quest for honesty in love and art, to his more recent, open-weave, semi-expressionist explorations of the roots of consciousness, the muscle tone of Kinsella's poetry has always been in perfect order."[37] Echoing Heaney's praise on the occasion of Kinsella receiving the Freedom of the City of Dublin in 2007, in recognition of his "enormous contribution to the city, in art and literature," Gerard Smyth expressed the hope that the honor would bring attention to "a body of work that is among the most outstanding in contemporary Irish and international poetry."[38] While most commentators and readers familiar with Kinsella would share Smyth's desire and also agree with Fitzsimons's assessment that "the range and reach of Kinsella's work is among the most extraordinary in contemporary poetry,"[39] widespread recognition of his achievements still lags behind such critical consensus. Given the enormity of Kinsella's contribution to the retrieval and preservation of our native Irish culture, and the extent of his incorporation of Irish mythology and the early bardic poets into his own poetry, it is perhaps not fanciful to read Kinsella as a contemporary Bard on the aesthetic periphery, situated in the continuing poetic pantheon of Gaelic Ireland with fellow poets Amergin, the mythical first poet of Ireland, and Aogán Ó Rathaille, the last great poet of early eighteenth-century Ireland, who chronicled the demise of the old Bardic order and the death of the Gaelic language.

It is our hope that this volume will stimulate further critical conversations on Kinsella's extraordinary literary achievements and demonstrate to a wider audience the enduring artistic, cultural, and historical value of his works.

Notes

[1] Seamus Heaney, *Finders Keepers: Selected Prose 1971–2001* (London: Faber and Faber, 2002), 240.

[2] See for example, *Fat Master* Peppercanister 28 (Manchester: Carcanet Press, 2011) and *Love Joy Peace* Peppercanister 29 (Manchester: Carcanet Press, 2011). In 2023 Carcanet released Kinsella's 2013 collection, *Late Poems*, which includes the five Peppercanisters not included in the UK or US version of his *Collected Poems*. This collection is retitled *Last Poems* to account for new material that the poet was working on in the years preceding his death on December 22, 2021.

[3] Kinsella resettled in Dublin during the period of 1968–69 as a result of obtaining a Guggenheim Grant to complete his translation of the *Táin Bó Cúailnge*.

[4] Adrienne Leavy, "'The Continuity of the Tradition': An Interview with Thomas Kinsella," *New Hibernia Review* 25, no. 1 (Spring 2021), 59. This article originally appeared in *New Hibernia Review* 15, no. 2 (Summer 2011).

[5] Thomas Kinsella, CP, 283. Unless otherwise stated in this essay and subsequent chapters, all poetry quotations are from Thomas Kinsella, *Collected Poems* (Winston-Salem, NC: Wake Forest UP, 2006).

[6] CP, 124.

[7] *Love Joy Peace*, 8; *Late Poems*, 82.

[8] Thomas Kinsella, *The Dual Tradition: An Essay on Poetry and Politics in Ireland* [Peppercannister 18] (Manchester: Carcanet Press, 1995), 91.

[9] Kinsella, *The Dual Tradition*, 63. Kinsella's close readings of these poems were published in *Poetry Ireland Review: A WB Yeats Special Issue*, ed. Vona Groarke, no. 116, 2015.

[10] Thomas Kinsella, "The Nineteen Thirties (1930–1939)," in *Flowing Still: Irish Poets on Irish Poetry* (Dublin: Dedalus Press, 2009), 34. This assessment did not blind Kinsella to the merits of Clarke or Kavanagh's poetry, notwithstanding the unevenness of their work. For example, Kinsella edited Clarke's *Selected Poems* after the elder poet's death in 1974, and as Maurice Harmon points out, Kinsella stated in his Introduction that Clarke's work "constitutes one of the most notable modern careers." Harmon, *Thomas Kinsella: Designing for the Exact Needs* (Dublin: Irish Academic Press, 2008), xvii.

[11] John Haffenden, *Viewpoints: Poets in Conversation* (London: Faber and Faber, 1981), 106.

[12] Leavy, "'The Continuity of the Tradition,'" 57. Responding to a question about his decision to abandon conventional poetic forms, Kinsella stated: "It's important not to impose form; let the content dictate the form and the form will emerge organically from the material. That is where Pound was a real example." 56.

[13] Eamon Grennan, "The American Connection: An Influence on Modern and Contemporary Irish Poetry," in *Flowing Still*, 112, 113.

[14] See Anthony Mellors, "Maximal extent: Charles Olson and C. G. Jung," *Late Modernist Poetics from Pound to Prynne* (Manchester: Manchester UP, 2005).

[15] Dillon Johnston, *Irish Poetry after Joyce*, 2nd ed. (Syracuse, NY: Syracuse UP, 1997), 99.

[16] CP, 162.

[17] In 2010 the British Government released the Saville Report, a 5,000-page document that took twelve years to compile, which dismissed the hastily written Widgery Report as a whitewash. After the Saville Report was published, Prime Minister David Cameron offered a formal apology to the Bloody Sunday victims and their families. In 2022 Carcanet published a Bloody Sunday 50th Anniversary Edition of *Butcher's Dozen* as Peppercanister 30, with a note on the poem by Thomas Kinsella.

[18] Seamus Heaney, "Meaning Business (1970–1979)," in *Flowing Still*, 59.

[19] Leavy, "The Continuity of the Tradition."

[20] As mentioned in note 2 and 17, Carcanet Press re-released *Butcher's Dozen* as Peppercanister 30 in 2022, and an expanded version of *Late Poems* was published by Carcanet in 2023 as *Last Poems*. This collection includes previously unpublished work.

[21] In 1996 Oxford UP published *Thomas Kinsella: Collected Poems 1956–1994*, which included Kinsella's work up through the publication of Peppercanister 17, *Open Court* (1991). The subsequent Carcanet and WFUP editions of the *Collected Poems* include five more Peppercanister sequences, nos. 19–23. Kinsella's two critical prose works, Peppercanister 18, *The Dual Tradition* (1995), and Peppercanister 25, *Readings in Poetry* (2006), were published separately. In 2013 Carcanet Press published *Late Poems*, which collects together the five most recent Peppercanister publications identified in the body of this introduction.

[22] David Lynch, *Confronting Shadows: An Introduction to the Poetry of Thomas Kinsella* (Dublin: New Island Books, 2015), 1. Other critics have also highlighted the paradox of Kinsella's critical reception. See for example, David Wheatley's review of Kinsella's

Selected Poems (Carcanet Press, 2007), in which Wheatley offered the following assessment: "For almost four decades, Kinsella has occupied an ambivalent position in the Irish canon: central but somehow marginalized, honored but insecure, like a dethroned god." Wheatley, "The dethroned god," *The Guardian*, July 7, 2007.

[23] Adrienne Leavy, "'As Clear as It Needs to Be': A conversation with Thomas Kinsella," *New Hibernia Review* 25, no. 1 (Spring 2021), 76.

[24] Seamus Deane, "Thomas Kinsella: 'Nursed Out of Wreckage,'" in *Celtic Revivals: Essays in Modern Irish Literature* (Winston-Salem, NC: Wake Forest UP, 1985), 140.

[25] Johnston, *Irish Poetry after Joyce*, 119, 120.

[26] See for example, Robert F. Garratt, "Poetry at Mid-Century 1: Thomas Kinsella," in *Modern Irish Poetry: Tradition and Continuity from Yeats to Heaney* (Berkeley: University of California Press, 1989); Dillon Johnston, "Clarke & Kinsella," in *Irish Poetry after Joyce*; Seamus Deane, *Celtic Revivals*; and Gerald Dawe, "Poetry as Example: Kinsella's Peppercanister Poems," in *Poetry in Contemporary Irish Literature* ed. Michael Kenneally (Dublin: Colin Smythe, 1995). See also, Thomas Kinsella Special Issue, *Tracks* 7 (1987), Special Issue: Thomas Kinsella, *Irish University Review* 31, no. 1 (Spring/Summer 2001) and *Irish Studies Review: Kinsella at Eighty* 16, no. 3 (2008).

[27] Derval Tubridy, *Thomas Kinsella: The Peppercanister Poems* (Dublin: University College Dublin Press, 2001), 1.

[28] Andrew Fitzsimons, *The Sea of Disappointment: Thomas Kinsella's Pursuit of the Real* (Dublin: University College Dublin Press, 2008), 10.

[29] James McCabe, "Thomas Kinsella: 'the most notable career performance since William Butler Yeats,'" *Irish Times*, May 17, 2016.

[30] Maria Johnston, "Walking Dublin: Contemporary Irish Poets in the City," in *The Oxford Handbook of Modern Irish Poetry*, eds. Fran Brearton and Alan Gillis. (Oxford: Oxford UP, 2012), 498.

[31] The modernist sensibility in Fiacc's works shares an affinity with Kinsella's poetry, as does the intensity of their profound disquiet in the face of violence: Kinsella's more general disillusionment with mankind; Fiacc in his reaction to the explosion of violence in Northern Ireland in the late 1960s. Another area of fruitful comparison would be a consideration of the unique manner in which each poet aesthetically remembers their father.

[32] Kinsella, *The Dual Tradition*, 90.

[33] Thomas Kinsella, "The Irish Writer," in *Davis, Mangan, Ferguson?: Tradition and the Irish Writer* (Chester Springs, PA: Dufour Editions, 1970), 60. In a recent interview Kinsella elaborated on this view, stating, "[the] change from Irish to English was brutal. It left a people separated from their own past." Adrienne Leavy, "As Clear as it Needs to Be," 71.

[34] Deane, *Celtic Revivals*, 137.

[35] Harry Clifton, "A true note on a dead slack string," *Irish Times*, Feb. 18, 2012.

[36] As Thomas Dillon Redshaw treats in detail the artistic partnership between Kinsella, Liam Miller, and Louis le Brocquy in Chapter 5, the visual, artistic, and aesthetic implications of Kinsella's *Tain* are not part of Tubridy's reading.

[37] Heaney, "The Place of Writing," 240.

[38] Gerard Smyth, "Thomas Kinsella," *Irish Times*, Feb. 6, 2007.

[39] Andrew Fitzsimons, "Thomas Kinsella," in *The Cambridge Companion to Irish Poets*, ed. Gerald Dawe (Cambridge: Cambridge UP, 2018), 227.

CHAPTER ONE

Thomas Kinsella

A TALE OF TWO CITIES

GERALD DAWE

I

This reading of Thomas Kinsella's poetry focuses upon a central thesis which is fairly straightforward and, in many ways, quite obvious to anyone with even the slightest familiarity with his writing. But like many "obvious" things it can be unfairly neglected. The point is that Kinsella is, to use the words of critic Maria Johnston, "unquestionably the pre-eminent poet of modern Dublin."[1] By extension, in my mind, he is also the pre-eminent poet of colonial Dublin (i.e., pre-Independence Dublin) because much of his poetry deals with or alludes to the urban villages that sprang up around inner-city Dublin during the nineteenth and early twentieth centuries, many of which can trace their own intensely "local" histories back to the earliest settlements along the Liffey and other rivers of what became Dublin as we know it today.

Kinsella, who was born in 1928 and grew up in one such village—Inchicore—has investigated its roots in terms of his own family history as migrants from Wicklow and Westmeath. This is how he describes his background in the wonderful series of poems, photographs, and prose collected in *A Dublin Documentary*:

> I am not, technically, a Dubliner, despite being born and reared in Inchicore. I am told that for the full qualification three generations born in the city are needed. My children would qualify, if they wished; my parents were born in Dublin. Their own parents were all born in the country.[2]

He also describes in his poetry the customs, lifestyles, and conditions of a hard-pressed working-class life based around the rail works, river, and allied industries of what had been a predominantly administrative port and capital city, the hub of political and cultural movements in the country going back to the eighteenth century. Kinsella's poetry sits, so to speak, on the threshold between several of these divergent points of reference: city life/the countryside, the national past/the unconnected present, the private self/the public arena. He registers these often through reproducing childhood memories as well as depicting the historical and natural landscapes of his home and upbringing.

Like Patrick Kavanagh's rural Inniskeen and the urban village which he subsequently found for himself around Baggott Street and the Grand Canal, Kinsella's village of family, friends, and social background is sourced roughly in the 1930s to the late 1960s, at which point Kinsella began his bi-located life, spending half of each year in the States as an academic and writer-in-residence. Except for a period of time living in Wicklow, he continued to live this bi-located life between Dublin and Philadelphia in retirement until the death of his wife Eleanor in 2017. Subsequently, he moved back to Dublin, living in the city until his death in December 2021. For many Irish writers of his generation, an aesthetic attachment to a specific geographic location was central to their writing. One can see this creative identification with place in writers such as Kavanagh (Iniskeen and later the Grand Canal area of Dublin), John McGahern (Cootehall), Jennifer Johnston (south county Dublin), John Montague (Garvaghey), Eilís Dillon (Galway), Brian Friel (the fictional village of Ballybeg), Edna O'Brien (Clare), Richard Murphy (Inisboffin), Eavan Boland (the Dublin suburb of Dundrum), and Padraic Fiacc (the inner-city Belfast of the Markets and Lower Falls). Kinsella's Inchicore—of Bow Lane, Phoenix, and Irwin Streets, the territory around Swift's hospital—forms a critical imaginative core to his writing life from which so much else of his writing radiates.

In what follows, I am going to unpick this core and point to a handful of poems which illustrate this point as directly as possible. But first, we need to understand Kinsella not only in the context of his place—the where of his life and his poems—but also, critically, in terms of his time. Because to adequately understand Kinsella we need to have some understanding of when he came to intellectual maturity (in the 1950s and 1960s) and to identify how he himself viewed the world then and the place of the poet within it. Terence Brown describes the environment of late 1940s and early 1950s Dublin, when Kinsella was in his late twenties and early thirties:

> By the 1950s, despite the slow rate of economic growth in the country as a whole, Dublin had been transformed from the elegant, colourful, and decaying colonial centre of English rule in Ireland into a modern if rather dull administrative and commercial capital. Where pre-Treaty Dublin, the Dublin of Joyce in *Dubliners* and *Ulysses*, was severely inhibited by a stultifying lack of economic and social opportunity for most of its citizens, the new Dublin, while scarcely the scene of major redevelopment or an economic boom, had become socially and economically more complex, less

> marked by its earlier preponderance of the laboring poor. . . . The Irish immigrants from the countryside or small town, with their firmly established distinctive mode of family life and social organization, encountered in Dublin precisely the same pressures as urban dwellers elsewhere.[3]

Brown notes that the problems faced by the country in the postwar period were "at root economic," and he describes how the Irish state—remember, barely 35 years old at this stage—sought to redress the economic problems besetting the nascent nation. He credits in large part the pioneering work of Dr. T. K. Whitaker, a senior civil servant in the Department of Finance where Kinsella himself was stationed as his junior, as responsible for the modernization of Ireland's economy:

> The author of [*First Programme for Economic Expansion*, 1958] which was to prove a powerful stimulus to new thinking on Ireland's economic future in a way which was to prove highly regenerative, was a T. K. Whitaker. He had been forced by the dismal circumstances of the 1950s to a radical reconsideration of his economic philosophy, which to date had been highly antagonistic to large-scale state involvement in the planning and financing of economic development . . . An Ireland that had espoused nationalism for a quarter of a century and employed manifold tariffs in the interests of native industry was to open its economy to as much foreign investment as could be attracted by government inducement. . . . Economic growth was to become the new national imperative, in place of the language and the protection of native values and tradition.[4]

Kinsella's early poems come directly out of this time, when he was reading W. H. Auden and meeting a group of like-minded men and women including his future wife, Eleanor, to whom much of this work was in one way or another indebted. They were part of a wider cultural response to the economic crisis that was encircling the fledgling republic. Figures such as Seán Ó Riada in music, Liam Miller with his new publishing venture, The Dolmen Press, the development of RTÉ as the national broadcasting network, among others, were actively establishing home-grown initiatives to combat critical problems. The major political issue of the time was how could the new Irish state (in which they had all grown up) sustain itself economically? And underlying questions about what kind of cultural and artistic expression was appropriate in these uncertain circumstances drew various different talents together at least for a decade or so in the 1950s and early 60s.[5] Their views contrast sharply with the irascible, mocking satire of what could be referred to as the Flann O'Brien generation, born in the 1910s and whose increasing disillusionment and distaste for "official" Ireland is inscribed in the many exchanges, for example, between O'Brien and his contemporaries, as one can see in his *Collected Letters*.[6] In contrast, Kinsella's generation seems to have shared a much greater animation and commitment to expanding their sense of "Irishness" alongside the modernist achievements of their immediate forebears and, crucially, linked the desire to modernize with their sense of the abiding Gaelic tradition, the latter a challenge met with such creative verve by the orchestrated traditional music by Kinsella's friend, Seán Ó Riada.

Brown captures this changing literary landscape of the period:

> Not only had a burgeoning publishing industry provided opportunities to Irish writers which even ten years earlier had not existed, but events like the Yeats International Summer School, mounted in Sligo each summer since 1960, the Listowel Writers Week, held each summer in County Kerry, and the Merriman Summer School held each August in County Clare and

> dedicated to the Gaelic literary and cultural tradition, all allowed writers the opportunity to read their works in public and gave literature a publicity, even if of a superficial kind, not enjoyed in the immediate past. Furthermore … contemporary literature played its part in schoolroom and university, and current Irish writers had their work represented in school anthologies and discussed in academic journals.[7]

Hardly a surprise therefore that Kinsella's first volumes published in the late 1950s and 60s—*Another September, Downstream,* and *Nightwalker*—registered some of this new-found confidence, as well as alluding to bigger issues and international questions. But crucially Kinsella also looked within himself for the necessary "answers." Describing the mood which he thought as general in postwar Europe, Kinsella stated the following in 1966:

> The most sensitive individuals have been shaken loose from society into disorder, conscious of a numbness and dullness in themselves, a pain of dislocation and loss … Everywhere in modern writing the stress is on personal visions of the world … The detailed exploration of private miseries is an expedition into the interior to find out what may guide us in the future. It is out of ourselves and our wills that the chaos comes, and out of ourselves that some order must be constructed.[8]

II

It is indeed possible to read Kinsella's poetry as a route through these changes and difficulties toward self-discovery, both for himself and for his city. First there was the commemoration of a way of life and a community that seemed to be disappearing in the poem "Dick King," and there was also the return to his own "self-hood" as an artist, as a poet, well-marked in the much-anthologized poem "Mirror in February." This was followed by the uncovering of his own family as a source of poetry-making in poems such as "Tear," "A Hand of Solo," and "His Father's Hands." During this time period Kinsella also extended his poetic gaze outward in the long meditative poem "Nightwalker," in which the nocturnal rambler broods on the country's violent past and materialistic present. Alongside the mapping out of this imaginative territory, Kinsella started to explore a much wider frame—of epic and historical myth in *The Tain* (1969),[9] for example, or the reclamation of the Irish language tradition in *An Dunaire 1600–1900: Poems of the Dispossessed* (1981).[10]

I am thinking here of Kinsella's finding a new language and form that—though it would change over time—achieved a sense of control and "constructed-ness" that allowed him to deal with his early experiences, though not in a confessional manner. There is also the documentary quality of this writing, which at times reads like a poetic investigation, followed by the achievement of his spoken voice and the local urban accent in the poetry—and, simultaneously, his attraction to an artistic force that is none of the above but is fascinated by the weird, ghostly, haunted, other-worldly, exiled, neglected figures such as one finds in the Peppercanister sequence, *St Catherine's Clock* (1987):[11]

> At the other end of the darkened market place
> a man's figure crossed over
> out of Francis Street
>
> reading the ground,
> all dressed in black
> like a madwoman.[12]

"Tear"[13] is a poem about experience, the growing into knowledge of the young boy as he visits his dying grandmother, retold through the lens of the older poet. Kinsella would have been in his mid-40s when he published this poem in *New Poems*, a volume in which many poems deal with the vanishing of a way of life and an older generation. The poem has a narrative to it, a storyline that takes us into the room of the old woman who has become almost creaturely, and it is through the lasting image of her spread hair, the smells, and darkening of the room that Kinsella commemorates the young boy's fear and growing realization that death is a part of life. And the "kiss," which he knows he is expected to give as a farewell, broods on the young boy's mind as it is remembered by the older poet. What surprises the boy and the remembering poet is the news of "an infant sister" who had died and, in whose recollection, the boy is made complicit:

> . . . her voice, soft, talking to someone
> about my father: 'God help him, he cried
> big tears over there by the machine
> for the poor little thing.' Bright
>
> drops on the wooden lid
> for my infant sister.
> My own wail of child-animal grief
> was soon done, with any early guess
>
> at sad dullness and tedious pain
> and lives bitter with hard bondage.
> How I tasted it now—
> her heart beating in my mouth![14]

Grief as a communal experience is shared and passed down through the family generation by generation and presents through the young boy's realization in the poem with a sense of the understanding, of resolution.

Dick King[15] is one of a number of characters who inhabit Kinsella's poetry—like the old WWI soldier, Mister Cummins in "38 Phoenix Street," or Miss Carney and Mr. Brown, the teachers in "Model School, Inchicore." The recreation of their lives, their shadow-lives more like, is part of the drama of the community which Kinsella imagines in the poems set in childhood landscapes. (*Downstream*, the volume from which the poem "Dick King" comes, is dedicated to Kinsella's mother and father). He is both interested in the places and people themselves but also, essentially, in the way in which the imagination is drawn back to the past and sifts through it in an effort to find some sort of meaning to life, even though the past is always quite simply that, the past—unrepeatable, irretrievable, gone. "Dick King" brings to life several aspects of the world that Kinsella knew unselfconsciously growing up. The man embodies a way of being that found no material reward but its own selflessness in caring for an invalid wife, befriending a young boy, carrying the Irish language and culture with him from his origins in the west of Ireland to work in Dublin, religious practice, and then the tragic passing of this life in "a Union ward." In *A Dublin Documentary* Kinsella recalls the neighbor and his "importance":

> He seemed to be always there: a friend of the family, a protector of my unformed feelings. I would visit him and his wife leaving the shop and crossing the yard. And he would visit us in our house in Inchicore, coming across from the Railway works; doing nothing, filling some kind of lack. He died years later, in the Union in James's Street. I wrote two poems for him, in

memory of his importance during those early years. Neither of the poems achieved completeness, but their parts came together.[16]

Kinsella's poem resists easy sentiment, or the sentimentalizing of Dick King's life (wide open to such exploitation), given what Kinsella calls in the poem "his dread years": "your voice, in a pause of softness, named the dead, / Hushed as though the city had died by fire, / Bemused, discovering."

While recreating the world of his upbringing forms a significant part of Kinsella's achievement as a poet, and the rendering of that world without illusion or a falsifying of reality, he has also produced poems which focus squarely upon what he, the poet, is doing. "Mirror in February," published in *Downstream* when Kinsella was in his mid-thirties, captures with unflinching focus a verbal self-portrait, the unadorned human gesture of looking at oneself as in a mirror and seeing through that image of "self" a glimpse of what life means. "Mirror in February" is a special poem in many ways. It defines a landscape immediately surrounding the solitary presence of the poet himself and, in a simple austere recognition, leaves the reader to see the portrait for what it is, nothing more, nothing less, than a moment of self-awareness: "It seems again that it is time to learn, / In this untiring, crumbling place of growth / To which, for the time being, I return." The meditative, somber tone of the poem, with its natural "awakening" and "brute necessities" of pruning back to allow growth to take place, has all the qualities of a self-portrait similar to what one associates with the artist Lucian Freud.

All the greater, then, the surprise when we come to the strange, elusive creature "Littlebody"—a figure that has hopped out of the mythical past, as if from a Grimm's fairy tale, or a text of Irish myths—a will-o'-the-wisp, or sprite from the classical underworld. Kinsella's shifting fascination over many decades is something rare in modern Irish poetry. Indeed, sometimes readings of Kinsella's poetry can become overly concerned with the magisterial, at times, bleak, almost anti-poetic nature of his writing and ignores the other unorthodox strains. The poem "Littlebody," from the 2000 Peppercanister of the same name, sits within a sequence called "Glenmacnass,"[17] the waterfall in the Wicklow hills, where the countryside is alive with deer, crows, and the life indoors of a family rhythm, breakfast, the playing of a cat. This natural world opens out as the poet takes a walk into "the quiet wood" and from there leaves behind that which is "real" and enters the realm of a magical realism, with its own supernatural customs and injunctions to follow: "I looked around the edge / – and it was Littlebody. Hugging his bag / under his left arm, with his eyes closed." So, with this quirky little estranging figure, completely out of any real or known place the poem changes tone: "'Demon dwarf / with the German jaw / surrender your purse / with the ghostly gold,'" and points to a less remarked-upon strain in Kinsella's work, an unorthodox, fable-like world. From the early extenuated (Dantesque) encounters of "Downstream" ("a ghost / That glimmered briefly with my gift of blood"), the poet characteristically walks through immanent landscapes—or makes sea-voyages—which anticipate dread or presentiments proffered from an unnatural world: Section V of "Glenmacnass," which precedes "Littlebody," offers another example of such off-center imagery: "Close up, on a patch of bark, a mouse body. / Upside down. Wings flat. / Meant only to be half seen / quick in the half light: little leather angel / falling everywhere, snapping at the invisible." In Kinsella's imagination, the bat belongs to a transgressive order of being: not simply itself but holding fast to that which is bizarre, unexpected, belonging to "the invisible" that lies beyond the rational conduct of everyday life and our ordinary workaday lives. And it is there, in the real, historical world where I will now turn in conclusion.

III

My title refers to a tale of two cities, why? There are the two cities of Kinsella's poetry: the one he grew up in, the actual city he experienced; and the one his poetry reimagines, a historical city in many ways. Both, however, stand in sharp contrast to the twenty-first-century city of today. But I am thinking about something else, entirely. In 2019 one of Kinsella's contemporaries, the Belfast poet Padraic Fiacc, born in 1924, died in his 95th year.[18] His passing brought to mind a comparison in the contrasting fates of both poets and the cities with which they are indelibly connected in the minds of the poetry reading public and a little beyond. In Kinsella's lifetime Dublin would become the capital of an independent republic and, bizarre as it is to say, the only English-speaking city in the European union—a most unexpected and ironic twist of fate, bearing in mind the hugely problematic historical relationship there has been between the language and its political baggage in Ireland. Belfast remains part of the union of British states—England, Scotland, and Wales—and is of course the capital of Northern Ireland: for how much longer these states will remain in union is beyond the remit of this essay, even though Kinsella has meditated upon these or related issues in his critical prose throughout his writing life.[19]

There are interesting parallels to consider in the light of these two poets' achievement and the contrasting nature of their critical recognition and reputation, both inside the country and internationally. The hundred miles or so of motorway that connects Dublin with Belfast skirts a common eastern seaboard. And though both cities share this common coastline, it is curiously absent from much of our literature, including Kinsella's and Fiacc's poetry. The northern city, much less northern society, is absent from Kinsella's poetry but for the political response to Bloody Sunday, contained in *Butcher's Dozen*. Kinsella also dismissed, in 1986, the very notion of northern poetry as being "largely a journalistic entity,"[20] a view clearly challenging at the time the critical reasoning behind the increasing public recognition of poets from the north of Ireland, such as Seamus Heaney, Michael Longley, Derek Mahon, and their younger contemporaries including Paul Muldoon, Tom Paulin, and Medbh McGuckian, whose work was being received with acclaim throughout Britain, the US, and elsewhere.[21]

Besides these pressure points of literary politics, there are fascinating comparisons waiting for examination whereby the urban experiences of growing up in Dublin and Belfast, returning after lengthy periods living in the US, link rather than separate the life experiences of Kinsella's poetic development with that of Fiacc. There is a generational sense of tradition, too, which they share and responded to in quite different and contradictory ways. However, Kinsella's Dublin had, by the late 1940s/early 1950s, settled into a deeply conservative Catholic society, but one effectively stabilized after decades of turbulence and political conflict. In contrast, Fiacc's Belfast, to which he returned to live in the 1950s, was on a knife-edge that, by the late 1960s, shattered into the turmoil of "The Troubles." Only since the late 1990s has that society stabilized itself and entered a period of post-conflict—whatever one can say about the possible impact of Brexit upon the still vulnerable politics of peace there.

In summarizing the achievement of Kinsella's generation, Brown made the telling point in relation to the publishing outlets that were flourishing in Ireland during the 1950s, whereby periodicals such as *Irish Writing*, *Poetry Ireland*, and *Envoy* gave new writers, including Pearse Hutchinson, John Montague, and Kinsella, "greater opportunities to see their work in print in Ireland than had existed for writers since the first decades of the century."[22] Fiacc, however, has not been identified with this original opening-up, although a selection of his poems was chosen for the AE Memorial Award in 1957 and, a decade later, his first full collection, *By the Black Stream: Selected Poems 1947–1967*, was published by Dolmen Press in 1969.

As Brown describes the cultural situation:

> A new iconoclasm was in the air, distinct from the satiric, antagonistic bitterness that had characterized the work of an earlier generation of writers ... Instead of assaulting the society they found so inhibiting, young writers simply got on with their work, stating what they thought to be obvious when occasion called for statement."[23]

Kinsella himself was passionate about this principle or attitude, as can be seen in various lectures of the period wherein he discussed the trauma of a society losing its language, and also in his civic engagements in regard to, for example, the public controversy in 1978 concerning the Wood Quay Viking Settlement site close to Kinsella's inner-city neighborhood.[24]

By contrast, the impact of the Troubles would in very many ways dominate, over the ensuing three decades, the artistic lives of northern-based writers such as Fiacc and lead to much debate about the nature of the poet's responsibilities in such a time of social division and political crisis. Regardless of the rights and wrongs of the critical debates of the 1980s, it is clear that, unlike Fiacc, Kinsella survived any adverse reputational impact in the following decades. He is without doubt the key poetic figure reconnecting mid-twentieth-century Irish poetry with European history, literary modernism, and American poetry while bridging his acts of epic translation with critical readings. However, like the society he came from, Padraic Fiacc's place remains largely unsecured and unresolved, a cruel contrast in the curious and challenging tale of two cities only a couple of hours apart.

Since the writing careers of his contemporaries continue to attract serious and extended critical and media interest, Fiacc largely remains the enigma and outsider he became in the early 1970s as the "Troubles broke." Belfast was reluctant to embrace this turbulent, questioning voice. The documentary aspects of Fiacc's life, paralleling the narratives of so many of his peers—in the family's movement from his father's roots in County Cavan to find work in urban Belfast (as a barman) and the experiences of inner-city working-class life Fiacc chronicles in his poetry, to the patterns on migration that followed—"Between the year of the slump and the sell out, I / The third child, am the first born alive . . . / My father is a Free Stater 'Cavan Buck'. / My mother is a Belfast factory worker," as Fiacc writes in "Son of a Gun."[25]

These social and historical experiences are all valued and given due recognition in Kinsella's Dublin in sharp contrast with Fiacc's treatment in the northern capital. The difference is also notable in terms of the literary and cultural understanding afforded both poets' distinctive poetic styles and the disruptive shifts in their imaginative efforts of adapting to modernity. Kinsella's poetry, for all its undoubted range and formal risk, delivers to the present an important and lasting artistic lesson on the tension and burden history can place upon the individual poetic imagination, or in Kinsella's own words from "Hen Woman": "there is no end to that which, not understood, / may yet be hoarded in the imagination / in the yolk of one's being, so to speak."[26]

Notes

[1] Maria Johnston, "Walking Dublin: Contemporary Irish Poets in the City," in *The Oxford Handbook of Modern Irish Poetry*, eds. Fran Brearton and Alan Gillis (Oxford: Oxford UP, 2012), 498.

[2] Thomas Kinsella, *A Dublin Documentary* (Dublin: O'Brien Press, 2006), 8.

[3] Terence Brown, *Ireland: A Social and Cultural History, 1922–2002* (London: HarperCollins, 2005), 207.

[4] Brown, *Ireland: A Social and Cultural History*, 202.

[5] Eibhear Walshe, "Censorship, Law and Literature," in *Irish Literature in Transition 1940–1980*, ed. Eve Patten (Cambridge: Cambridge UP, 2020), 169–184.

[6] *The Collected Letters of Flann O'Brien*, ed. Maebh Long (Dallas, TX: Dalkey Archive Press, 2018).

[7] Brown, *Ireland: A Social and Cultural History*, 214.

[8] Roger McHugh, "Poetry Since Yeats: An Exchange of Views. Stephen Spender, Patrick Kavanagh, Thomas Kinsella, W. D. Snodgrass," *Tri-Quarterly* 4 (1965), 108.

[9] *The Tain*, translated from the Irish epic "Táin Bó Cuailnge" by Thomas Kinsella with brush drawings by Louis le Brocquy (Dublin: Dolmen Press 1969; London: Oxford UP, 1970).

[10] *An Duanaire 1600–1900: Poems of the Dispossessed*/curtha i láthair ag Seán Ó Tuama, with translations into English verse by Thomas Kinsella (Mountrath: Dolmen Press, 1981).

[11] Thomas Kinsella, *St Catherine's Clock* (Dublin: Peppercanister, 1987); *Collected Poems* (Winston-Salem, NC: Wake Forest UP, 2006).

[12] CP, 271.

[13] Thomas Kinsella, "Tear," *New Poems* (Dublin: Dolmen Press, 1973), 25–27; CP, 106. It is interesting to compare "Tear" with Seamus Heaney's poem "Mid-Term Break," *Death of a Naturalist* (London: Faber and Faber, 1966), 28, for such a moving contrast in expression of similar experiences of such early filial loss.

[14] CP, 106.

[15] Thomas Kinsella, "Dick King," *Downstream* (Dublin: Dolmen Press), 1962, 20–21; CP, 36–37.

[16] Thomas Kinsella, *A Dublin Documentary*, 17.

[17] Thomas Kinsella, *Littlebody*, (Dublin: Peppercanister/Dedalus, 2000), 15–18; CP, 352–355.

[18] See Padraic Fiacc, *Ruined Pages: New Selected Poems*, eds. Gerald Dawe and Aodán Mac Póilin (Derry: Lagan Press, 2012). Also, *My Twentieth Century Night Life: A Padraic Fiacc Miscellany*, ed. Patrick Ramsey (Belfast: Lagan Press, 2009).

[19] Thomas Kinsella, *Prose Occasions: 1951–2006*, ed. Andrew Fitzsimons (Manchester: Carcanet Press, 2009).

[20] Thomas Kinsella, ed. *The New Oxford Book of Irish Verse* (Oxford: Oxford UP, 1973), xxx.

[21] See, for instance, Gerald Dawe, "History Class: On 'Northern Poetry,'" in *The Proper Word: Collected Criticism, Ireland Poetry Politics*, ed. Nicholas Allen (Omaha, NE: Creighton UP, 2007), 312–323.

[22] Brown, *Ireland: A Social and Cultural History*, 214.

[23] Brown, *Ireland: A Social and Cultural History*, 215.

[24] See https://www.historyireland.com/volume-22/heritage-outrage-wood-quay/.

[25] Fiacc, "Son of a Gun," *Ruined Pages*, 122.

[26] CP, 99.

CHAPTER TWO

Childhood and Psychic Geography in *A Dublin Documentary*

HUGH HAUGHTON

We look at the world once, in childhood. / The rest is memory.
—Louise Glück, "Nostos"

I

In an interview Thomas Kinsella said: "The final poems in *Downstream* are poems of uprooting and resettlement. And it was at the same time that I began writing clearly about Dublin memories."[1] Seamus Heaney has an important essay on "Place and Displacement in Contemporary Northern Irish Poetry" about the sense of displacement arising from the dual British/Irish allegiances in the province, but it is clear from Kinsella's words that the "uprooting and resettlement" he describes involves a comparable (though different) vision of place and displacement. Kinsella's work, nonetheless, involves a similar investment in what he calls "Dublin memories" and identity, framed in terms of a drastic "uprooting" of some kind, in his case partly the result of his new experience of bi-location as a poet with one foot in the Irish Republic and the other in the United States, and partly due to other kinds of intellectual unsettlement and resettlement. As he writes in "Phoenix Park," the final poem in *Nightwalker* (1969), "One stays or leaves. The one who returns is not / The one, etcetera."

One also leaves and returns to childhood, and since *Downstream* (1966) Kinsella has written a series of resonant poems of "Dublin memories," embodying "the savour of our days restored"[2] in what one Peppercanister pamphlet calls *Personal Places* (1990). As is the way of Kinsella's work, fragmentary poems and the memories speak to each other in the sequences they occur in as well as creating a discontinuous continuity over time, visibly embodied in the *Collected Poems* of 2006. 2006, however, also saw the publication of Kinsella's *A Dublin Documentary*, a rather anomalous book that is formally unique in his oeuvre: a *sui generis* selection of poems framed by prose observations and black-and-white illustrations. It gathers key "Dublin memories" of childhood composed across his career, interspersing them with autobiographical commentary and fifty or so photographs, as well as a historical print of St. Catherine's Church and reproductions of family manuscripts. The description on the inside cover of the book describes it as "Kinsella's personal account" or "case study" of his origins in "old Dublin, a window into a world that has since disappeared." Noting it is made up of "poems and interlinking prose," the dust jacket says that it "gives his own first, child's impressions of the world around him, and describes his growing awareness and expanding horizons from the yards and whitewashed walls in the back lanes of the Kilmainham/Inchicore area to the bustling centre of Dublin and beyond."[3]

This hybrid account of a city childhood offers a new construction from earlier first-person poetic accounts of "first impressions." It is both a quasi-Wordsworthian poetic autobiography and a "case study" (suggesting something more scientific or psychoanalytic), a story of honing in but also of "growing awareness" of "expanding horizons." Calling it a "Documentary" differentiates it from comparable life-writing such as the sustained autobiographical dialogue of Seamus Heaney's *Stepping Stones* or the self-conscious prose poetics of Eavan Boland's *Object Lessons: The Life of the Woman Poet in Our Time*, both of which are as much critical essay as personal memoir. It also reads very differently from the essayistic recollections of Michael Longley in *Tuppenny Stung* or the mnemonic fireworks of Ciaran Carson's *The Star Factory* about his childhood Belfast. Kinsella's sparse prose is reminiscent of a quasi-scientific record, not unlike the experiments he says he did as a science student at University College Dublin "watching certain solvents reacting in their glass phials."[4] Indeed, Kinsella's poems about personal places and childhood memories are often reminiscent of scientific rigor, and the prose of his *Dublin Documentary* is as studiously unpoetic as a Civil Servant's briefing paper. Nonetheless, the book is an elaborately created work in its own right, offering a radical reconstruction of the dispersed poems of childhood scattered in other collections, embodying his chronic quest for origins and destinations in a topology of its own.

With their investigative rigor, Kinsella's poems of childhood memory tap into a long tradition, going back to the Romantic period of Rousseau, Wordsworth, Coleridge, and Stendhal, and the fictive modernist memoirs of Proust, Virginia Woolf, and Joyce, particularly the Dublin "epiphanies" of Joyce in *Portrait of the Artist as a Young Man*. They also owe something to Austin Clarke's account of a Dublin childhood in *Around the Black Church* and the lyric life-writing inaugurated in the US by Robert Lowell's *Life-Studies*. On another front, they also bear the impress of psychoanalytic accounts of childhood memory, particularly by his chosen model Jung, recalled in "C. G. Jung's 'First Years,'" where "dreams broke in succession and ran back / whispering with disappearing particulars." Like Freud, D. W. Winnicott, and Marion Milner, Kinsella's texts seek to identify the legacy of the earliest recoverable experience as well as intimating what cannot be recovered (or recovered from).

In their more disturbing ontological mode, the autobiographical vignettes of childhood that begin with Kinsella's *New Poems* (1973) also work in dialogue with other signature poems about Irish childhoods written by Heaney, Boland, Longley, Ní Chuilleanáin, Muldoon, and others. Though Kinsella may have been resistant to recognizing the link, they indirectly reflect the impact of—and counter—Heaney's childhood poems in his first volumes, *Death of a Naturalist* (1966) and *Door into the Dark* (1969), with their glimpses of his first life in rural County Derry. Such comparisons intensify the uniquely discomforting frequency that Kinsella's poems of early memory operate on, a frequency that is simultaneously quasi-surgical in its investigative precision and uncanny in its imaginative resonances. There is nothing like the beneficent resonance of Heaney's "Personal Helicon," for example, with its trusting colloquial opening, "As a child they could not keep me from wells," and self-affirming conclusion "I rhyme / To see myself." [5] Though Kinsella's poems also offer doors into the dark, their darkness opens on a less hospitable and reassuring place than Barney Kiernan's "altar / Where he expends himself in shape and music." [6] Closer analogues are to be found in Proust's *A la recherche du temps perdu*, with its many moments of "involuntary memory," desire, and humiliation, or Wordsworth's *2-Part Prelude* of 1799, with its combination of self-inventing form and disquieting sense of "unknown modes of being."[7] All the same, the culture of Kinsella's working-class Inchicore is a world away from the Swiss mountains, lakes, and castles of Jung's "First Memories," Proust's affluent historic Combray, or Wordsworth's English Lakes.

In 1998 Kinsella said he was re-reading Wordsworth and admiring him for "the scale of his apprehensions, his emotional range, and great linguistic gift." Quoting him, he said his own poems were also born out of memory: "Emotion recollected in tranquillity ... The importance, and the impulse to record, felt later."[8] Like Wordsworth's, the best of Kinsella's poems are built around specific sites of memory, and this gives their reappearance in *A Dublin Documentary* a new topographical currency, countering the often esoteric mythopoeic resonances foregrounded in the volumes they are taken from. Like other Irish poems of childhood, they are in the first place poems of place, and mark a bond between our first places and identity, like Heaney's "Mossbawn," returning to his first world in rural County Derry, Mahon's Belfast-inflected "Autobiographies," the Cork City in Ní Chuilleanáin's "Early Recollections," or the Armagh of Muldoon's "The Right Arm" and *Yarrow*. Like these other poets, Kinsella is interested in the topology of memory, though of a generally more opaque and enigmatic kind. He recreates individual places, objects, subjects, people, or moments in a de-familiarizing light that feels less securely tethered to mappable places than the accounts of childhood in these other poets. His childhood lyrics focus on tiny, fragmentary particulars, pitched against an unsettling background of receding darkness and unknowability. They often revolve around a version of the "miniature" discussed by Susan Stewart, which she sees as "located at a place of origin" or "the childhood of the self," tending towards "tableau" rather than "narrative," and "towards silence and spatial boundaries rather than towards expository closure."[9] They are often disturbingly "uncanny" in Freud's sense of the *Unheimlich* (the "unhomely" or "uncanny"), which he argues exerts its haunting power over us because it is actually an estranged version of that which is most *Heimlich* (or homely), a displaced and estranged projection of our first family world, shot through with infantile desire and fear, and subsequently repressed.[10] The effect is often of a violently condensed or miniaturized sublime. *A Dublin Documentary* documents how Kinsella's charged childhood memories of family and home in Dublin can be mapped against knowable geographical markers, but not contained by them. They generate an aura of unknowability, of unnameable forces lurking in boxes, passages, drawers, and cupboards, like the almost illegible iconographic markers in "38 Phoenix Street" with its "strange room" where "the Sacred Heart / leaned down in his long clothes over a red oil lamp / with his women's black hair and his eyes lit up in red, / hurt and blaming."[11]

A Dublin Documentary is a very selective *Selected Poems* but creates a new sequence of "strange rooms" built out of early Dublin memories. Derval Tubridy has documented the revisions and reconstructions Kinsella subjected his Peppercanister pamphlets to when he incorporated them in Oxford Press volumes and his *Collected Poems*, illuminating Kinsella's obsessional reconfigurations of the same material. Something comparable happens in *A Dublin Documentary*, as it reconfigures texts from *Collected Poems*. Boland's later volume, *A Poet's Dublin*, edited by Paula Meehan and Jody Allen Randolph, also combines a selection of her poems with photographs, though in her case the photos are her own and the text has been curated by editors in dialogue with the poet. *A Dublin Documentary*, by contrast, is an independent hybrid, made up of Kinsella's own texts and other people's photographs, uprooting poems from familiar published contexts into a new topographical space, framed by the Joycean "scrupulous meanness" of Kinsella's prose. The result confirms Kinsella's view in the interview quoted earlier that:

> The self is the basic unit, an awareness in the personal psyche of the immediate reality. This opens into wider areas of significance under imaginative pressure. With total commitment and precision, there is really no limit to the significant relevant world.[12]

Like the title poem of *Downstream*, the poems are projected against a specific nameable geography but travel into unnameable territory, "Searching the darkness for a landing place."[13] In *A Dublin Documentary* remembered places like 38 Phoenix Street are not so much landing places, however, as sites of embarkation, or what he calls in *Songs of the Psyche* (1985) "a series of beginnings."

II

The first and largest section of *A Dublin Documentary* is entitled ". . . imaginative beginnings . . ." (complete with its trail of crucial punctuation marks). Its first poem is "A Hand of Solo," originally one of a suite of poems of early memory from *New Poems* (1973), where it follows "Hen Woman" and is followed by "The High Road," "Ancestor," "Tear," and "Irwin Street," all of which are scattered in a different order across this first section. ". . . imaginative beginnings . . ." opens, however, with a close-up photo of shining coal-black pavement followed by a little prose fragment., which begins drily: "I am not, technically, a Dubliner, despite being born and reared in Inchicore." It then offers a brief outline of the family history of the Kinsellas who came to Dublin from County Wicklow and of his mother's family, the Casserlys, from Westmeath. The poet's curt prose supplements the account of migration to the city in "Ritual of Departures": "Farther South:

landscape, with ancestral figures" as "their children's children vanished in the city lanes." In "The Divided Mind," his diagnosis of the traumatic "rift" in Irish culture, Kinsella talked of feeling "the discontinuity in myself" and of "coming from a broken and uprooted family, of being drawn to those who share my origins."[14] In the prose of *A Dublin Documentary* topography and employment are to the fore in this "uprooted family" world. He mentions his Cafferly grandfather as a "collector" for an Insurance Company "unreliable on his bicycle," and his quieter Grandfather Kinsella, "long retired from Guinness's," who is "a repairer of shoes," but the real emphasis is on the wives of these men, "formidable women" who both "managed shops in their houses." They preside over the interiors that follow. It is only having tersely established these familial and topographical coordinates (one shop is located in Basin Lane, off James Street, the second on "the other side of James's Street, close to the end wall of Swift's hospital, and at the start of the road leading to Kilmainham"), that Kinsella opens a door onto his imaginative beginnings:

> It was in a world dominated by these people that I remember many things of importance happening to me for the first time. And it was in their world that I came to terms with these things as best I could, and later set my attempts at understanding.[15]

Possessive pronouns do a lot of work here. On the one hand, *these* people, *their* world—and on the other, "things of importance happening to *me* for the first time," and "*my* attempts at understanding." Time also matters intensely, in particular when and where things happen "for the first time," then when he "came to terms with these things as best I could" and where he "later set my attempts at understanding." These dry words offer a condensed poetics of memory, with poems as retrospective "attempts at understanding" within an autobiographical inquiry into primal scenes. This is like an outgrowth of Kinsella's re-reading of Wordsworth's "spots of time" in the late 1990s.

With the brilliantly named "A Hand of Solo," Kinsella hones in on one of these places, "the Casserly home, in a room behind the shop," where the family gathered for cards at weekends, and where he situates "Some of my first awarenesses" (a fascinating plural that recalibrates Wordsworthian "spots of time" or Joycean epiphanies). Having mentioned "the firelight on the shelves of the dresser and on the card table" and "the voices of the players familiar and mysterious," the prose introduction abruptly breaks off with a colon—a colon that is followed by a blank quarter-page and then a page devoted to a studio photo of the Casserly family—and then, overpage, the appearance of the first poem. The colon, the empty space at the foot of the page, the mid-page family portrait opposite, and the turning page, all give a topological force to the solo poem, situating it in a complex mnemonic space. Another studio photograph, this time of the infant Kinsella standing on his mother's knee (given the legend "Mother and child" in the acknowledgments) appears to the right of the opening stanzas of "A Hand of Solo." This gives the poem's opening account of the primal oral satisfactions of a baby a new (or old) life in this documentary context: "Lips and tongue / wrestle the delicious / life out of you," words that take on a new resonance when we see the little Kinsella on his mother's lap. After the poem, another photo is a portrait of the artist as a young toddler with his mother and her three sisters. It gives this uncanny poem a couple of very *Heimlich* bookends, grounding it in a familial space very different from the archaic Irish mythological contexts of *Notes from the Land of the Dead* with which it is associated in *New Poems*.

Brian John, commenting on "A Hand of Solo," says that, "as the poem's title suggests, the experience contributes to the self's evolution into a 'solo' or 'one,' just as the scene in the Dublin shop kept by the grandmother takes on mythological significance through the portrayal of the old women as a Hecate figure, presiding over the underworld" (he is referring to her saying "You'd think I had three heads!"), a mythic reading based partly on the pomegranate (or "Indian apple") the boy devours so sensually in the text ("I drove my tongue among them").[16] If so, the photographs, and the documentary context, foreground the incongruity between the solidly prosaic Dublin world of the photos and the poem's account of the young boy's psychic initiation into an underworld dominated by powerful women and their bodies, culminating in the post-Kleinian celebration of his primitive Keatsian oral pleasure in eating the "Indian apple" at the end:

> I drove my tongue among them
>
> and took a mouthful, and slowly
> bolted them. My throat filled
> with a rank, Arab bloodstain.[17]

After the poem, Kinsella comments that: "Indian apple was our name for the pomegranate. There was a strangeness about it. And about many things: the two rooms at the end of a dark passageway, where the grandparents spent of a lot of their time, and seemed very dark in themselves." The poem's many estranged but implacably physical things include the "red heart and black spade" (of the playing cards), the "box of Indian apples," the "first traces of the blood" (of the fruit), the "tin ghost" of Mick McQuaid over the fireplace, the Freudian grandmother's "key / in the pocket of her apron," and that final "rank, Arab bloodstain." There is an eerie but visceral sense of misogynistic and racial othering (as in "Arab" here), generating a sense of bizarre psycho-drama that is intensified—but also "placed"—by the following black-and-white snapshot of Kinsella as a toddler beside his crouching mother in front of her three sisters in their backyard.

Kinsella's prose then takes us from that "dark passageway" to the "silent square courtyard at the back," with its "whitewashed cottages," "cats and hens and a feel of the country" (clearly related to the photo). This creates a bridge to the dream-like archetypal world of "Hen Woman," one of the most uncanny of his epiphanic poems of childhood, which is entirely built around the memory of seeing "a beetle like a bronze leaf" moving a "dungball" and a neighbor's hen laying in the "noon heat of the yard":

As I watched, the mystery completed.
The black zero of the orifice
closed to a point
and the white zero of the egg hung free,
flecked with greenish brown oils.[18]

The flat word "mystery" covers both the child's fascination with sexuality, birth, and creation and also the Catholic "mysteries of the rosary" and classical "Eleusinian Mysteries," interpreted in Kerenyi and Jung's *Science of Mythology: Essays on the Divine-Child and the Mysteries of Eleusis* (1951), which discusses the child-motif in relation to others like "the golden egg," seeing it as representative of "the preconscious, childhood aspect of the collective psyche."[19] At the heart of Kinsella's poem is the persistence of that remembered egg and the continuing imaginative nourishment it provides:

I feed upon it still, as you see;
there is no end to that which, not understood,
may yet be hoarded in the imagination,
in the yoke of one's being, so to speak,[20]

The poem flips from past to present, making the egg a metaphorical embodiment of Kinsella's memory of it, and giving a primitive oral pleasure to the memory that also recalls Yeats's play on Pythagoras in "Among School Children," where he talks of the unity created by reciprocal love as "a sphere from youthful sympathy, / Or else, to alter Plato's parable,/ Into the yolk and white of the one shell," a phase eerily evoked in the poem's later reference to the egg as still falling, "alive as the yolk and white of my eye." The egg-eating in reference to what he calls "an egg of being" gives a different resonance to an idea that goes back to the premier poet of autobiographical imagination, Wordsworth, who in "Tintern Abbey" records the pleasure owed to early memories of the Wye valley, saying: "oft, in lonely rooms, and 'mid the din / Of towns and cities, I have owed to them, / In hours of weariness, sensations sweet, / Felt in the blood, and felt along the heart." In Kinsella, they are felt in the mouth, and in the uncomfortable "yolk and white" of his eye.

The poem is followed by the self-conscious comment: "A scene ridiculous in its content, but of a serious early awareness of self and of process: of details insisting on their survival, regardless of any immediate significance." The passages of bare interlinking commentary in *A Dublin Documentary* connect the poems along an austere narrative thread much as the prose of Bashō's *haibun* lends new frames to pre-existing *haiku*, locating them in space and time. This makes it read very differently than in *New Poems*, where it follows after the Faustian narrative prelude, chronicling the questing poet's dream-like fall into a nameless pit, haunted by "countless forms," "Poor spirits" or "a vapour of forms." In *A Dublin Documentary*, this shadowy Shelleyan mythography gives way to a pedestrian topography in which "Hen Woman" is paired with "Dick King," originally published much earlier in *Downstream* (1962) but introduced here as "another permanent finding in the same whitewashed yard." Interestingly, Kinsella introduces it as "two poems," neither of which achieved "completeness," but "came together." It is a tribute to another near neighbor associated with the same backyard space who died penniless in a Union ward and whose vocal ghost teaches him to "read / That death roams our memories igniting / Love." "Dick King" is cast in the present tense of ignited memory:

Clearly now I remember rain on the cobbles,
Ripples in the iron trough, and the horses' dipped
Faces under the Fountain in James's Street,
Where I sheltered my nine years against your buttons
And your own dread years were to come.[21]

An almost photographic memory, it offers a child's-eye view up the neighbor's waistcoat buttons, rippling with a sense of movement (with "ripples" and "cobbles" almost rhyming across the line-break). In *Documentary*, the poem is printed after a photo of the Catholic Church in James's Street and beside another of the James's Street Fountain mentioned here, a Georgian obelisk in the Liberties with a drinking fountain dating back to 1790. This suggests a rather different architecture of commemoration to the homemade elegiac quatrains Kinsella modulates into in the latter part of the poem ("He clasped his hands in a Union ward / To hear St James's bell. / I searched his eyes though I was young, / The last to wish him well.") In the memoir, topography and photography give a new charge to the poem's account of Dick King's move from "the salt seaboard" where he grew up "To bring a dying language east / And dwell in Basin Lane," and of his invalid wife, who "prayed her life away," whose "whisper filled the whitewashed yard / Until her dying day." The whitewashed yard generates a Dublin lyrical ballad.

After the poem and photo of the Fountain, as in a film documentary, Kinsella segues via one prose sentence "down Bow Lane, across James's Street and nearer the river" to make "discoveries on the Kinsella side of the family," as Proust divides life into Swann's way and that of the Guermantes. He takes us via a photo of Bow Lane descending under trees to the poem "Bow Lane," which involves jumping a decade or more in time of composition to *Songs of the Psyche* (1985) as well as removing it from its rarefied mythopoeic world. In an interview, Kinsella said "the past has a psychic geography which is vitally important to the present," something Tubridy develops in her chapter on "Psychic Geography," focusing on Kinsella's archaic mythical topography in *One* and other Peppercanister pamphlets.[22] Peter Denman has proposed that *Songs of the Psyche* "has as its object an engagement with the inner life, in an attempt to disengage from the contingent world and to enter the realm of pure spirit."[23] If so, *A Dublin Documentary* situates the psyche firmly back in the contingent world. Real places frame the poem's account of poking about in "the back corner / of the wardrobe," of the blind that "rustled / like a bat trapped inside," and "the Blessed Virgin on the shelf / over the grandparents' bed" while the poem is now juxtaposed with the even more uncanny evocation of what the prose calls "the grandmother Kinsella" in the otherwise anonymous "Ancestor," with its evocation of her profile in the shop "old, and dark like a hunting bird's," "Her black heart," "brushing by me in the shadows" on her way "down to the back room." The street photos don't reveal the rooms, but the book juxtaposes the two different Bachelardian rooms side by side, anchored in a space where fascination and repulsion, the *Heimlich* and *Unheimlich*, are intimately allied. For Kinsella, as the phenomenological Bachelard says, the childhood house maps "the topography of our intimate being" and provides a key to the inner self, since "it is our first universe, a real cosmos in every sense of the word."[24] In the 'topoanalysis' of *The Poetics of Space* Bachelard explores "a series of images which may be considered the houses of things: drawers, chests and wardrobes," and exclaims "What psychology lies behind their locks and keys! They bear within themselves a kind of aesthetics of hidden things."[25] This leads to what he calls "a phenomenology of what is hidden" that bears closely on Kinsella's own.

After the poem "Tear," "imaginative beginnings" changes key at this point, as Kinsella turns his attention from these presiding women to the absent figure of his father, saying it was only "later in life" that he began to be aware of his importance in relation to the way "the generations" succeed each other (this is clearly a patriarchy, though women are more powerful presences). We then cut to a paternal diptych consisting of "His Father's Hands" from *One* (1974), about his father and grandfather—transposed from its original context within a fragmentary archaic myth about the arrival of anonymous settlers in Ireland—followed by the long Peppercanister poem *The Messenger* (1978) in his father's memory, which tells "the story out of Guinness's" of his father working for the brewery and presents him in his first Post Office job as "the new messenger boy" with his "uniform, in shining belt." Spread out over twenty-six pages in *Documentary*, these two poems are interspersed with photographs of sheets from an MS record of Kinsella family history relevant to "His Father's Hands" and with several images of the Guinness brewery where his father worked, including of barges and dray horses associated with the brewery along with documents recording him being laid off and being given a loan for a child's funeral. There's also a picture of the Oblate Church, Inchicore, where the poet remembers being "squeezed against a cold pillar" as "A Bull-voice rang among the arches" (and in the original pamphlet told them how to vote). Though there is no actual photo of his father, and he doesn't re-use the

Mercury image from the Peppercanister cover, the various images frame the poem's filial evocation of his father's life in the most circumstantial way, situating and counter-pointing the poem's very different claim that "The Self is islanded in fog." These images stand beside but do not correspond with such charged details in the poems as the nail-studded cobbler's block in "His Father's Hands." The block survives the craftsman's death, and stands focally as not only a memorial to his grandfather but an embodiment of the act of memory itself:

> Extraordinary . . . the big block – I found it
> years afterwards in a corner of the yard
> in sunlight after rain
> and stood it up, wet and black:
> it turned under my hands, an axis
> of light flashing down its length,
> and the wood's soft flesh broke open,
> countless little nails
> squirming and dropping out of it.[26]

The block is Kinsella's equivalent of the unfinished sheepfold in Wordsworth's *Michael*, or the farmyard pump Heaney calls his "Omphalos." Kinsella's poem sifts through memories of his grandfather's hands, holding plug tobacco or a fiddle, filters phrases from "The Wind that Shakes the Barley," and fans out from the 1798 ballad to take in reflections on the Kinsella family helping the Croppies in 1798 and their "Men Folk" who were "either Stone Cutters / or masons," involved in "dispersals or migrations" from the North of Ireland to Wicklow, and an image of the poet as a boy working at the "rude block, his bench" (now also a figure for poetry). The block recalls the jutting stone Jung describes in his autobiography as "my stone," which had a "secret relationship to me." Jung describes his memoir as chiefly about "inner experiences" including "dreams and visions," saying it is written in the belief that "there are archaic psychic components" which enter "the individual psyche" without "any direct line of transmission."[27] Something comparable is articulated in Kinsella's *One*, where memories of his grandfather are associated with the split log. Resituated in *A Dublin Documentary*, however, the poem draws away from the archaic world of myth to focus on an actual place, the block in "the corner of the yard" being part of the city geography of Dublin, coming to life again in the poet's hands as "an axis / of light" (with its light pun on "axes"), and those uncannily animate "countless little nails / squirming and dropping out of it" that make it so unlike Heaney's monumental omphalos and still full of swarming life.

"The Messenger" also gains a grainier documentary value, with the allusions to "the barge captain," the river running "fast / into the middle span of the last bridge," the ship's "funnel" and "the Liffey wall" all confirmed in the photographs of working barges on the Liffey, as the photo of the "Oblate Fathers" frames the account of his father leaving the church in protest at being denounced by the priest with his "black mouth shouting / Godless Russia after us." We don't follow his parents to the primal scene of their lovemaking by the river bank in Wicklow, where the displaced seminal "gossamer ghost" is a "pulsing" worm, whose "tail-tip winces and quivers" and the poet says "I *think* this is where I come in." Nevertheless, the solid black-and-white of the photographs offers a riverine city context for the elusive and fragmentary memories of his father's life as young messenger, cobbler, and Marxist Union man, ending with his funeral, with the "oak box / paused gleaming in the May morning air." Kinsella then guides us to "Irwin Street" which revolves on "another image from the same neighbourhood, later in the same time," which he describes as an account of "my father encountered for the first time as an equal," a reference to the poem's uncanny Heine-like *Doppelgänger* effect:

> He was coming toward me, my maker,
>
> in a white jacket, and with my face.
> How could he be there, at this hour?
> Our steps hesitated in awkward greeting.[28]

In *New Poems* "Irwin Street" was associated with the other family memory poems like "Hand of Solo" and "Tear" and led into *From the Land of the Dead*, while here it is grouped with poems associated particularly with his father and segues into "The High Road" (also from *New Poems*), which Kinsella, in his prose introduction to it, describes as "only the remains of what it was," locating the street precisely on the map, and talking of walking home by it from the Kinsella grandparents, "crossing the small bridge over the Carmac," starting on the High Road "on the way to Kilmainham." Though the road still keeps "traces of its rural past," it has "no reason to be recorded, except for its place in the rhythm of those earliest years, insistent in the memory." It is "like the grandfather Kinsella's cobbler's block or the grandmother's apron, giving a shape of its own to what happened there." The poem's account of the gift and loss of the "silvery / little mandoline, out of the sweet-box," of "the parapet of the bridge / at the end of Granny and Granda's" where "the brown water bubbled and poured" and of how "stony darkness / trickled down Cromwell's Quarters step by step" is complemented by a series of photographs of the High Road, Bow Bridge, and the steps of Cromwell's Quarters, giving the poem's eerie account of the "mob of shadows," of "watching the pitch drain out of their wounds," of "man's dung and bluebottles," and of "the big hole, full of fright" a new topographical intensity, and projecting, as Kinsella says, "a shape of its own to what happened there" (and/or vice versa). Like Wordsworth in the Lakes, Kinsella's account of inner-city childhood is rooted in experiences of fear, awe, trespass, and guilt, as "Irwin Street" ends with "my feet on the bare boards, / my hand in my pyjama trousers" and "The High Road" with the account of "a sin happening" when he lets go of the miniature mandoline, "turning over with little flashes / silveryshining with loss."

In between the photos, Kinsella's prose takes us from these walks past "the great gate" of Kilmainham gaol towards "Inchicore" ("island of berries"), and to the "triangular playground" of the School, taking us back to two key poems from "Settings" in *Songs of the Psyche*, "The Model School, Inchicore" and "38 Phoenix Street." The book generates a kind of eerie frictional *frisson* between psychic geography and actual Dublin topography, bringing out something integral to the poems while establishing their topology in a different register altogether. "Model School" is Kinsella's equivalent of Heaney's "Anahorish," Mahon's "Autobiographies," or Muldoon's "Anseo" or "Geography," an evocation of the primal scene of education. As so often, Kinsella's school memories boil down to tiny, stained instants and instances: a ball of plasticine rolled into "a snake curling / around your hand" that leaves a "stain" on paper, a "white dot" chalked on the blackboard in maths, a "fat bee" in the schoolyard as a teacher invokes "History," and finally "the taste / of ink off / the nib" of a pen (a sharp reminder of the bond between literacy and orality). His initiations into art, maths, history, religion, and writing flicker through these minute details, with the greatest focus being on his internalization of the culture of Catholic surveillance ("Will God judge / our most secret thoughts and actions? / God will judge / our most secret thoughts and actions"), reminding him of "the Day of Judgement." First and last things go hand in hand in Kinsella.

In *A Dublin Documentary*, the text is framed by a snapshot of the school and school photos of boys in ranks, while a passage of local geographical prose leads us from the "shed" at school via a reflection on names and places like "The Khyber Pass" to "our house on Phoenix Street," where he says, "Beside the Liffey, looking across the Fifteen Acres in the Park," he "spent the best part of my own beginning." The "best part" is ambiguous, perhaps, but it gives force to the following photo of the terrace house "38 Phoenix Street," where he says he made his "first encounter as an infant with people outside the family" while "Staring at the stranger" or "at the other" across the dividing wall between 37 where his family lived and their neighbors. The abrupt opening of the poem, with its equally abrupt shift of tenses from present imperative to past ("Look. / I was lifted up") reads differently in tandem with the photograph which we are looking at. The logic of the Freudian uncanny is at work throughout, with the image of the Sacred Heart held out "with his women's fingers" casting a shadow back over the heart of the Kinsella household. This chimes with the Catholic eschatology captured in "Model School, Inchicore," offering a counterpart of the interplay between domestic and religious iconography you find in the Swiss Protestant childhood in Jung's "First Years." Photos on the opposite page of a stern unnamed mother figure, a uniformed soldier (presumably the wounded Mister Cummins of the poem), and three children sitting on stones against a crumbling wall, lend a documentary graininess and specificity to the strange autobiographical hauntology of the poem which turns the sight of the home into the site of otherness. Summing up his childhood after it, Kinsella says that beyond the two districts mapped out in the poem and prose, Dublin seemed "threatening and strange," noting that all these poems show "a tendency to look inward for material—into family or self," suggesting a blurring of any boundary between family and self. In his essay on "Blood and Family," Gerald Dawe's remarks on the questions in play in poems like these:

> How do we articulate the past and what we see round us "now"? What has brought us "here" in the first place? What our family "means" and how we gather all such "things" into our "selves"? These issues are questions at the very heart of Kinsella's poetry.[29]

A Dublin Documentary gives such questions a local habitation and a name.

Having arrived at the Phoenix Street poem, Kinsella offers a rushed summary of the rest of his early life, with his brief uprooting to the wartime Manchester of air-raids, sirens, and shelters, a return to Dublin, Basin Lane, and Christian Brothers school, and a scholarship to study science at UCD, "watching certain solvents reacting in their glass phials" (a later equivalent of the Sacred Heart). Recounting his subsequent enlistment in the Civil Service in the Land Commission and then Department of Finance, Kinsella ends the first part of the *Documentary* with the move to "a dark and unhealthy single room" in an attic on Baggot Street, the site of his encounter with Auden, his discovery of poetry as "a meaningful human activity" and his "first serious attempt at writing verse." At this point, we re-encounter "Baggot Street Deserta," which Brian John calls the "single most significant poem" in *Another September* (1958) and from the earliest stage of his career, first published in *Irish Writing* in 1956 in a much longer version. It reflects another Dublin as well as another September, and, with its views of "doctored recollections," "the Past" as a "fairy bog," and "the sting of memory's quick, the drear / Uprooting." The poem not only documents Kinsella's self-conscious initiation into the medium but casts a new light on the later poems of "doctored recollections" we have read earlier. With its alternating rhyme "Baggot Street Deserta" operates in a more formal, urbane, and Audenesque world than the fluid poems of childhood we have been looking at, but remarkably, we realize how consistent their vision is with the strange ontology of Dublin. John observes that "Dublin, only barely perceptible in the poem" was "to prove increasingly the distinctive Kinsella landscape: urban, nocturnal at times numinous, frequently a land of the dead, always a setting for spiritual pilgrimage."[30] At the end of "imaginative beginnings," that signature poem of poetic arrival is followed by "The Familiar," or rather the first three poems from that seven-poem sequence of 1999, recording another initiation, this time to love, experienced in "my cell, up under the roof / Over Baggot Street," where his future wife moved in with him, and became "Muse on my mattress." After it, Kinsella cuts away to invoke a different range of affairs: of family life in the Southern suburb of Sandycove, "years of service in the Department of Finance" and "a growing—and conflicting—commitment to poetry," ending with a shadowy photo of the high terraces of Baggot Street, the site of his apprenticeship as a poet.

III

There is a sense in which the seventy-five pages of "imaginative beginnings" are the heart of *A Dublin Documentary* and lay down the groundwork for Kinsella's oeuvre. The Civil Service years and Sandymount don't figure in this memoir. Instead Part II ("... second roots ...") focuses on the new family home "in a pleasant house in the city centre," on Percy Place beside Huband Bridge, where he set down "second roots" across the canal from "the Peppercanister Church, within sound of the church bell on Haddington Road, and with a coalman and his horse in our mews on Percy Lane." Only five poems figure in this second part, ending with the longer sequence "St Catherine's Clock" which had been published as an independent Peppercanister pamphlet in 1987 before its inclusion in *Blood and Family*. The last sequence in particular gives us Kinsella's take on the Georgian and Victorian capital, offering a haunted view of the terrace, the canal, the "squat front of St Catherine's," the Emmet Fountain, and ending with "1740" with its closing Goya-like image of a man's figure ("another disturbed figure like Swift's" as he says, introducing the poem) "reading the ground, / all dressed in black / like a madwoman." Like the Stranger, this last is an uncanny figure of memory and of the poet as a disturbing other (or the other as poet). We realize that *A Dublin Documentary* is itself a sustained instance of "reading the ground" in many senses—of re-reading and re-treading the ground in Dublin but also the ground of his identity, as the poet reconstructs his doctored recollections of places and anchors his ambitious over-arching poetic project in this geographically objective but also fiercely subjective Dublin. With its two parts, its "reading of the ground" has a strong claim to be read as a work in its own right, Kinsella's hyper-condensed equivalent of Wordsworth's *Two-Book Prelude* offering an account of "the growth of the poet's mind" in a consistently *unheimlich* Home in Dublin.

"St Catherine's Clock" marks time as well as place, as all of these poems do, revolving around the building that gives the name to his Peppercanister poems, and returning to earlier moments in Irish history associated with the place, including the murder of the Chief Justice Lord Kilwarden, the execution of Emmet, and Swift's founding of St. Patrick's Hospital, but also memories of the places and people of his childhood, recorded in Part I, which are re-framed in the long section "1938." The poem sets historical dates against historical prints, but among them the date "1938" returns us to Kinsella aged 10, again looking at the family world from a child's angle, and returning to the grandmother's shop, with its "tin tea boxes out of India," its "brass pans ... hanging in their chains," before moving to the "back room" where he kills flies, culminating in an eerie close-up of a fly "on the face of the Sacred Heart" which is "Twining and wiping its thin paws," a particularly weird instance of the miniature sublime or perverse epiphany which provides the currency of childhood memory. This particular poem winds between a series of such luminous (or tenebrous) epiphanies, memories of stuck-up aunts overcome with laughter or "looking down through our shadows into the water / for the sign of a striped perch," feeling the "little eggs" of his brother and himself, and of setting rubbish on fire as "The Night crept / among our chalk signs on the path." The poem's account of his aunt Bridie who "knelt down quickly beside me" for a "hurried hug" is set beside the last photo of the book, which records this moment, giving us a last glimpse of the poet as infant, staring at the camera from a receding Dublin alleyway. These memories of family, sex, and place, of both being "dressed properly" and of boyish "wickedness" end with a report of being alone, first in bed "lain inert, the flesh in nightmare" and then sitting "solitary / outside, on the low window-sill, / a brutal nail nagging out of nowhere." These "chalk signs" are mustered among many others—an uncanny portrait of the world seen through the eyes of a ten-year-old, mesmerized by splintery details that redefine the relationship between terror and beauty. Kinsella's Schumann-like *Kinderszenen* dwell on the psychic significance that crystallizes in the tiniest things: the minute, if not the miniature. That single "brutal nail nagging out of nowhere."

As Tubridy notes of the Peppercanister version, "By focusing on a single location: the area around St Catherine's Clock, Kinsella is able to explore his sense of self in terms of the family history that takes place around Bow Lane and Basin Lane, and also in terms of the national history which takes place at Bridgefoot Street and Thomas Street."[31] Single places are permeable, and like single objects, radiate outwards towards "expanding horizons," like the "fumbled clang" of "The Bell" that is "audible in Inchicore." As Bachelard said, "For a knowledge of intimacy, localization in the spaces of our intimacy is more urgent than determination of dates."[32] This is particularly so within the "psychic geography" of *A Dublin Documentary*, which vividly embodies the truth announced in "Personal Places" that "*There are established personal places* / that receive our lives' heat / and adapt in their mass, like stone" as they "absorb in their changes / the radiance of change in us." Collected together in this Dublin psycho-topology, the poems offer a new sense of "The radiance of change" and the uncanny nuclear radiance of Kinsella's memories of a Dublin childhood.

Notes

[1] Ian Flanagan, "Thomas Kinsella: An Interview," *Metre*, No.2 (Spring 1997) 108–15.

[2] Thomas Kinsella, "Westland Row," CP, 60.

[3] Thomas Kinsella, *A Dublin Documentary* (Dublin: O'Brien Press, 2006).

[4] *A Dublin Documentary*, 69 (henceforth, DD).

[5] Seamus Heaney, "Personal Helicon," *Open Ground: Selected Poems 1966–1996* (New York: Farrar, Straus and Giroux, 1998), 14.

[6] Heaney, "The Forge," *Open Ground*, 20.

[7] William Wordsworth, *The Two-Part Prelude of 1799*. First Part, line 122. Jonathan Wordsworth, M.H. Abrams and Stephen Gill, eds., *The Prelude, 1799, 1805, 1850* (New York: Norton, 1974), 4.

[8] Donatella Abate Badin, "From 'An Interview with Thomas Kinsella,'" Special Issue: Thomas Kinsella, *Irish University Review* 31, no. 1 (Spring/Summer 2001): 114; originally published in *European English Messenger* 8, no. 1 (1999).

[9] Susan Stewart, *On Longing: Narratives of the Miniature, the Gigantic, the Souvenir and the Collection* (Durham and London: Duke UP, 1993), 66–68.

[10] See Sigmund Freud, *The Uncanny*, ed. Hugh Haughton (London: Penguin, 2004).

[11] CP, 169.

[12] Ian Flanagan, "Thomas Kinsella: An Interview."

[13] CP, 50.

[14] Thomas Kinsella, "The Divided Mind," in *Irish Poets in English*, ed. Seán Lucy (Cork: Mercier Press, 1972), 208–9.

[15] DD, 8.

[16] Brian John, *Reading the Ground: The Poetry of Thomas Kinsella* (Washington, DC: Catholic University of America Press, 1996), 128.

[17] CP, 102.

[18] CP, 98.

[19] C. G. Jung and C. Kerenyi, *Science of Mythology: Essays on the Divine-Child and the Mysteries of Eleusis*, trans. R. F. C. Hull (London: Routledge, 1951), 95.

[20] CP, 99.

[21] CP, 36.

[22] Daniel O'Hara, "An Interview with Thomas Kinsella," *Contemporary Poetry* 4, no. 1 (1981), 16; Derval Tubridy, *Thomas Kinsella: The Peppercanister Poems* (Dublin: University College Dublin Press, 2001).

[23] Peter Denman, "Significant Elements: 'Songs of the Psyche' and 'Her Vertical Smile,'" Special Issue: Thomas Kinsella, *Irish University Review* 31, no. 1 (Spring/Summer 2001): 109.

[24] Gaston Bachelard, *The Poetics of Space*, trans. Maria Jolas and with a New Foreword by John R. Stilgoe (Boston: Beacon Press, 1994), xxxvi.

[25] Bachelard, *The Poetics of Space*, xxxvii, 4.

[26] CP, 173.

[27] Carl Jung, *Memories, Dreams, Reflections*, trans. Richard and Clara Winston (London: Collins, 2019), 14, 37.

[28] CP, 108.

[29] Gerald Dawe, "Blood and Family: Thomas Kinsella," in *Against Piety: Essays in Irish Poetry* (Belfast: Lagan Press, 1995), 122.

[30] Johns, *Reading the Ground* (Washington, DC: Catholic University of America Press, 1996), 40.

[31] Tubridy, *The Peppercanister Poems*, 164.

[32] Bachelard, *The Poetics of Space*, 9.

CHAPTER THREE

Kinsella's Dublin

GERARD SMYTH

After Swift, Dublin has two laureates, Joyce and Kinsella.
—James Liddy

After Joyce, any writer seeking to place Dublin as a central component in their work faced a challenge. With *Dubliners* and *Ulysses* Joyce had devoured the very fabric of the city, had sucked its marrow, leaving little or nothing for those who came after him. Or so it might have seemed until the poet Thomas Kinsella succeeded—and brilliantly—in placing many of the city's landmarks and something of its character and essence as significant co-ordinates in his poetry. Joyce's most recent biographer Gordan Bowker sees the writer as someone who was "riveted and possessed . . . by the Dublin of his youth."[1] That other Dubliner, Kinsella, seems similarly "possessed" in the many poems that retrieve from memory the city of his first and defining experiences. He stands pre-eminent among the writers who have given Dublin to the world.

The poet's urban imagination matches and mirrors Joyce's in many ways, and for both writers, it was the city that sparked their artistic consciousness. This is everywhere evident in Joyce, and in Kinsella, the Dublin locations and backdrops giving charge to many of his major poems and sequences.[2] Neither writer allowed himself to be aesthetically circumscribed by his local boundaries or the local quotidian, but instead saw within those boundaries possibilities for expansion into more universal themes and the opportunity for a wider discourse. Thus, what we find in the work of both writers is that local forces and perceptions are shifted and extended into much wider frames of reference. The observation by Padraic Colum that Joyce had decided to be "as local as a hedge-poet"[3] is equally true of the Kinsella whose work is rooted in his Dublin origins and whose discernment of local character began among family and neighbors. In these Dublin poems Kinsella reveals exactly the same quality that Colum noted in Joyce, namely, that "only the things that have been encountered day after day in the same definite place can be given with their own atmosphere, their own motion."[4]

Looking back at poems that evoke the world and atmosphere of his childhood, Kinsella himself had made a corresponding statement recognizing the importance of his own "definite place":

> I had been wondering at the insistence of certain subjects: detailed memories of random places and happenings, gestures and voices, distinct as though they were there. A phrase heard only once, a glimpse through a doorway that would never go away, always part of my daily thoughts, with these insistent memories it was not enough to leave them as recorded memories. There was a need to put them in intense words—words that would try to remake the memory and my response so as to make it possible always to re-experience the exact memory and the response.[5]

While Joyce, in a letter to his publisher in May 1906, states that he chose the city as the scene for his short stories because it "seemed to be the centre of paralysis," for Kinsella, Dublin was "the umpteenth city of confusion," according to his journey poem "Phoenix Park." However, as he recalled on the occasion when he was granted the Freedom of the City of Dublin in 2007, it also "gave many important things their first shape and content for me." Those "important things" infiltrated his voice and established him as a poet having a close affinity with his native city, one who has delved deeply into the "rich reality" of its history, its buildings, and its people, who, according to Kinsella, were "happy to be where they were."[6] He discovered a city in which "one age can be peeled away to reveal another" and was fascinated by it.[7] That fascination with time and the city is particularly evident in the Peppercanister sequences *The Messenger* (1978), *St Catherine's Clock* (1987), and *The Pen Shop* (1997). In these, and other poems, the city reveals its past to the poet's observant eye.

Dublin has continually entered into the particulars of Kinsella's poetry, especially his inner-city world of Inchicore, Kilmainham, James's Street, and the nearby River Liffey; places where he first found his bearings and out of which he remembered "many things of importance happening to me for the first time,"[8] all of which were hoarded in his young imagination, put aside in the memory vault. In his brief but revealing statement of thanks for his Freedom of the City honor, Kinsella looked back to the role of that childhood setting in words that explain his adherence to the local life in so many of the Dublin-focused poems:

> I have tried over the years to get my findings in these areas recorded distinctly, as I remembered them: so that anyone who might be interested would know exactly what I meant; and even share some of these experiences—I believe that is one of the things art is for.[9]

In essence, the poet became an artistic custodian of the urban topography of his childhood and of the virtues of that childhood, all of which would become central to and vividly represented and evoked in the work of the mature poet.

Kinsella's titles signal the autobiographical tendencies in much of the poetry and its Dublin *dinnseanchas*: "Baggot Street Deserta," "Phoenix Park," "The Liffey Hill," "St Catherine's Clock," "38 Phoenix Street," "Irwin Street," "Model School, Inchicore," "The Pen Shop," and those places that perhaps only the locals might have been familiar with, such as "Cromwell's Quarters," "the Furry Glen," and the "the Robbers' Den," the latter of which also was known to Austin Clarke, who mentions it in *Mnemosyne Lay in Dust* as "the Robbers' Cave / Beyond Kilmainham." Like Kavanagh's Monaghan poems, the use of place-names and landmarks gives these poems added voltage. While Joyce might have needed a copy of Thom's directory of 1904 beside him to guide his construction of Leopold Bloom's itinerary, Kinsella's topographical reference points seem ingrained in the memory, part of his DNA. The city first enters his work somewhat obliquely in his early portrait of the artist, "Baggot Street Deserta," from *Another September* (1958). Away from his working-class roots, or perhaps freed from them, the apprentice poet making his way in the world in more cosmopolitan environs was experiencing an aesthetic reorientation "in the quiet of my attic" and absorbing a vastly different urban atmosphere. The Scottish poet Douglas Dunn recalled that on his first visit to Dublin in 1963 the effect of this poem compelled him to seek out Baggot Street to complete his appreciation of the poem, much as Joycean pilgrims once did in making their way to Leopold Bloom's fictional northside residence at 7 Eccles Street. Dunn describes it as a "poem of the nocturnal window, a poem of the room and of solitude."[10] The restless young poet (Kinsella) is very much located in the city in this poem but keeping his distance from it, sequestered in "the quiet of my attic" and contemplating what lies beyond, directing his gaze at "a crawling arch of stars." Yet the city's waft was making its way into both his physical and psychological space, making him aware that "A mile away the river toils / Its buttressed fathoms out to sea."

"First Night," a much later memory poem from *Marginal Economy*,[11] recalls "Baggot Street Deserta," if only in faint echoes. Though its intention is different, this later poem evokes a similar atmosphere and perhaps the same sense of ennui in the voice of the speaker-poet. The will to work is again "laid aside," but on this occasion there is no wish to stay sequestered as the poet is drawn by the seductive "lights of the bar opposite," and the company of a stranger there who is central to the purpose of the poem. The mood of introspection that overtakes the poet in the earlier poem is replaced in "First Night" with a convivial engagement with the world beyond his window. Nevertheless, it does capture a recognizable and broody Kinsella moment of contemplation when the poet looks out "across the old roofs, back toward the edge of the city / the new slum I had just left. . . ." This "new slum" would seem to refer to one of the city's newly-built suburban housing schemes to which the Kinsella family had moved from the inner city. It appears to be the one residence or Dublin location that the poet eschewed in his work and for which he appears to have had no great affection. In "Baggot Street Deserta," the poet is conscious of the heads of dreamers in their "Dublin beds," and similarly "First Night" has him thinking about other existences. Peering down at a "night street . . . absorbing a new view of the world," he becomes aware of a condition that besets many urban dwellers: "City loneliness."

While the long ruminative perambulation-poem "Nightwalker" traces a suburban journey of deep introspection and close observation, it is perhaps "Phoenix Park"—from the same 1968 Dolmen collection—that marks a Dublin occasion of great significance in his early work and identifies Kinsella as a poet who would follow Joyce in attending to the minutiae of city life. Here he becomes the recorder of moments when the surroundings of the parkland become emblematic in the personal life of the poet. The naming of its landmarks is essential to the evocative power of the poem: *Chapelizod Gate, St Mary's Hospital, the Furry Glen, Knockmaroon Gate, Strawberry Beds.* As the poet with his wife Eleanor continue their journey through the park, having stopped in "a back bar in Lucan," the poet's more personal places holding family associations, places that would become familiar and pivotal in later work, make their first call:

> The road divides and we can take either way,
> Etcetera. The Phoenix Park; Inchicore,
> Passing Phoenix Street – the ways are one, sweet choise,[12]

"Phoenix Park" is not the only example in *Nightwalker and Other Poems* of Kinsella as a definitive Dublin poet following the Joycean path. Maurice Harmon has pointed to the Joycean technique of the title poem, the meditation-walk poem "Nightwalker," remarking that "some sections of the poem resemble the stream of consciousness technique used in certain parts of *Ulysses*." Harmon observes the same fluidity of movement in both *Ulysses* and "Nightwalker" through incidents, memories, ideas, and images, and he notes that, "as the walker approaches the Martello tower in Sandycove he appeals to the prose master James Joyce rather than the master poet W. B. Yeats."[13] Similarly, Gerald Dawe echoes Liddy's bracketing of Kinsella with Swift and Joyce in his commentary on *Nightwalker*, pointing out that "In tackling such intransigent material, Thomas Kinsella calls into being an invigorating alignment of Swift and Joyce, where the latter's support is summoned:

> Watcher in the tower, be with me now
> At your parapet, above the glare of the lamps.

Turn your milky spectacle on the sea
Unblinking; cock your ear.[14]

Apart from this invocation to the master, the kind of attention to detail and precise etching that Joyce demonstrates in his Dublin narratives is also evident throughout Kinsella's many poems evoking scenes from childhood, which are often presented through recall of memories of encounters with older generation family members. In "Ancestor," the grandmother figure in her Bow Lane setting holds a stark presence: "Her profile against the curtains / was old, and dark like a hunting bird's." On her death-bed, a dying grandmother's grey hair is remembered in "Tear" as being "loosened out like a young woman's / all over the pillow, / mixed with the shadows / criss-crossing her forehead." That far reach into memory is worth recalling, for example, in the context of the poem "Model School, Inchicore," in which the poet returns with great exactitude to an extraordinary Joycean moment of self-knowledge and self-awareness, the beginning of self-identity in his young mind:

In the second school we had Mr Browne.
He had white teeth in his brown man's face.

He stood in front of the blackboard
and chalked a white dot.

'We are going to start
decimals.'

I am going to know
everything.[15]

There is the intriguing possibility that both Kinsella and Joyce looked at the same blackboard in O'Connell Christian Brothers Schools in North

Richmond Street. While Joyce was famously educated by the Jesuits in Clongowes and later Belvedere College, he briefly attended O'Connell school in 1903 with his brother Stanislaus. Kinsella was a student there in the 1940s.

Among these poems of remembrance is "38 Phoenix Street" from *One* (1974). Viewed from the vantage point of time, Kinsella here revisits deeply embedded scenes from childhood, which take the reader into a personal psychic terrain, beginning with that breakthrough moment of encounter with the wider world outside the sanctuary of home, a moment of entry into knowledge that reminds us how vital the poet's "local watchfulness" has been to creating the kind of attention we find in his poetry: "Look. / I was lifted up / past rotten brick weeds / to look over the wall." As Andrew Fitzsimons reminds us, Kinsella visits and revisits this particular site, his first nurturing ground, in *Notes from the Land of the Dead* (1972) and throughout the Peppercanister series, particularly in *The Messenger* and *St Catherine's Clock*. Citing "Dick King" as an early poem containing "the first indication of where Kinsella's work eventually finds vital and nourishing material,"[16] he quotes from an early draft held in the Kinsella papers in Emory University that gives us a Dublin scene that could almost come straight out of a short story in *Dubliners*:

> Around the fountain fifty years ago
> My cold-eyed father with his schoolboy's stare
> Watches their black cabs careering, watches them throw
> Their bowler hats in the water, and the bare
> Heads burning with Saturday's night bacchanal
> Poke through the windows, shouting on the horses.
> The wheels on the cobbles died . . .[17]

The poem "Phoenix Street" demonstrates how Kinsella can go back to retrieve and reclaim even what might appear to be the most banal of domestic details: "banisters, draped with / trousers and pullovers," as well as a reference to that vital logbook to be found in most working-class Dublin homes of the period, "the insurance collection book / in a fat elastic band." He never fails to pick out such minutiae as a resource of importance, giving them a primary place in the Dublin poems. As a recorder of such random detail, he is, like Joyce, fastidious in what he coaxes from memory:

> Over the parapet of the bridge
> at the end of Granny and Granda's
> the brown water bubbled and poured
> over the stones and tin cans in the Camac,
> down by the back of Aunty Josie's.[18]

The shift away from the more traditional forms of his first books, poems that were perhaps subservient to the influence of Auden, to the loosening of language, plainer speech, and starker rhetoric found in *New Poems* (1973), coincided with an awakening of Kinsella's Dublin memory and its empowering role in some of the keynote poems of that volume's opening section, *Notes from the Land of the Dead*. Recognizing the close connection between memory and imagination, one folding into the other, he tells us in "Hen Woman": "I feed upon it still, as you see; / there is no end to that which, not understood, / may yet be hoarded in the imagination." From what was hoarded in the imagination, Kinsella has drawn his memory map of the specific Dublin places of his origin and authentic self: The High Road, Irwin Street, The Liffey Hill, Bow Lane. These retrievals from memory also generated a liberation of the poet's imagination, a refreshing of his inventiveness. In such places on his map of the city "A few ancient faces / Detach and begin to circle. . . ." Though the mood is often dark, closed in—a child forced to enter the den of a dying grandmother, the sight of "old knuckles"—the power of memory in these poems elicits the kind of honest and clear description that became a hallmark of Kinsella's style, his insistence on keeping the record straight when it comes to the particulars. He shares with Joyce a determination to be authentic in his representation of the city and those of its citizens he commemorates, as well as the places that became part of his inheritance.

Dublin is also intrinsically linked with another of Kinsella's major themes: family, or "blood and family" as the title of one of the Peppercanister publications more emphatically declares it.[19] His own private world and the city are bound together, and in much of his writing his creative power seems directly derived from that relationship. His Dublin childhood, one he seems to have inhabited with great intensity and closeness of attention, has yielded the materials for many of the poet's psychic explorations of a sense of self. Kinsella's handling of this autobiographical material, his reclamation of a personal past, has always been meticulous in its scraping away of the layers to reach the most vital components, to fulfill the task of what Adrienne Leavy describes as "his life-long preoccupation with both eliciting order, and imposing order, on the direct experience of life."[20] In poems such as "The High Road," "38 Phoenix Street," and "Model School Inchicore," Kinsella recreates the abundance of detail that caught his attention as a young and perceptive observer. The comment by Flannery O'Connor—that we have gathered enough material by the age of eight for a lifetime of writing—comes to mind when reading these poems of his inner-city childhood. The child's dreamworld, in which he appears to have comfortably felt at home, and the emergence of his acute urban consciousness seem to have come together in a way that would later appeal to his artistic instinct and benefit the work of the mature poet.

My first encounter with his work, in a Dublin 8 library where the poet himself had been a book borrower in his youth, presented me with a revelation. To come across his poem "Dick King" in his second major collection *Downstream* (1962) triggered a moment of liberation in my understanding of what a poem can be and can achieve, and into what territory it can fruitfully venture. This was a poem of images and references quite unlike the school text poetry that relocated my imagination to Xanadu, Dover Beach, and Tintern Abbey, but set firmly in the actualities of the Dublin world just outside the library window, part of the living day, conjuring an immediately recognizable series of images: the bell in James's Street could be heard from my classroom, the fountain was a familiar place of rendezvous, and the rain on the cobbles was as Dublin as a coddle dinner. Poetry announced itself as something to be found on my own streets. The experience and my feelings of response were not unlike Kinsella's own when he first opened the pages of *Dubliners*: "Above all, finding Joyce's *Dubliners*—the opening paragraph of 'Araby,' electrifying in its accuracy and immediacy. I had been there, every day . . ."[21] Joyce's scene-setting depiction—"North Richmond Street, being blind, was a quiet street except at the hour when the Christian Brothers School set the boys free"—mirrored Kinsella's own lived-in experience of that area of the city. The immediacy of "Dick King" came to me, particularly in the topographical descriptions: I had been there every day. Since first opening that library book to discover "Dick King," I have again and again heard in the pages of Kinsella his utterly recognizable natural register of the Dublin dialect which W. J. McCormack characterized as Kinsella's "uncanny preservation of a Dublin idiom, which seems at times ink running through a gravelly accent."[22] This accent, which is not only gravelly but sonorous, is vital to the authority of his poetic voice. Whenever I heard Kinsella's speaking voice it took me back among the remembered childhood voices I heard in the parlor and on the street corners of my own Dublin in the 1950s and 60s.

Dublin provided the poet not only with the materials of memory and imagery but with modes of expression that deal directly with the particulars and the facts. Perhaps because he once was a public servant trained in the Department of Finance he developed to become a poet of precision when it came to assembling these poetic materials. The speaker of *St Catherine's Clock* not only inhales "the granite lamplight" but also the vivid vernacular of his native city. The texture of his verse owes much to that vernacular. As Dennis O'Driscoll has reminded us, when childhood memory is evoked it is often in language into which "everyday Dublin phrases are woven equally wittily and authentically."[23] For example, in "A Hand of Solo" the speaker's grandmother admonishes him thus: "'Shut the kitchen door, child of grace. / Come here to me. / Come here to your old grandmother.'" That familiar endearment, *child of grace*, rings true to my Dublin ears. In an interview with Kinsella, John F. Deane noted that the voice in his translations from the Irish "had a strongly Dublin ring to it, a directness and sharpness."[24] Those latter qualities are hinted at as being the characteristics of the "formidable women" of his childhood, celebrated in *A Dublin Documentary*, who managed small shops in their houses in Basin Lane and Bow Lane and who were the strongest early influencers in his life. Thomas McCarthy has described this closed community as Kinsella's "hermetic space; a place of Guinness workers and desolate civil servants, but also a space that seems to remain behind the locked gates of St. James's Brewery. One can never enter this space without an invitation."[25]

Kinsella is aware that his childhood working-class districts of Inchicore and Kilmainham were not only populated by native Dubliners, but also by others forced there from rural communities by economic need. Among them, Dick King, that fondly-remembered neighbor and man of toil, had to quit his familiar "salt seaboard ... its rock and rain" and settle in more alien urban terrain where "... his second soul was born / In the clangour of the iron sheds, / The hush of the late horn." That powerful depiction of a countryman leaving his west of Ireland roots to find work in Dublin expresses a common situation in post-independence Ireland. In "Ritual of Departure" the same awareness of the city's role as the place of destiny and settlement for many whose origins are elsewhere in rural Ireland is acknowledged: "And their children's children vanished in the city lanes." While the "upright man" Dick King worked on the nearby Great Southern Railway (many of the homes in The Ranch in Inchicore were built for railway workers), the poet's own grandfather had moved from the hill country of Tinahealy in County Wicklow to work in the Guinness brewery.

The poet's idealistic father, the subject of *The Messenger*, also worked for Guinness and became active in the labor movement during his tenure. That citadel of Old Dublin, the Guinness brewery in James's Street, is a dominant landmark on the poet's first skyline and stands at the heart of this powerful portrait of the artist's father. The sequence combines a moving elegy with searing anger in its portrayal of the life of the poet's father, whose trials included conflict with the Guinness establishment on matters of principle as well as other "hammerblows." David Lynch is one of many critics who reads *The Messenger* as a key poem out of the poet's memory of a "Dublin urban experience,"[26] and more than any other of his Dublin poems it evokes and illuminates Kinsella's working class identity. The qualities the son sees in the father, a champion of certain ideals, appear to have been pivotal in the character-forming of the poet who as a child witnessed his father "on an election lorry . . . shouting about the Blueshirts" and making a protest exit from Mass in a local church. Again this biographical and personal material emanates from home ground: the poet returning to scenes "outside the Black Lion, in Inchicore" and in the church of the "Oblate Fathers" (also in Inchicore).

The poet of "Nightwalker"—and later, *The Pen Shop*—achieves what poet and translator Jennie Feldman sees in the work of the Parisian flaneur poet Jacques Réda: an "equipoise between internal and external awareness."[27] Kinsella makes for a less than leisurely and somewhat unsettling flaneur in "Nightwalker," eventually reaching and leading his readers to his "Sea of Disappointment," while delivering his Joycean analytical discourse on the political and social changes he senses taking place in national identity and values. The same rage and indignation at the failures of the disappointing and flawed Republic and what he sees as betrayal of the ideals of its revolutionary founders is voiced in "A Country Walk." Rage and indignation surface again in later poems but in a particular Dublin context: the destruction of the city's heritage and the remnants of its past. In the reflective poem "One Fond Embrace" Kinsella's anger is renewed by the erasure of the site of Dublin's Liffeyside Viking origins on Wood Quay. His "umpteenth city of confusion" has become the "bungled city" and the blame for that is squarely placed on the shoulders of "our city fathers" whose action is seen by the poet as the creation of an enduring monument to themselves, an office car park sunk deep in history. The admonishment continues:

> Invisible speculators, urinal architects,
> and the Corporation flourishing their approvals
> in potent, compliant dance;[28]

The poet's role, with other artists and campaigners, in the onsite protests and sit-ins against the building of the City Council Headquarters on the site is evoked in the short poem "Night Conference, Wood Quay: 6 June 1979." City officials are berated as "white-cuffed marauders" in an image that conflates their wonton destruction of an important historical site with the destruction wrought by their Viking ancestors.

Referring to the poems in *Notes from the Land of the Dead* that emerged out of childhood memory, Kinsella has declared that "the poetry is set mainly in inner-city Dublin."[29] However, those excavations of time and place did not exhaust his fascination with the city or his use of it as subject material. Other "Dublins" would enter his imaginative space, not least what he considered to be his "second roots," the home he set up with Eleanor in Percy Place that "faced down the Georgian vista of Mount Street, and south Merrion Square, toward Government Buildings. The same vista, in the other direction, and ending perfectly in the Peppercanister Church."[30] Like Joyce, whose youth was spent moving from house to house, location to location as the family fortune waned, Kinsella too experienced transfer from place to place: Phoenix Street in the Inchicore area known as The Ranch, later to what he describes in *A Dublin Documentary* as "short stays in strange houses—one of them in Irwin Street," close to relatives in Bow Lane and then a "tiny house in Basin Lane," adjacent to the Guinness Brewery. His "second roots," not many miles but still a world away from working-class Dublin 8—the Grand Canal replacing the River Camac, the bell on Haddington Road instead of the chimes of St. James's Bell—opened a new vista into which the poet directed his scrutinizing gaze. *Poems from City Centre* (1990) articulates the impact of the shift into a cityscape far different to the one in which he grew up, though even at such a remove from them he cannot quite get away from his origins, telling us in "The Bell" that the ringing sounds of "The Bell on Haddington Road" were "audible in Inchicore." Similarly, in "The Back Lane" he notes his awareness of "the slovenliness of the City and its lesser works." The milieu of these poems takes Kinsella into a different world to the one in which he spent his childhood and formative adolescence—the brewery and railway workers give way to the "Administrator," in the poem of that title, who is "Accustomed to property and its management" as well as "people from the new Canal Hotel," observed as they boarded “their fat, fashionable barges.” And here by the waters of the canal, Kinsella finds a “nighttown” that matches Joyce’s:

A pair of shades. One, in a short skirt,
stirred herself; the other, in black leatherette,
waited back against the railings,
the tip of her cigarette red. Her eyes
and her oyster mouth wet to my thoughts.[31]

In “The Stable” we encounter a practice that lasted in some areas of the city until the late 1960s: the housing of horses in back lane stables. There is a note of lament in his recollection of this feature of local life coming to an end when in the poem, O’Keeffe, a custodian of this horse-keeping tradition, gets sick and can no longer care for his horse:

the wife and the helpful son-in-law
manoeuvred it out for the last time.
She waited in the stable, crying.
They both knew well the kind of hold
they were handing over with the key.[32]

Another poem from the same zone of Kinsella’s city life that is shadowed by the erosion of old ways is “The Back Lane” (also from *Poems from City Centre*). This is the poem in which Kinsella invokes the Lord to “grant us a local watchfulness”—a watchfulness, of family, neighborhood, and the wider universe, that has yielded much of the local knowledge informing and augmenting his poetry—as well as giving it the “bite and sting” that Kafka demanded from literature. This local watchfulness and knowledge is pertinent to a poem such as “The Stranger” in which the figure, “a clerk from somewhere in the area,” is repeatedly observed by the poet “crossing over from Mount Street,” and “once in Baggot Street.” The passing figure, odd and mysterious as many are in the poems of Kinsella, derives his memorability because of the Dublin settings and situations in which the poet encountered him.

The river that toils "a mile away" in "Baggot Street Deserta," the same "Anna Livia Plurabelle" that appears so often in Joyce, winds its way through a later Joycean inspired sequence, *The Pen Shop* (1997). Here, the river Liffey, "dirty and disturbed," comes "From Islandbridge. Under Kingsbridge" with "the black currents turning among each other / among the black piles at the lower Brewery gates." Kinsella's description of "the loaded barge settling itself on the river / and starting downstream" bears a Joycean echo (for example, when the young protagonists in the *Dubliners* short story "An Encounter" catch sight of the same Liffey barges as they signal "from far away by their curls of woolly smoke"), and the Liffey scenes in this poem are also a reminder of the river's familial association. His grandfather worked on the same brewery barges that carried barrels of porter to the docks where the Guinness vessel, "the Lady Patricia moored beyond butt Bridge," waited to transport the dark brew across the Irish Sea.

Routes and the journey-time they afford for introspection have been important to Kinsella's searching curiosity. In *The Pen Shop* the poet's city meanderings are presented as a scrupulously structured itinerary through "the heart of the Hibernian metropolis," as Joyce called his Dublin. An itinerary that surely must now echo with the poet's footsteps:

> Down Dame Street, by Thomas Davis slack and sad.
> By the Castle; and the Fountain; and the Forty Steps;
>
> toward Kilmainham, heading Westward.
> Past Inchicore.
> Toward the thought of places

beyond your terminus.
By the pale Western shore where I have seen
the light of cities under the far horizon.

I crossed over, more calm
under the eyes of Burke and Goldsmith.
To the corner of Grafton Street,

the shops at the far end opening towards the South:
toward Wicklow; toward Wexford, and the company of women.
Toward Finistere.[33]

This extended sequence, which reverses in part the trajectory of Leopold Bloom's wandering through Dublin in *Ulysses*, follows a pathway not only through the central cityscape but also through moments in history that are identified in the statuary figures encountered along the way including "Sir John Gray, of *The Freeman's Journal*," Daniel O'Connell, and Smith O'Brien, who is "Dead thirty years, to the day, / when Mr Bloom unclasped his hands in soft / acknowledgement."

The poet's own "established personal places" are perhaps most explicitly mapped out in *St Catherine's Clock*, a sequence in which Kinsella again points to the connection between history and place through the act of naming and commentary on scenes from history: the execution of Robert Emmet in front of St. Catherine's Church on Thomas Street and the assassination of Lord Kilwarden, Ireland's Lord Chief Justice, in the same street during the 1803 rebellion are key moments in the sequence. The poem interweaves these historical events with family memory, or as Kinsella described it, "family history and some of the bloody history of the early nineteenth century are tangled together in that poem."[34] Here once more we enter territory that is at the core of his imagination, places that belong not only on the map of Dublin but within the poet's own psyche and have been central to his preoccupations. If the clock on the Ballast Office, as the Stephen of Joyce's *Stephen Hero* announces, "is capable of epiphany," so too is the St. Catherine's Clock and its surrounding byways and landmarks in the Kinsella poem:

> Past the Watch House and Watling Street,
> beyond St James's Gate, a pale blue
> divides downhill into thin air
>
> on a distant dream
> of Bow Lane
> and Basin Lane.[35]

James Liddy has noted that Kinsella possesses "a late great style, and it is an urban one like Joyce's."[36] Liddy, a fellow Dolmen Press poet and an astute observer of his contemporaries, recognized some defining qualities in Kinsella's work: "He is an introspective challenger of depth, an anxious recorder of interior space, an inhabitant of native Catholic tensions laced with the appropriate fears."[37] He is also, as O' Driscoll reminded us, "a true dissident: obstinate, inconvenient, discomforting, essential,"[38] one who has never been afraid to challenge either himself or his readers, as the poem "At the Head Table" tells us:

> . . . I have devoted
> my life, my entire career,
> to the avoidance of affectation,
> the way of entertainment[39]

Terence Brown has pointed out in his essay "Dublin in Twentieth-Century Writing" that for both Joyce and Yeats the city "is an element in a debate about the nature of Irish life."[40] Kinsella's portrayals of the city serve a similar purpose. He has been foremost among those post-Independence writers who, as Brown put it, incorporated Dublin into their writing "as something more than a setting for their work," and instead treated the city "as a subject which allows them to reflect on the nature of the Irish mind and imagination." Perhaps Kinsella's task or purpose as a writer—corresponding somewhat with Joyce's—has been, as he revealed in an interview with Donatella Abbate Badin, "to preserve what I can and give it a longer hold in life."[41] His overall achievement makes him not only a quintessential Dublin writer but also one who, on a wider canvass, has engaged in the most profound inquiry into and speculation about the human condition and its attendant ordeals. In attempting to fathom these ordeals, Kinsella has in so much of his work remained close to home, beginning with that compassionate gesture that was his poem "Dick King," in memory of his childhood neighbor who "always seemed to be there: a friend of the family, a protector of my unformed feelings."[42]

In tracing the Dublin aspects of his work, Kinsella's comments on the later poems of his fellow Dublin poet, Austin Clarke, strike me as something he might have felt about many of his own poems, that they were "written in the key of reminiscence, of autobiographical-summing up, a developing autobiography of ideas, feelings, significant scraps, the darts and twists of life."[43] In recording so much of the Dublin life of his family, as well recognizing his roots and the laboring classes of his old neighborhood, Kinsella has fulfilled the poet's duty to rescue what might be discarded or forgotten. The accumulation of local knowledge—another Joycean trait—that was part of the poet's inheritance has been well matched by his vitality of mind in recording that knowledge and turning it to art. But more than that the poems that are weighted by their Dublin dimension—and Dublin *dinnseanchais*—show how "Kinsella's archaeology of self, family and nation is a powerful reminder why, if the Joycean mantle is anyone's in Irish poetry, it is his."[44]

*

THOMAS KINSELLA'S DUBLIN

in memory

We sat in the half-dark, never noticed dusk seeping in
from the Booterstown marsh.
We had a list of places to get through—
some of them gone from the map.
One of them, you said, was dust at your feet
when you returned with a friend but couldn't find
the beginning or end of Basin Lane
or the harbour where the barges once came with barley
to leave at the brew master's gate.
Further away, the old school was still there,
as solid as when you were learning to read
new words chalked on a blackboard.
So too was *The High Road* and *The Forty Steps*
where Cromwell's army slept
during a pause in the conquest.
In boyhood you found adventure ground:
a bridge, a river, brown water that *bubbled*
and poured at the end of Bow Lane.

Blood ran from the shambles, a pigyard
had troughs full of neighbourhood slops.
At the back of the shop where card players met
an ancestor kept to her chamber—
(all this stayed in the memory and would not go away).
To get to city centre you had to walk the broad street
of history's defeats, past Emmet's *ghost scaffold*.
These were the places where first things happened.
Along the way you met the watchful and the watched,
and read the ground for local knowledge.

Notes

[1] Gordon Bowker, *James Joyce: A New Biography* (New York: Farrar, Straus and Giroux, 2012), 6.

[2] See, for example, poems such as "Baggot Street Deserta," "Dick King," "Phoenix Park," "Nightwalker," "The High Road," "Irwin Street," "Ely Place," "38 Phoenix Street," "Model School Inchicore," "Phoenix Street," "Bow Lane," "The Bell," "The Back Lane," "The Stranger," "First Night" and the Peppercanister sequences, *The Messenger*, *St Catherine's Clock*, *One Fond Embrace*, and *The Pen Shop* in Thomas Kinsella, *Collected Poems: 1956–2001* (Winston-Salem, NC: Wake Forest UP, 2006).

[3] Padraic Colum, introduction to *Anna Livia Plurabelle* by James Joyce (New York: Crosby Gaige, 1928).

[4] Colum, introduction.

[5] "Thomas Kinsella in conversation with Adrienne Leavy," *Reading Ireland: The Little Magazine* 11 (Winter 2019), also in *New Hibernia Review* 24, no. 4 (Spring 2020).

[6] Thomas Kinsella, "Address on Occasion of being Awarded the Freedom of the City of Dublin," May 2007.

[7] James Liddy, "George Moore's Dublin" in *Perspective*, ed. Janet Egleson Dunleavy (Dublin: Colin Smyth, 1984), also in James Liddy, *On Irish Literature and Identities* ed. Eamonn Wall (Dublin: Arlen House, 2013).

[8] Kinsella, *A Dublin Documentary* (Dublin: O'Brien Press, 2006), 8.

[9] Kinsella, "Address on Occasion of Being Awarded the Freedom of the City of Dublin."

[10] Douglas Dunn, "Baggot Street Deserta," Thomas Kinsella Special Issue, *Tracks* 7 (1987), 14–18.

[11] Peppercanister 24 (2006), *Late Poems* (Carcanet Press, 2013).

[12] CP, 92.

[13] Maurice Harmon, "Thomas Kinsella: Poet of Many Voices" in *Maurice Harmon, Selected Essays*, ed. Barbara Brown (Dublin: Irish Academic Press, 2006), 159–177.

[14] Gerald Dawe, *In the Violent Zone, the World as Province: Selected Prose, 1980–2008* (Belfast: The Lagan Press, 2009). Kinsella revised this stanza in his *Collected Poems* to read as follows: "Watcher in the tower, / Be with me now. Turn your milky spectacles / On the sea, unblinking." CP, 80.

[15] CP, 221.

[16] Andrew Fitzsimons, *The Sea of Disappointment: Thomas Kinsella's Pursuit of the Real* (Dublin: University College Dublin Press, 2008), 49.

[17] Kinsella Papers, box 2, folder 27.

[18] CP, 103.

[19] *Blood and Family* (Oxford: Oxford UP, 1988), collects together the following five Peppercanisters in one volume: *Songs of the Psyche* (Dublin: Peppercanister Press, 1985); *Her Vertical Smile* (Dublin: Peppercanister Press, 1985); *Out of Ireland* (Dublin: Peppercanister Press, 1987); *St Catherine's Clock* (Dublin: Peppercanister Press, 1987) and *One Fond Embrace* (Dublin: Peppercanister Press, 1988).

[20] Adrienne Leavy, "An Interview with Thomas Kinsella," *New Hibernia Review* 15, no. 2 (Summer 2011), 136.

[21] Michael Smith, "Thomas Kinsella in interview with Michael Smith," *Poetry Ireland Review* 75, (Winter 2002/2003), 110.

[22] W. J. McCormack, "Politics or Community: Crux of Thomas Kinsella's Aesthetic Development," Thomas Kinsella Special Issue, *Tracks* 7 (1987): 61–77.

[23] Dennis O' Driscoll, "His Wit: Humour and Satire in Thomas Kinsella's Poetry," Special Issue: Thomas Kinsella, *Irish University Review* 31, no. 1 (Spring/Summer 2001): 1–18.

[24] John F. Deane, "A Conversation, Dublin, September 1986," Thomas Kinsella Special Issue, *Tracks* 7 (1987): 86–91.

[25] Thomas McCarthy, "Journals, 1974–2014," *New Hibernia Review* 23, no. 3 (Autumn 2019), 28.

[26] David Lynch, *Confronting Shadows: An Introduction to the Poetry of Thomas Kinsella* (Dublin: New Island Books, 2015).

[27] Jennie Feldman, introduction to *Jacques Réda, Treading Lightly: Selected Poems 1961–1975*, trans. Jennie Feldman (Manchester: Carcanet Press, 2005).

[28] CP, 274.

[29] Adam Hanna, "An Interview with Thomas Kinsella," *PN Review* 44, no. 6 (2018): 35.

[30] Kinsella, *A Dublin Documentary*, 90.

[31] CP, 294.

[32] CP, 296.

[33] CP, 326, 327.

[34] John F. Deane, "A Conversation."

[35] CP, 264.

[36] James Liddy, "Nationalist and Worker in the Poetry of Thomas Kinsella and Thomas McCarthy" in *On Irish Literature and Identities*, ed. Eamonn Wall (Dublin: Arlen House, 2013).

[37] James Liddy, "Thomas Kinsella, Freeman of the City of Dublin." Draft lecture sent in correspondence to this writer.

[38] Dennis O'Driscoll, "His Wit: Humour and Satire in Thomas Kinsella's Poetry."

[39] CP, 310.

[40] Terence Brown, "Dublin in Twentieth-Century Writing," *Irish University Review* (Spring 1978), 7–21.

[41] Donatella Abbate Badin, "From 'An interview with Thomas Kinsella,'" Special Issue: Thomas Kinsella, *Irish University Review* 31, no. 1 (Spring/Summer 2001): 113–115.

[42] Kinsella, *A Dublin Documentary*, 17.

[43] Kinsella, "The poetic career of Austin Clarke," in *Prose Occasions 1951–2006*, ed. Andrew Fitzsimons (Machnester: Carcanet Press, 2009).

[44] David Wheatley, "The Dethroned God," *The Guardian*, July 7, 2007.

CHAPTER FOUR

Altered Mass

LANDSCAPE AND LANGUAGE IN THOMAS KINSELLA'S POETRY

MARY O'MALLEY

Thomas Kinsella is one of the great poets of cityscape, of place, but also of landscape, from Ballydavid to the route of the Táin. For many years, I felt that I had only ever seen my own place and the life of the sea in English poetry in the work of Richard Murphy. I recognized the place, and the people, as he recognized the place and people in my own colonized child's sequence from *Where the Rocks Float* (1993). "They weren't that grand," he said to me with that slightly amused look. "They were to me," was all I could say in my defense, but of course he was right, and the fine distinctions of snobbery and degree that held sway in the "Descendency," as we called it, were as foreign to me as I was to them. Yet Murphy gave me a place I recognized in poem after poem, with lines such as "On a patrician evening in Ireland / I was born in the guest room: she delivered me," and he could shift to mimic the local voice so accurately in poems such as "Pat Cloherty's Version of *The Maise*" that Cloherty's lines might well be a quote: "That's the way the sea found her / and the sea never came in / near that mark no more ..." Murphy's mannered poems were, for the most part, successful, and I loved his work in part because I recognized the territory as resembling, and sometimes coinciding, with the place I knew.

Eamonn O'Chonaile, better known as Eddie Bheartla, is a priest in Connemara. He is no longer young, and his parish stretches over many miles of fairly challenging terrain. A local historian and fine folklorist, he sees the nature of place in the way the poet does. He understands its elasticity. Some years back, after the Celtic Tiger came to its catastrophic end, I mentioned to him that his must be a fairly big parish. "Oh getting bigger every day," he said. "From Tir an Fhia to Taiwan, I have parishioners in New York and Carna, in Mexico and Australia." We went on to discuss the new names that had entered the lexicon with the most recent emigrant wave, places such as Beijing, Hong Kong, Cusco, names as familiar in Connemara now as Pittsburgh and Long Island were to me as a child. When I came across Kinsella's *Song of the Night and Other Poems* (1978), I read the poems with a shock of recognition. Philadelphia, with its city roar so reminiscent and so different from the sound of the sea, was a place at once alien and familiar, unknown but not foreign. American cities would never be foreign to the Irish child from a coastal background, if only because we learned our geography from being shown where an aunt or uncle or cousin lived, and asked to find it on the map.

Now in "Song of the Night" it was a city composed mainly of noise, "a skytrain waning in a line of thunder" outside the poet's window. It was still in the next parish, but now I could hear it. This poem is a fine example of soundscape as cityscape, with its telling reference to "... terrible pressure ..." pressing on the reader's eardrums. The auditory quality is one of the defining qualities of place and the lack of rhythm noted in the city's ceaseless noise is one of the striking features of this poem. It prepares us for the final line, the opened atlas, "The Atlantic curved on the world." The line is calming, the sea mother reassuring us. Water, not land, defines this world. The line prepares us for the move back, across the Atlantic to the poet's summer home in South Connemara.

Carraroe was placed up against Philadelphia, logically and without strain. There was no mythic load, no romantic vision. Only Wittgenstein has caught the essence of Connemara so well, when he called it "the last pool of darkness in Europe," although Murphy comes close in his Cleggan poems, most famously "The Cleggan Disaster." Murphy wrote as an outsider who knew the territory well and, insofar as his background allowed, as an insider who made his home in the West for many years, whereas Kinsella's poetic authority renders any such distinction redundant.

"Carraroe" opens quietly: "Our far boundary was Gorumna island / Low on the water . . ." the use of the word "on" giving the sense of floating so essential to that particular landscape, lifting the poem beyond the surface beauty of its quiet description: "On our shore, among a tumble of boulders / on the minced coral . . ." The stanza on the "silvery sand eels" picked up by the poet's children "in wet small palms, in an iodine smell" is like a scene from a film or play, defined as it is by the light of a camping lamp. "Carraroe" is also a love poem to the poet's wife, Eleanor:

> She was standing in a sheltered angle,
> urgent and quiet.
>
> 'Look back.'
>
> The great theatre of Connemara,
> dark.[1]

The poem moves through the quiet summer night, "blazed with child voices," as the couple move to a rocky point where "A new music came on the wind," underscored by "... a soft inner-ear roar / blown off the ocean; a persistent / tympanum double beat ..." This is no pastoral symphony, as a "long horn call" is answered by a curlew overhead, and the poet allows one brief lyric response, "'... hauntingly beautiful ...' Yes!" before shifting, as Connemara does:

A part of the mass
grated and tore, cranking harshly,
and detached and struggled upward
and beat past us ...[2]

to the final note-perfect line: "bat-black, heron slow." There is no myth-making here, but instead, a refreshing acknowledgment of the impenetrable.

Perhaps it is in tone, above all else, that the landscape poems succeed so well. This is not surprising in a poet so well-versed in the tradition—if it is fanciful to suggest that landscape is made pervious to language, it is less so to suggest that the Irish language still sung and spoken along the West coast was pervious to its particular landscape. In "The Shoals Returning," a poem in memory of Gerry Flaherty, a *sean-nós* singer and fisherman from Dingle, the solidity of a big sea is captured in the first few lines, spare as a sung lament:

I dip the oar and lean
Supported and opposed
On the green flesh of a wave.[3]

The imagery is restrained: the sea "swallows / My strength like a stone," and death surfaces "face upward." In the final stanza of this first section of the poem, a fisherman "... stoops and flings out / The body of a cod." Here again is a seascape in flux, an acknowledgment of circularity: a body floats to the surface, a fisherman throws his catch up on the quay. The Atlantic also features prominently in a poem based on the bardic poet, Aogán Ó Rathaille (c. 1675–1729), as he nears the end of his life. In "The Poet Egan O' Rahilly, Homesick in Old Age," the ocean offers no comfort to the ailing poet as the "stony crash" of the "West's rhythmless waves" destroys his sleep. Kinsella leaves nature and landscape alone. He lets it speak for itself. Rereading "Tao and Unfitness at Inistiogue on the River Nore," I wonder if this refusal to romanticize landscape has its roots in a Taoist vision of life. Maurice Harmon's observation on Kinsella's poem is instructive:

> For the Taoists, the universe is a living organism, its woods and rivers infused with a mysterious spirit, its rocks and mountains endowed with a life force. . . . To perceive the stillness, they say, one must cultivate stillness. Kinsella's poem is a parable of such perception, underlined by a sequence of quiet directives, such as 'Move, if you move, like water.'[4]

Kinsella's poems of place and landscape are not bare streets and hills waiting passively like blank canvases for the poet to develop to his purpose, but poems of the inhabited city and country. The litany of his place poems moves with him, from Baggot Street in Dublin through St. Gobnait's Graveyard in Ballyvourney, to Philadelphia in the US and back, places marked by the lives of the people who lived there and those who had gone before:

> *There are established personal places*
> that receive our lives' heat
> and adapt in their mass, like stone.[5]

As Julia Obert has noted, Kinsella's poems describe "a sentient space" that is constantly changing, arguing that Kinsella resists what she refers to as "fantasies of cartographic coherence."[6] There is no scope here for a further exploration on Kinsella's commentaries on cartography, except to say that he refuses to see place as somewhere to be "owned," pinned down and stamped with the poet's signature. Paradoxically, it is this recognition of the questionable use of place as cultural container, a sort of designer branding of particular places, that gives his place poems their authority. Kinsella's place poems move with him, without condescension or sentimentality. He moved out, to Philadelphia. Always a foot here, and one there, as the best place poets have, the eye clarified and refined by the view from the far shore, the voice as sure as ever. This bi-location has given the work great independence from what Kinsella identified as "our own rather cramped tradition" and enabled the sort of leverage he himself attributes to hearing in the American voice of William Carlos Williams, and to the *Cantos* of Ezra Pound. In an interview with Adrienne Leavy, he says, "In the understanding of the poetic medium, the enabling example was Ezra Pound."[7] Pound's influence on Kinsella's poetics is frequently cited, but I have always wondered if the direction of his own explorations was already set, and whether his vision was perhaps illuminated and expanded by Pound's aesthetic concerns. Whatever impulse directed his escape from the elegance of the Audenesque beauty of his early work, the experimental journey was a logical development toward mapping the flux. At any rate, Pound helped, as he did so many of us struggling free from the long shadows. As did Joyce, who escaped Dublin only to construct the city so accurately that you could build it from scratch by reading *Ulysses*, a quantum Dublin rich in the musings of one long day.

I thought of Joyce when I first read "Finistère." I did not find the poem "difficult" as it has sometimes been described. Quite the opposite, I read it as a companion poem, an extension, of the musical ending to "Carraroe." A song from the end of the mapped territories, it begins with the incantation,

"I smelt the weird Atlantic. / Finistère . . . / *Finisterre* . . ." and ends at a place of discovery, "(I went forward, reaching out)." In a small house in Connemara, quietened for the Shipping Forecast, I first heard of "Finistère." It remains talismanic, a potent symbol of possibility and storms, and as I read it, I always hear the same opening bars of a traditional tune. This is the only poem of Kinsella's I can think of where the poet lets go and dives in, stripped of his customary iron restraint, into

    gale gullet
salt hole
    dark nowhere
calm queen[8]

The poem is rooted in the source of *Lebor Gabála Érenn* (*The Book of Invasions*), which is comprised of a series of poems and prose narratives about the original peoples of Ireland. It doesn't describe the place; it is more of a transmitter, encoding the turmoil and possibility, the madness and courage of leaving the known world behind and striking out in a new direction. Kinsella's poem is thus a journey of self-discovery as well as a meditation on the mythical discovery of Ireland through successive invasions.

Dublin, for many of my generation in the West, was where you went for the visa to America, the boat to Hollyhead or to visit relatives. It was administrative, irrelevant, and foreign except as a site of history that housed the Dáil, the GPO, and the National Museum. It was not "our" city in the way Boston or Chicago, or London was. Although I started school in Dun Laoghaire, due to reasons of family health, Dublin remained as neutral as a map, without resonance. I knew it was there, but except for Dun Laoghaire Pier and my aunt's house, it made no impact. Kinsella's poems and Joyce's books allowed me to see Dublin as a real place, another country, granted, but with a landscape inhabited by people and creatures I could believe in:

She came along the passage in her slippers
with a fuzz of navy hair, and her long nails
held out wet[9]

and

Bright gulls, gracefully idling
in the blue and wholesome heights
above our aerials;[10]

Kinsella's "Memory of W. H. Auden" with "the dark channel of Baggot Street" and its vexed reference to the poet's fingers "with the taint upon them" seemed to me to refer to the taint of that part of the city, its houses crudely cut up into bedsits, as much as to the need to distance himself from the Audenesque beauty and flow of his own early poetics. Those lines are imbued with loss and have the hard edges of the streets. I had no place in this city, whose culture was different from mine. My capitals were Lisbon and New York, Paris, and to a lesser extent, London. Whatever the reasons for this sense of exclusion, the sense of being a cultural outsider confers neither confidence nor entitlement. I needed, without knowing that I did, a bridge between the Gaelic world of *An Duanaire* and these unfriendly streets. Up to then, only Joyce and Beckett and Behan made Dublin comprehensible, or rather made it into a city I might come to know. Looking through their lenses, I could see a world I understood—surreal, funny, tough, and mad. *Ulysses* had shown me a great detailed slice of the city Joyce didn't like but seemed to love. Through Kinsella's *Poems from Centre City* (1990), I was beginning to see another layer, and look into its villages through poetry.

The long chronicle of decay in *Poems from Centre City*, with its hyssop-drenched opening salvo in "A Portrait of the Artist," coincided with what

I knew of developers and renewal. Of course I found the poems relentless, but when I read "The Back Lane" and "The Bell" I entered small, personal spaces I could believe in, if not long for. "Baggot Street Deserta" was at least known territory, since it seemed to consist mainly of houses hammered into bedsits, where students, nurses, and guards lived side by side with young couples and, if the books were anything to go by, poets. "Model School Inchicore," from *Songs of the Psyche* (1985), with Miss Carney handing out "blank paper and marla" and the wonderful child's line, "I am going to know everything," could have been the first school I entered in Dublin, though mine was in Dun Laoghaire and I had no friends there, being a "culchie" and new. I too remembered the ink in my mouth, or I re-remembered it when I read that surprising final stanza, but that is incidental. The shift in tone is unexpected and it moves the poem inexorably towards adulthood.

The Pen Shop (1997) brought places I was getting to know, as a visitor to what RTÉ refers to as "the Capital," into sharp focus. The sequence opens in the GPO, where the act of posting a letter will set, or re-set the course of a friendship, and moves out onto O'Connell Street where the poet sees the statue of the great trade union leader James Larkin, "with his iron arms on high, / conducting everybody / in all directions, up off our knees." In the second section of the poem, *To the Coffee Shop*, figures from history such as Daniel O'Connell, with his "dealer's eye," and Smith O'Brien mingle with Leopold Bloom. Kinsella's poem draws attention to the typography of the city, as he walks "toward College Green, / by the pillars of the Bank of Ireland," then "down Dame Street," and into "Nassau Street," where he reaches his final destination, the Pen Shop. The River Liffey is as central to the poem as the Dublin streets: "The river poured in dirty and disturbed," and the poem follows its movement backwards, through parts of Dublin I didn't know but, for the first time, wanted to discover, even if many of the details were already disappearing. The essence of a place is in the detail, and *The Pen Shop* is attentive to all the mundane details that the poet encounters along his walk, from the Number 21 bus hurtling around Trinity College, its "green backside swaying and settling / with an organic blast" to the "great grinder" in Bewley's coffee shop, where he stops for coffee, and, in a detail which recalls that Kinsella's father and grandfather worked for Guinness Brewery, the barges on the Liffey, with "the long body" of one he observes "sliding in / under the bridge under my feet, / starting to slow down for the Lady Patricia."[11]

The shifting life of its inhabitants makes a place what it is, and *Poems from Centre City* and *The Pen Shop* snatch something of the life of the city, challenging cliché and stereotype in which Dublin abounds and making the city, for this reader, real, concrete, interesting. I was already tired of the hard man anecdotes about Behan and Kavanagh and Flann O' Brien, all of whose work I admired. I wasn't sorry to have missed out on McDaid's. I would never have fitted in there, but somehow in Kinsella's poems, I found a place more vital and resonant than the worn anecdotes about "literary life." I was beginning to learn that certain groupings are doomed to be consigned to marketing and cliché, but it would be difficult to fit a Thomas Kinsella poem on an Irish literary tea towel.

"There are places where history is inescapable, like a highway accident—places where geography provokes history," Brodsky wrote in his essay "Flight from Byzantium."[12] And history influences language, and sometimes robs us of it. In 1986 I came back from the Continent after ten years away in search of my tradition. It was a conscious decision, because I wasn't sure where I stood in relation to Irish poetry in English as a potential writer. I had tried to suppress the need to write poems but wrote secretly for years without submitting anything, or mentioning them to anyone. I knew this lack was connected to a sense of failure connected with the Irish language, a kind of literary shame. I also correctly believed I had not yet served my apprenticeship. Since leaving University, I had been reading mostly the French and Latin poets, excited by Pessoa with his heteronyms and literary games, still mad about Lorca, Paz, Neruda, and Machado, poets who spoke my language in foreign tongues. I came across *An Duanaire 1600–1900: Poems of the Dispossessed* (1981) in Kenny's bookshop in Galway later that year. I opened the book and read the introduction, then the contents. My eye was snagged by the heading "Filiocht Idir Dhá Ré," meaning "Transitional Poetry." I had little money, but I asked Mrs. Kenny to put a copy aside, and I bought it as soon as I could. This was my bridge over troubled waters, across that bothered passage to repossession and reclamation. It helped me to come to grips with the written parts my own tradition, leading "the eye left across the page, back to the Irish" as Heaney wrote, but also leading the eye to the right, from the Irish to the English translations which were unfussy and mostly unrhymed. This left the ear free to hear the echoes of the deeper, more knotty rhythms of the originals, their elegant ease, a difficult but successful balancing act between readability and fidelity which Seán Ó Tuama and Kinsella had reached in no small part by deciding to sacrifice the seductions of rhyme to the different tunings of the older, complex rhythms. That aim was signposted in the introduction, which in itself serves as an accurate divining rod for the lineaments of the original syllabic and accentual rhymes, the bardic meter. It occurred to me, reading those translations for the first time, why Hopkins's poems, with their odd accents and turnings within the line, their powerful build-up of energy had seemed strangely familiar to me, even before I had much idea what they were about.

An Duanaire, co-edited by Ó Tuama, has rightly been called the "re-education of our poetry," and many of our contemporary writers are indebted to both men for this mine of poetry and translation. With its scholarly tracking of a nation's making sense of itself, this *Duanaire* or anthology is one of the essential books for any Irish poet with an eye to the origins and trajectory of our poetic heritage. As Kinsella describes it, the anthology is a selection, with new English translations, of poetry from "the troubled centuries from the collapse of the old Gaelic order to the emergence of English as the dominant vernacular." The preface is short, a little over half a page. On the left, the opening paragraph states: "Anuas go dtí an naoú haois déag b'fhéidir a rá grub í litríocht na Gaeilge litríocht na hÉireann." On the right-hand page, the English translation reads: "The literature of Ireland, in prose and poetry, from the earliest time until the nineteenth century, is predominantly in the Irish language."[13]

Another rendering might be: "Until the nineteenth century it could be said that literature in Irish was the literature of Ireland." The difference in emphasis and the distinction between prose and poetry have always struck me as particularly eloquent. In that small gap between those facing pages lies history, misunderstanding, and the shame of linguistic failure. In that gap lay, if only I could find it, permission "to dwell without cultural anxiety among the usual landmarks of your life," as Seamus Heaney wrote about his own empowerment on reading Patrick Kavanagh.[14] In her review of An *Duanaire* Patricia Craig described the anthology as not only invaluable to "every student of Irish literature," but also, given its inclusion of so much unfamiliar material, "instructive and absorbing to everyone else."[15] Compiling it was an act of generosity as well as creative imagination, the opposite of the sort of linguistic shaming that often went on in Universities, much of it unintentional, yet nonetheless withering for all that. It was the book that helped me come to grips with my own tradition, the map back to the source, forever connected with shame and guilt, the shining restrained unromantic Irish language I was separated from by one generation on my mother's side and two on my father's. Any permission to write the poems I wanted to write, and much of the impulse to write them, came from a life lived between languages.

Perhaps my dilemma arose from the lack of a recognizable literary tradition, and not alone from my ignorance of such a tradition. Perhaps it arose in part from that split or rip in a tradition provoked by the suppression and loss of a language. Poets after all pick up the electromagnetic waves such shocks produce long after the event is over, like light traveling from exploded stars. Yeats, as ever, perceived the reality and stated the case which Kinsella acknowledges at the onset of *The Dual Tradition*, his prose essay on this linguistic conflict:

> In *Ideas of Good and Evil*, Yeats remembers standing on the side of Sliab Echtge looking out over the Galway plains, thinking of the continuing generations of poetry and poetical life:
>
>> There is still in truth upon those great level plains a people, a community bound together by imaginative possessions, by stories and poems which have grown out of its own life, and by a past of great passions which can still waken the heart to imaginative action. One could still, if one had the genius, and had been born to Irish, write for these people plays and poems like those of Greece. Does not the greatest poetry always require a people to listen to it?[16]

Kinsella comments thus on Yeats's dilemma:

> '. . . if one had the genius'—one was hoping for the best—'. . . and had been born to Irish . . .'. There was nothing to be done about that. One might go

further out into Galway and learn Irish—others were doing so. Even turn away from English. But one does not usually hope to make 'the greatest poetry' in a second language. Aware of the losses involved, Yeats returned inside the gates of Coole Park, and continued the cultivation of another audience.[17]

And there, genius aside, was the poet's dilemma. "One" was Irish, but had not been "born to it." Where that left the contemporary poet and poetry was mapped by Kinsella in this seminal essay, an essay which helped me feel less lonely in my own quest.

As well as making choices, Kinsella was mapping the ground on which we stand even as he was moving outwards, leaving the safety and constraints of the lyric tradition for the exacting sea of Pound and the great Americans, to where his cool voice broadened and deepened his own poetic explorations. "Wyncote, Pennsylvania: a gloss" is one of the few poems Kinsella has written about America. This is surprising, considering how long he lived there. The "wet crimson berry" in the mockingbird's beak is as tantalizing and vivid as William Carlos Williams's tantalizing plums, and I was intrigued that the poem didn't end with

Under that copper light
my papers seem luminous.[18]

The last two lines, "And over them I will take / ever more painstaking care," mystified me. In a lesser poet, they might have seemed superfluous, but the poet's gaze rests where it does for a reason, and Wyncote was where Pound spent most of his formative years. I first read this poem, which is composed with the concision and elemental expression of a haiku, as reminiscent of the glosses between the lines of the earliest Irish manuscripts, but what was the gloss illuminating and to what did it refer? They may well be a subtle reference to Pound's insistence on the need for a rigorous aesthetic, a kind of "note to self" at the end of one of Kinsella's most luminous poems.

Joseph Brodsky, writing about Rilke, makes the claim that ". . . . economy is art's ultimate *raison d'etre*, and all its history is the history of its means of compression and condensation."[19] In poetry, he says, language is itself a highly condensed version of reality. This is true of much of Kinsella's work, which is also an unending process of psychic cartography. This is a poet suspicious, as Joe Heaney was in his *sean-nós* singing, of too much ornamentation. I rarely think of Kinsella's poems in relation to other Irish poets, but often a certain spare style of unaccompanied singing, or the spare, lone interpretations of some of the best fiddle players come to mind. There is a tonal similarity, a like authority and loneliness, and like the best of musicians, the poet also sings, and when he does, the lines soar, appealing, to paraphrase Borges, not to reason but to the imagination:

At the dark zenith a pulse beat,
a sperm of light separated
and snaked in a slow beam down
the curve of the sky . . .[20]

Accuracy, in an age when lies and counter-lies have become the *lingua franca* of commerce and politics, is crucial, and few poets have done more to preserve the truth of language; and the choice of words to describe the interior aesthetic process says as much about Kinsella as it does about the musician Seán Ó Riada to whom the above poem is dedicated.

Notes

[1] CP, 207.

[2] CP, 208.

[3] CP, 67.

[4] Maurice Harmon, *Thomas Kinsella: Designing for the Exact Needs* (Dublin: Irish Academic Press, 2008), 80.

[5] CP, 283.

[6] Julia C. Orbert, "Space and Trace: Thomas Kinsella's Postcolonial Placelore," *New Hibernia Review* 13, no. 4 (Winter 2009).

[7] "Thomas Kinsella in Conversation with Adrienne Leavy" *New Hibernia Review* 24, no. 1 (Spring 2020), 145.

[8] CP, 163.

[9] CP, "Dura Mater," 290.

[10] CP, *One Fond Embrace*, 275.

[11] CP, 325.

[12] Joseph Brodsky, *Less Than One: Selected Essays* (New York: Farrar, Straus and Giroux, 1987).

[13] *An Duanaire 1600–1900: Poems of the Dispossessed*, ed. Seán Ó Tuma, trans. Thomas Kinsella (Dublin: Dolmen Press, 1981), vi, vii.

[14] Seamus Heaney, "The Placeless Heaven: Another Look at Kavanagh" in *Finders Keepers: Selected Prose 1971–2001* (London: Faber and Faber, 2002), 140.

[15] Patricia Craig, "Playing to Empty Pockets," *The New York Review of Books*, May, 13, 1982.

[16] Thomas Kinsella, *The Dual Tradition: An Essay on Poetry and Politics in Ireland* (Manchester: Carcanet Press, 1995), 18.

[17] Kinsella, *The Dual Tradition*, 18.

[18] CP, 130.

[19] Joseph Brodsky, *On Grief and Reason: Essays* (New York: Farrar, Straus and Giroux, 1997).

[20] CP, *Vertical Man*, 144.

CHAPTER 5

The Moment of a Poem

KINSELLA'S "BAGGOT STREET DESERTA" AND BEYOND

ANDREW FITZSIMONS

The spring 1956 edition of *Irish Writing* is one of the most extraordinary single issues of a literary journal ever published in Ireland.[1] A mere 64 pages, it commands perennial attention for a special section devoted to Samuel Beckett, "late of Dublin," the man of the literary moment.[2] The section features an extract from the yet-to-be published English translation of *Malone Meurt*, an article called "Waiting with Beckett" by Denis Johnston, to mark the first British edition of the English translation of *Waiting for Godot*, and another, "Mr. Beckett's Everymen," by the New Zealander Dan Davin, on Beckett's prose from *Molloy* to *Nouvelles et texts pour rien* (1955). This special section is a snapshot of a moment: Beckett, a quondam local, entering the realm of global literary phenomenon through work not "local" in any easily accommodatable sense, doubly estranged, through imagination and through dint of achievement. In the drama of the journal's special section, we see the local (*Irish* Writing) attempting to grapple with the phenomenon of Beckett, we see the local gathering to itself, or finding itself gathered into, significance at the very moment of its arrival. The articles on Beckett all quiver around the question of moment in the two senses that I want to explore in this essay: "moment" as period in time and "moment" as significance, importance, and consequence. What is good *now*? Which of the things we think good now will *last*? This doubleness to, and questioning of, moment generated one of the other contributions to this issue of *Irish Writing* that makes it so compelling a document, and indeed an issue in itself illustrative of this tension within the meaning of the word: *Irish Writing* saw the first publication of "Unfinished Business" by Thomas Kinsella, a poem that would go on in revised form to become "Baggot Street Deserta."[3]

Coincidences abound. I would like you to keep in mind that the editor of this issue of *Irish Writing* was S. J. White, that "Unfinished Business" is epistolary in form, addressed to a character named "Brendan," and, less significant in terms of the poem but very significant in terms of Kinsella's writing life, that the typographer of the issue was Liam Miller, founder of the Dolmen Press, Kinsella's publisher and the most significant Irish publisher of poetry until Miller's death in 1987. In this same issue, alongside a review of Philip Larkin's *The Less Deceived*, Donald Davie reviewed Elizabeth Jennings's *A Way of Looking*. From October 1955 to October 1958, when he was first composing and then revising "Unfinished Business"/"Baggot Street Deserta"—a poem which worries at the falseness of the "finish" given by memory and poetry to things caught up in the flow of time—Kinsella was the regular poetry reviewer for the *Irish Press* and, in June 1956, also reviewed Jennings's book. He wrote, "The style is very like that of a report. It has a steady pace, *an illusion of completeness*, an unobtrusive competence."[4] He quotes these lines: "A love is worn away not by the one / Who leaves but by the one who stays and hopes," one of, he says, "a number of phrases which come back continually to mind as having summed up something once and for all."[5] Jennings's lines would appear later, re-imagined, in

"Phoenix Park": "One stays or leaves. The one who returns is not / The one, etcetera." In another coincidence, which shows the intimacy of the literary circles of the time, only a few months before *Irish Writing* appeared, in the *Irish Press* on October 8, 1955, Kinsella had written dismissively of another contributor to the issue, the South African-born poet and critic Laurence D. Lerner, then a lecturer at Queen's University, Belfast: "His six short poems are intelligent and efficient. They make little impression beyond that, nor are they intended to."[6]

Less of a coincidence and more telling in one local effect on "Baggot Street Deserta" is Kinsella's reading of Wallace Stevens's *Collected Poems*.[7] At the end of a laudatory review, he writes of "Not Ideas About the Thing But the Thing Itself": "The final poem is one of awakening: he hears a 'scrawny cry' at daylight or before, in the early March wind."[8] In Stevens the bird's cry is "like / A new knowledge of reality;" in Kinsella's "Unfinished Business" the bird's "threadbare cry" is "wild," "lost," "desolating" and of a piece with the speaker's "curlew-call of exile, half- / Buried longing, half-serious / Anger" and "Dangerously near the spurious, / Commonplace."[9] In "Unfinished Business" the speaker's voicings and the bird's cry are intimately linked, each as "dry / A dose for the discriminating" listener as the other. In the revisions made for "Baggot Street Deserta," the speaker's voicings and the curlew's cry have been separated; the bird and speaker encounter each other, the bird bringing a knowledge of reality to which the speaker compassionately, but inadequately, responds:

> A cigarette, the moon, a sigh
> Of educated boredom, greet
> A curlew's lingering threadbare cry
> Of common loss. Compassionate,

I add my call of exile, half-
Buried longing, half-serious
Anger and the rueful laugh.
We fly into our risk, the spurious.[10]

The reviews in this issue of *Irish Writing* give an insight into the wider literary moment of the mid-1950s and the poetic language to which Kinsella was reacting in such tightly-clipped, Audenesque lines. The "tight beat" of the poem is reminiscent of Eliot's "Burnt Norton" and Yeats's "Easter 1916," but the urbane, un-illusioned tone is most closely modeled on Auden, as he writes in the drafts, "To borrow a manner from our agile friend across the water."[11] Pearse Hutchinson, then resident in Barcelona, with three poems of multi-lingual capaciousness also in the issue, reviewed Blanaid Salkeld's *Experiment in Error*, calling it "the finest collection by an Irish poet since [Patrick Kavanagh's]" and, remarkably, in the same piece reviewed the Sri Lankan poet Patrick Fernando's debut, *The Return of Ulysses*, the first book by a Sri Lankan poet to be published in London, the beginning of an eminent career as Sri Lanka's major English-language poet.[12] Hutchinson remarks of Fernando (1931–1983) that "there have been few new poets for a long time with half as sound an eye, brain, and ear," favoring his work over his "contemporaries in Kirkup-and-Orton-land."[13] Hutchinson's dismissal of the excesses and influence of Joe Orton and James Kirkup, is of a piece with Donald Davie's dismissal, in his review of Larkin and Jennings, of the "turbulent expressiveness" of much of the English verse of the day.[14]

To compare, and to get sense of what he considered the good and bad in contemporary poetic modes, we have Kinsella's own review of Davie's *Brides of Reason* in the *Irish Press* in November 1955. Kinsella writes:

> These poems and their diction, like the poet himself, know where they stand, and refuse to take too much on themselves. They are conscientious, and sober; they reject, deliberately and explicitly, the temptation to soar. The poet shrugs away from flights of fancy, feeling perhaps that they may cheat him or his reader.
>
> In this it is probable that he underrates his capabilities. His belief that "a neutral tone is nowadays preferred" appears to arise, in part at least, from a sense of embarrassment at the linguistic and emotional excesses of some recent poetry. The ruthless clipping of his verse's wings may be some kind of atonement for this.[15]

What Kinsella says of Davie could equally be said of the tensions underlying the reserved poetic mode of "Baggot Street Deserta," with one key difference. Though Kinsella's lines are as rinsed of lyrical fancy as Davie's, he wants to take on more, wants flight, not of fancy, but toward contact with meaning, the "main / Mystery," *the* business:

> Out where imagination arches
> Chilly points of light transact
> The business of the border-marches
> Of the Real,[16]

The poem as an act of mind is, Wallace Stevens wrote, "a violence from within that protects us from a violence without. It is the imagination pressing back against the pressure of reality."[17] Stevens was writing in 1942, just after the US entry into World War II, reflecting on the turmoil of the 1930s and the lingering effect of the "Great War": "for more than ten years, the consciousness of the world has concentrated on events which have made the ordinary movement of life seem to be the movement of people in the intervals of a storm."[18] Kinsella re-worked this idea of poetry as countervailing response in his remarks about *Nightwalker and Other Poems*, published in 1968, a year of political tumult and violence, globally and locally, when he described his poems as "trying to find a balance in the violent zone, between the outer and inner storms, where human life takes place."[19] For Stevens, the pressure of reality was "the pressure of an external event or events on the consciousness to the exclusion of any power of contemplation."[20] The early twentieth century, he wrote, had seen the pressure that reality exerts through the wash of external events become increasingly similar in substance and form.

"Baggot Street Deserta" is a poem of uneasy peace in the aftermath of violence, told through the metaphor of a poem about making poems:

> Lulled, at silence, the spent attack.
> The will to work is laid aside.
> The breaking-cry, the strain of the rack,
> Yield, are at peace. The window is wide
> On a crawling arch of stars, and the night
> Reacts faintly to the mathematic
> Passion of a cello suite
> Plotting the quiet of my attic.[21]

It is a poem deliberately and self-consciously located in a named, specific place, an attic flat on a street in the heart of Dublin, a few minutes' walk from the centers of Irish public life and administration,[22] and concerns what happens when the world of events enters the meaning-making requirements of a head, or a poem. The conflicting meanings of the word "filter" captures something of the tensions the poem explores, "filter" as the sifting out of the inessential, and "filter" as falsifying sheen. When Kinsella was composing and revising "Baggot Street Deserta," what pressures was the poem a response to? Why is the poem so concerned with its own procedures? Were these pressures similar to pressures being felt by poets elsewhere, in English, but also in non-English-speaking cultures? In other words, I want to survey the personal and historical moment within which Kinsella was writing. At another level, the poem in its "plot" concerns a particular moment, a moment of reflection lasting the length of a smoked cigarette. The poem's lines are a long disquisition on a moment in a room, a reflection of, and on, the mental habits of the speaker. This disquisition is one, though, which delves into another layer of meaning contained within the word "moment": what, if any, is the significance of the speaker's seemingly inescapable mental habits? The speaker of the poem is questioning the value of rumination, of thought, and ultimately, of a poem. What is the moment of a poem?

To begin to answer the question, I want to look briefly at the contemporary scene between 1955 and spring 1956 in Ireland, and in elsewheres immediately available in Ireland, namely the UK and the US, when the first version of "Baggot Street Deserta" was published in *Irish Writing*. I will then go on to look at areas not immediately within earshot of an Irish poet in 1955 but which show how the frequencies picked up by Kinsella, the dilemmas with which he was engaging, specifically in "Baggot Street Deserta," were in touch with anxieties about the claims and capabilities of the poetic act to which poets far removed from Ireland were also responding. I will argue that Kinsella's poem, the moment of its moment, is a perennial one in that he is exploring the quintessential poetic dilemma, as figured by Allen Grossmann in an essay entitled "My Caedmon: Thinking About Poetic Vocation." "Baggot Street Deserta," though a poem of a particular moment, reveals how Kinsella's poems issue "from a special state of mind rather than occasional inspiration" as Kinsella himself said of the verse of his first major influence, W. H. Auden.[23]

To contemporary Irish readers, Kinsella's original title, "Unfinished Business," would have been read as an allusion to a phrase used in nationalist discussions of the partition of Ireland in 1921, a political context that the poem itself deliberately undercuts and qualifies through its concern with personal and poetic self-definition. By 1955, there had been significant moves in the "unfinished business" of Irish statehood. The Irish Free State had become the Republic of Ireland, the Republic of Ireland Act 1948 having come into effect in 1949. In response, the UK Parliament had passed the Ireland Act 1949, for the first time legally ensuring that Northern Ireland would not cease to be part of the UK without the consent of the Parliament of Northern Ireland. Sean T. O'Kelly was President of the Republic, and the Taoiseach was John A. Costello of Fine Gael, at the head of a minority government, the second of its kind, that would be in power from June 1954 until March 1957. By the 1950s, the politics of the state had begun to move, slowly, away from the Civil War toward social issues: employment, housing, and healthcare. This last issue, with the Church hierarchy's reaction against the "Mother and Child Scheme," had resulted in the collapse of the first inter-party government in 1951. Though the "unfinished business" of the state had receded from view in the practical affairs of the running of the state, the IRA had not, however, gone away, and after a dormant period in the 1940s, by the end of 1956 had initiated the "Border Campaign," a series of attacks against military and infrastructure targets in Northern Ireland. Kinsella's "the border-marches / Of the Real" captures something of the sense that the border remained an issue, distant though insistent, in the minds of those in the Republic.

In Northern Ireland itself, Prime Minster Basil Brooke, of the Ulster

Unionist Party, had been in office since May 1943 and would remain in office until 1963. In 1955, a regular television service was launched by the BBC, the transmissions of which could also be received in parts of the Republic. The fears of the undue influence of these transmissions would eventually lead to the establishment of a native television service, Telefís Éireann, in 1961. Popular forms of outside influence were, however, present, and, in film and music, growing in reach and appeal.[24] In Britain, it was a time in which there was a spate of films devoted to heroic World War II exploits: *The Colditz Story, The Dam Busters, Above Us the Waves, The Cockleshell Heroes*, all produced in 1955 and all screened in Irish cinemas. With the apparent settling down of the "Troubles," Ireland had also been the setting for British-made films on Irish political turmoil, featuring prominent British actors in the role of conflicted IRA men. The most famous, Carol Reed's *Odd Man Out* (1948), starring James Mason, is a drama of excoriating power, but there were others, including *The Gentle Gunman* (1952), starring two of the most popular British actors of the day, John Mills and Dirk Bogarde. Historical distance from actual events had allowed such sympathetic, even glamorous, portrayals, a process of falsification that "Baggot Street Deserta" adumbrates with scorn.

It was very much a provincial affair, and the reason for invoking such details of the time is that "Baggot Street Deserta" reflects this, in its atmosphere of "educated boredom," but also in its sense of "lull," of "spent attack," and of a heroic past for which the speaker is a latecomer. The speaker at the window, smoking, listening to Bach, is dealing with a lull after work, but also, in a sense, the lull after heroic history ("'History / Is that which antedated ME'").[25] The speaker is conscious of being late for something of consequence, a momentous past that qualifies and undermines the present moment. He has, though, heard the tales. And these tales are of a kind as the actioners and melodramas being produced out of commercial film studios. The falsifications of historical memory are both social but also, produced out of the self's act of memory, "Looking backward, all is lost; / The Past becomes a fairy bog."

And yet, at the time of composition, Kinsella was at the heart of developments within government, working in the Department of Finance, where he eventually rose to become assistant to the secretary of the Department, T. K. Whitaker, architect of the First Programme for National Expansion, 1958–1963. The alienation of the speaker, the questioning of the prerogatives of the artistic act, the contrast between high culture (the "cello suite") and barbarism (the grave-robbing Burke and Hare, the "horror-stricken" eyes of frightened children), derive out of and figure the anxieties of post-war intellectual life. The violence of the metaphors used to describe the inner life of the cultured speaker—burying, prising apart, grave-robbing, cadavers—imply that the buried life is barely buried, and the savage and the civilized, as the horrors of World War II had shown, reside each within the other. The legacy of "coming to conscience on that edge of dread" ramifies through Kinsella's work as early as *Downstream* in "Old Harry," a poem concerned with the dropping of the atomic bomb on Hiroshima, and in "Nightwalker," a poem that intimated that the civil surface of Irish life, dominated by the precepts of the Catholic Church, had concealed from view horrors much closer to home.

In the US in October 1955, in response to hearing a first reading of *Howl*, Lawrence Ferlinghetti sent his famous telegram to Allen Ginsberg, quoting from Emerson's words to Walt Whitman, "I greet you at the beginning of a great career."[26] Ginsberg was later included in Donald Allen's anthology *The New American Poetry 1945–1960*, published by Beckett's American publisher, Grove Press, which presented the work of poets in the "make it new"

Pound/Williams tradition from the loosely-affiliated groupings of the day: the "Black Mountain Poets," the "New York School," and the "San Francisco Renaissance."[27] Allen's anthology was a deliberately contrary response to *The New Poets of England and America* (1957), edited by Donald Hall, Robert Pack, and Louis Simpson, an anthology of "Academic" poets, so called not only because many had third-level connections and occupations but for their adherence to "make it anew" traditional metrics. It included Richard Wilbur, Anthony Hecht, John Hollander, May Swenson, and Donald Justice. In 1955, Hall had published his first book, *Exiles and Marriages*, an example of verse as much under the influence of Auden as Kinsella's, and one could argue that, at this stage, Kinsella would have fit well in Hall's anthology, while the post-*Nightwalker* Kinsella would be a better fit within Allen's. Though he was speaking specifically of the Beats when accepting the National Book Award for *Life Studies* (1959), these anthologies present more generally the division in American poetry between what Robert Lowell termed the "cooked" and the "raw." Kinsella was listening in to American poetry, in particular after he began traveling there in the early 1960s, and eventually living there for part of the academic year from the mid-1960s. Lowell's attempt to incorporate elements of the "raw" into *Life Studies* served as an example to Kinsella in his own poetic development. But poets elsewhere were also questioning the modes and manner of their poetry, and the poetic act itself, feeling what Donald Davie termed, though much later in his writing life, the "insufficiency of lyric," and in a world wider than English.[28]

Davie's writing on Czesław Miłosz and the Polish experience of poets such as Zbigniew Herbert, Tadeusz Różewicz, and Wisława Szymborska is exemplary of what I want to now discuss with reference to two other poetic traditions outside English, namely the Italian and the Japanese. In Italy, the triumvirate of Eugenio Montale, Giuseppe Ungaretti, and Salvatore Quasimodo, the renovators of post-D'Annunzio Italian poetry, were in their different ways in the post-war period taking stock of, or in the case of Ungaretti, coming to an accommodation with, their experience and conduct during the years of fascism. In "Intentions (Imaginary Interview)," first published in January 1946, Montale could be describing just as well the impulse behind the work of Ayukawa Nobuo[29] in Japan, as we will see, and Kinsella in Ireland:

> Volevo che la mia parola fosse più aderente di quella degli altri poeti che avevo conosciuto. Più aderente a che? Mi pareva di vivere sotto a una campana di vetro, eppure sentivo di essere vicino a qualcosa di essenziale. Un velo sottile, un filo appena mi separava dal *quid* definitivo. L'espressione assoluta sarebbe stata la rottura di quel velo, di quel filo: una esplosione, la fine dell'inganno del mondo come rappresentazione. Ma questo era un limite irraggiungibile. E la mia volontà di aderenza restava musicale, istintiva, non programmatica. All'eloquenza della nostra vecchia lingua aulica volevo torcere il collo, magari a rischio di una controeloquenza.[30]
>
> [I wanted my speech to be closer than that of the other poets I had read. Closer to what? I seemed to be living under a bell jar, and yet I also felt I was close to something essential. A subtle veil, a thread just separated me from the definitive *quid*. Absolute expression would have meant the breaking of that veil, that thread: an explosion, the end of the illusion of the world as representation. But this was an unattainable goal. And my desire for closeness remained musical, instinctive, unprogrammatic. I wanted to wring the neck of the eloquence of our old aulic language, even at the risk of a counter-eloquence.] (*Translation mine*)

Dissatisfaction with the prevailing poetic language, the desire to get closer to experience than inherited language permitted, motivated the radical renovations of Italian verse enacted in Montale's poetry. Yet the violence of the terms Montale uses, the desire to *wring the neck* ("torcere il collo"), intimates the desire for a language that would overcome the alienated personal experience he describes, derived also from "a violence without," in Stevens's terms. Writing in 1946, in the immediate aftermath of the war, the "old aulic" Italian language had seemed complicit in recent events, had been hollowed out by extreme experience, by fascism, and by the human and cultural catastrophe of the war, by history. Pier Paolo Pasolini's *Le ceneri di Gramsci* ("Gramsci's Ashes"), first published in 1954, and collected in the book of that title in 1957, offered the desolate summation of the 1950s generation, the poets younger than Montale: "Ma come io possiedo la storia, / essa mi possiede; ne sono illuminato: // ma a che serve la luce?"[31] ["But just as I possess History / it possesses me; I am enlightened by it: // but what use is such light?"] (*Translation mine*).

"Baggot Street Deserta" expresses Kinsella's desire for a language that would come closer to the "definitive *quid*," and as with Montale, initially at least, the prevailing poetic language is the only means available, the medium through which this desire is perforce expressed. Thus the moment of a poem is, in a sense, a "predicament," in the sense gleaned by Georges Duthuit from Beckett's position in the famous "Three Dialogues" published in *transition* in 1949: "the occasion of his [Bram van Velde's] painting is his predicament, and [. . .] is expressive of the impossibility to express." Beckett clarified: "It is obvious that for the artist obsessed with his expressive vocation, anything and everything is doomed to become occasion."[32] Montale's figure of the "subtle veil" recalls Yeats's (via Mallarmé) "trembling of the veil" and that moment in Heaney as Sweeney readies himself for flight when "goldfinch or kingfisher rent / the veil of the usual."[33]

The figure of reality as veiled, at a remove, or at a framed distance through a window, engenders the perennial poetic quest. The moment of poetry is perennial, tied to its historical moment but also to a moment in art that is ever the case. In his poem "Keisen Hoteru no Asa no Uta" ("Morning Song at the Marine Hotel"), Ayukawa Nobuo writes:

窓の風景は
額縁のなかに嵌めこまれている
ああ おれは雨と街路と夜がほしい
夜にならなければ
この倦怠の街の全景を
うまく抱擁することができないのだ[34]

[The landscape out the window
is set in a picture-frame
Ah I want rain and city-streets and night
Until after night falls
the full view of this listless city
to well embrace I'm incapable] (*Translation mine*)

Ayukawa (1920–1986), born, as he says later in the poem, between "the two great wars of West and East," was the leading figure of *sengo-shi* ("post-war poetry"), a generation clearing and cleaning out, like Montale, a compromised, venerable tradition. Ayukawa was part of an Eliot-inspired grouping known as *Arechi* ("The Waste Land") and, like Miłosz's Catastrophists in Poland, found Eliot's metaphoric desolation literalized by the war, and he felt, too, the insufficiency of the personal lyric: "Individuality doesn't accomplish much. Neither gradual advances nor dramatic leaps can be expected from poets who rely on the lyrical quality of language and use words as tools to express the atmosphere of nature and the emotions aroused by it."[35] Ayukawa's *Arechi* group gave way in influence to poets such as Tanikawa Shuntarō (b. 1931) and Ōoka Makoto (b. 1931). Tanikawa's first book *Nijūoku kōnen no kodoku* (*Two Billion Light-Years of Solitude*) appeared to great acclaim in 1952; Ōoka's first, *Kioku to genzai* (*Memory and the Present*) in 1956, initiating bodies of work central to mid- and late-twentieth century poetry in Japan. Both poets arose out of a 1950s generation, too young to have served in the war that had, it was said, "calmed down" (*ochitsuita*): reappraising, rather than rejecting outright, Japanese values compromised by the catastrophe of militarism, and, while the wider society was busy building the Japanese economic miracle, creating new syntheses out of native traditions and imported forms of modernity.[36] The parallels with Ireland are instructive. Kinsella was part of what might also be termed an *ochitsuita* generation in Ireland: born into an independent state, reappraising received forms of literary Irishness and the "unfinished business" of the Irish past, aware of, and receptive to, modern realities and modes of expression, with exemplars such as Yeats, Joyce, and, readily at hand in the middle of his great outpouring, Beckett.

In "Reflection of a Poet," an early uncollected poem, Kinsella outlines the moment a poem begins to happen:

> Perhaps you've just been reading and a thought,
> Stirred by the sentences, has taken fire
> And burned away the meaning that you bought
> And all that's left is this ash-grey desire,

A mental passion, like a painless sore
That vaguely is, and waits for its relief.
You might, to find your poem, try any door,
House-breaking outward, an upended thief.[37]

The negative metaphors for the poetic act resemble "Baggot Street Deserta," where the poetic act is likened to, among other nefarious acts, grave-robbing à la Burke and Hare, the notorious "resurrection men" of nineteenth-century Edinburgh. This trope of thievery continues in "Reflection of a Poet":

You, like a thief, have got a tender tip
That reaches to and shrinks from things around
And you, like he, crouch, fingering a lip,
And steal selectively from what you've found.

The idea that selection, the artistic act *par excellence*, is problematic bespeaks a relationship between poetry and the world, art and the world, within which the world is primary. The poet attends to a world which demands, for some unarticulated reason, true account, and the falling short of that world is rendered in guilt-laden terms: thievery, house-breaking, grave-robbing. And yet:

But what is it to be? There is so much
That here and there a reckless hand has hurled.
Will you with your intimate or prouder touch
Settle a mood or make another world?

Why should this world, so badly-made by a recklessly bad maker, demand so much? The poet can make another world. But is the world really the be-all and end-all of a poem?

Take what you like, but count yourself the true
Item of spoil; the rest is a game you play.
Moulding by candle-light a mask like you,
You in the mirror will know what to say.

The self in the reflected world, the mirror of self-reflecting art, will know what to say. The gap between "know what to say" and "will know" returns us to the world of "ash-grey desire" and unwritten poems. In the world of the perennial poetic moment, we are left "danc[ing] round in a ring," as in Robert Frost, while "the Secret sits in the middle and knows."[38] The knowledge is somewhere to be had, to be achieved. And so we go on:

Versing, like an exile, makes
A virtuoso of the heart,
Interpreting the old mistakes
And discords in a work of Art
For the One, a private masterpiece
Of doctored recollections. Truth
Concedes, before the dew, its place
In the spray of dried forgettings Youth
Collected when they were a single
Furious undissected bloom.[39]

One of the many contradictions of the poem is that, though the speaker decries the absence of poetry and the failure of his poetic act, the reader can't, for the reader is receiving this news via a highly-wrought lyrical, aesthetically pleasing, structure. This is most definitely poetry.

At the forefront of Kinsella's poetic practice is the "bitter logic" of poetry itself, the paradox that the poetic principle is "nonidentical" with actual poems, even as it acts as a guide and goad. It is the drama of, and in, the poems. Kinsella's work enacts over and over what Grossman called the "impossible demand"[40] of poetry, as figured in the story of Caedmon, the demand from an exterior force, God, or a schoolmaster, say, to sing, to say something, and how the song actually produced always falls short of what the external force requires, what the moment demands: "The goddess who had light for thighs / Grows feet of dung and takes to bed."[41] "Baggot Street Deserta" concerns poetic vocation almost precisely in the terms supplied by Grossman. The poem finds the speaker at precisely that moment of concession to the impossibility of the demand. Yet this is the classic subterfuge played by all poets, Grossman argues. When Grossman writes of "first" experience being a catch-all term for experience that reaches back generation after generation to "no beginning," he parallels Kinsella's own questioning of origin in his preparatory notes for the poem. Here is Grossman:

> What I speak of as "first" experience is very likely the supply of terms for many experiences that came before the "first" one: in fact, a sequence of first experiences collapsing backward toward the beginning of conscious life; and, then, backward again to the beginning of the world; and then, at last, to the great receptacle of all there is—the figure of no beginning.[42]

And here is Kinsella:

> Who are they? (the Garrison) The dead? My many fathers whom I don't know. Cobblers, sailors, [p]oor farmers on a hill; from that into the mist sheep minders, peasant soldiers (98), priest-fearers, seeking truth in the shadow of a hedge at night, non-dancing race ... back to where God knows what began, ... the apes, the oceans, the first amoeba. The pulse keeping in touch all the time with the beginning, which is always with us ~~being itself~~. The pulse recording all changes. How alien the thing is which we carry with us, which caused us to be here. We are not more distant from the beginning than from our own fathers.[43]

The concerns in these preparatory notes emerge in "Baggot Street Deserta" as these supremely lyrical, closing lines:

Fingers cold against the sill
Feel, below the stress of flight,
The slow implosion of my pulse
In a wrist with poet's cramp, a tight
Beat tapping out endless calls
Into the dark, as the alien
Garrison in my own blood
Keeps constant contact with the main
Mystery, not to be understood.
Out where imagination arches
Chilly points of light transact
The business of the border-marches
Of the Real, and I – a fact
That may be countered or may not –
Find their privacy complete.[44]

The moment of the poem is an *interregnum* in the Gramscian sense: "The crisis consists precisely in the fact that the old is dying and the new cannot be born."[45] "Baggot Street Deserta" is a poem that presents, through negation, a vision of poetry seeable only through seeing what it is not, articulatable only through saying what it is not, forever unattainable, unfinishable. The poetry that is described is a failure ("the spent attack," "doctored recollections"); if a poem does achieve the status of "masterpiece," that masterpiece is unsatisfactory, morally, aesthetically, spiritually. What instead does this speaker want? Is "Baggot Street Deserta" the "spent attack" itself, the "private masterpiece / Of doctored recollections"? Or has it overcome the impossible demand of its moment by its own momentum, the concatenation of its disappointments? Through incorporation and articulation of its own negative conditions, as Beckett outlined to Duthuit, has artistic sleight of hand managed to afford a visionary moment, one akin to Krapp's in *Krapp's Last Tape*? A moment we can never quite grasp because Krapp, as we know, never *finishes* its articulation; we are not allowed to hear him finish, the vision in the raging storm. Kinsella's storm is an "inner storm" and an "outer storm," and the poem a moment of balance, ever unachievable. In the notes to the poem, he writes:

> (I, plus my effect on life) is a column standing lonely in a storm, beaten upon by events and eroded by them, but nonetheless forever lonely and uninvolvable—retaining its separateness in the midst of bitternesses, joys, and love—responsible for itself, unescaping, poignant, (itself its own source, dwelling in its own night, its own dream), an exile, most absent in the midst of all.[46]

On January 26, 1958, around the same moment "Baggot Street Deserta" was published in its final form in *Another September*, Paul Celan gave his "Speech on the Occasion of Receiving the Literature Prize of the Free Hanseatic City of Bremen." The reachable, the distant, and the lost haunt Celan's work, as much as, in a different key, they haunt Kinsella's work in "Baggot Street Deserta" and beyond. Celan captures the limit and the reach of the moment of a poem; the moment is the medium through which a poem seeks to achieve its moment: "For a poem is not timeless. Certainly, it lays claim to infinity, it seeks to reach through time—through it, not above and beyond it." He addresses, at the end of his speech, "other lyric poets in the younger generation," among whom Kinsella figures, not only, and not merely, because of age. He could indeed be speaking of "Baggot Street Deserta":

> And I believe that ways of thought like these attend not only my efforts, but those of other lyric poets in the younger generation. They are the efforts of someone who, *overarced by stars* that are human handiwork, and who, *shelterless* in this till now undreamt-of sense and thus most uncannily in the open, goes with his very being to language, stricken by and seeking reality.[47] [emphasis added]

Celan's perspective—"stricken by reality": the historical moment, "seeking reality": moment—is reflected in the Kinsella of "Baggot Street Deserta," and also of "Downstream" ("Searching the darkness for a landing place"),[48] and of "Nightwalker" and beyond. Another coincidence that carries us forward and further into Kinsella's later work: "S. J. White," the editor of that extraordinary edition of *Irish Writing*, was none other than Seán J. White, the addressee "Brendan" in "Unfinished Business" who, as the drafts reveal, is the model for the nameless co-shadow in "Downstream," whose native Durrow and whose tale of a dead body found in the woods cast the pall of the past over the speaker's sense of the present moment. "Baggot Street Deserta" points to a poem beyond itself in such specifics, in its questioning of poetic vocation, and in the rueful resolve of its final couplet, revealing how, as Grossmann writes, "a poem is always other than the impossible work that it replaces but shows what such work will be like."[49]

> My quarter-inch of cigarette
> Goes flaring down to Baggot Street.[50]

Notes

[1] S. J. White, ed., *Irish Writing* 34 (Spring 1956).

[2] Denis Johnston, "Waiting with Beckett," *Irish Writing* 34 (Spring 1956): 23.

[3] The poem first appeared under the title "Unfinished Business" in *Irish Writing*

(Spring 1956) and, later in the year, in a revised version with the title "Baggot Street Deserta," in *Poetry Now*, ed. G. S. Fraser (London: Faber, 1956), 102–03. It appeared in its present form in Kinsella's first full volume, *Another September* (Dublin: Dolmen Press, 1958). For an excellent reading of the revisions to the poem, see Brian John, *Reading the Ground: The Poetry of Thomas Kinsella* (Washington, DC: Catholic University of America Press, 1996), 36–43.

[4] Thomas Kinsella, *Prose Occasions 1951–2006*, ed. Andrew Fitzsimons (Manchester: Carcanet Press, 2009). Henceforth PO.

[5] PO, 159.

[6] PO, 138.

[7] Irish Press, June 23, 1956.

[8] PO, 164.

[9] Thomas Kinsella, "Unfinished Business," *Irish Writing* 34 (Spring 1956): 52.

[10] CP, 12.

[11] Kinsella Papers, Box 4, Folder 10. The archive material in this essay can be found in the Thomas Kinsella Papers (MSS 774), Special Collections and Archives Division, Robert W. Woodruff Library, Emory University.

[12] Pearse Hutchinson, review of *Experiment in Error* by Blanaid Salkeld and *The Return of Ulysses* by Patrick Fernando, *Irish Writing* 34 (Spring 1956): 60.

[13] Hutchinson, review, 61.

[14] Donald Davie, review of *The Less Deceived* by Philip Larkin and *A Way of Looking* by Elizabeth Jennings, *Irish Writing* 34 (Spring 1956): 62.

[15] PO, 142.

[16] CP, 13.

[17] Wallace Stevens, "The Noble Rider and the Sound of Words," in *Collected Poetry and Prose* (New York: Library of America, 1997), 665.

[18] Stevens, *Collected Poetry and Prose*, 655.

[19] Kinsella, "Thomas Kinsella Writes . . ." *Poetry Book Society Bulletin* (PBS) 55 (December 1967).

[20] Stevens, *Collected Poetry and Prose*, 654.

[21] CP, 11.

[22] Kinsella's flat was at 9 Lower Baggot Street (since demolished), near Merrion Row, a short walk to both Government Buildings on Merrion Street, and Leinster

House, the meeting place of the two houses of the Oireachtas, Dáil Éireann, and Seanad Éireann.

[23] PO, 149. The review of Auden was almost exactly contemporaneous with the publication of "Unfinished Business": "Auden and Achilles." Review of *The Shield of Achilles*, by W. H. Auden (Faber). *Irish Press*, February 18, 1956; *Irish Writing* was published on February 22, 1956.

[24] For a detailed background to the cultural atmosphere of the 1950s in Ireland, see Terence Brown, *Ireland: A Social and Cultural History* 1922–2002 (London: Fontana Press, 2004).

[25] Kinsella, "Unfinished Business," *Irish Writing*, 52.

[26] Bill Morgan, ed., *I Greet You at the Beginning of a Great Career: The Selected Correspondence of Lawrence Ferlinghetti and Allen Ginsberg* 1955–1997 (San Francisco: City Lights, 2015), 1.

[27] The "Black Mountain Poets" in the anthology included Robert Creeley, Robert Duncan, Denise Levertov, Charles Olson, and Ed Dorn; the "New York School" included John Ashbery, James Schuyler, Frank O'Hara, Kenneth Koch, and Barbara Guest; and the "San Francisco Renaissance" included, alongside Ginsberg, Gary Snyder, Jack Spicer, Philip Whalen, and Michael McClure.

[28] Donald Davie, *Czesław Miłosz and the Insufficiency of Lyric* (Cambridge: Cambridge UP, 186).

[29] I use the Japanese order of names: Ayukawa is the family name, and Nobuo his given name.

[30] Eugenio Montale, "Intervista immaginaria," *La rassegna d'Italia: rivista di letteratura*, January, 1946. Republished in *Per Conoscere Montale: Antologia corredata di testi critici*, ed. Marco Forti (Milano: Mondadori, 1986), 156–157.

[31] Pier Paolo Pasolini, *Le Ceneri Di Gramsci* (Milan: Garzanti, 1957).

[32] Samuel Beckett, *Disjecta: Miscellaneous Writings and a Dramatic Fragment*, ed. Ruby Cohen (London: Calder, 1983).

[33] W. B.Yeats, *The Trembling of the Veil* (London: Privately printed for subscribers only by T. Werner Laurie Ltd., 1922); Seamus Heaney, *Station Island* (London: Faber and Faber, 1984), 104.

[34] Ayukawa Nobuo, *Shishū (Collected Poems)* 1945–1955 (Tokyo: Arechi Shuppansha,

1955). In roman script the lines read: "Mado no fūkei wa / gakubuchi no naka ni hame komareteiru / ā ore wa ame to gairo to yoru ga hoshī / yoru ni naranakereba / kono kentai no machi no zenkei o /umaku hōyō suru koto ga dekinai no da." Ayukawa Nobuo: *Shishū* ["Collected Poems"], 24. The poem was first published in the journal *Arechi* ("The Waste Land") in October, 1949.

[35] Janine Beichman, ed., *101 Modern Japanese Poems*, compiled by Makoto Ōoka, translated by Paul McCarthy (London: Thames River Press, 2012), xix.

[36] See Geoffrey Bownas and Anthony Thwaite, trans., *The Penguin Book of Japanese Verse* New edition (London: Penguin, 1988), lxxiv.

[37] Kinsella Papers, Box 3, Folder 35. The poem was published in the *National Student* 112 (October 1951), 15.

[38] Robert Frost, "The Secret Sits," in *The Poetry of Robert Frost: the Collected Poems, Complete and Unabridged*, ed. Edward Connery Lathem (New York: Henry Holt, 1969), 362.

[39] CP, 12.

[40] Allen R. Grossman, "My Caedmon: Thinking About Poetic Vocation," in *The Long Schoolroom: Lessons in the Bitter Logic of the Poetic Principle* (Ann Arbor: University of Michigan Press, 1997), 1–17.

[41] CP, 13.

[42] Grossman, "My Caedmon: Thinking About Poetic Vocation," 2.

[43] Kinsella Papers, Box 4, Folder 10.

[44] CP, 13.

[45] Antonio Gramsci, *Selections from the Prison Notebooks*. Edited and trans. Quintin Hoare and Geoffrey Nowell Smith (London: Lawrence and Wishart, 1971), 276.

[46] Kinsella Papers, Box 4, Folder 10.

[47] Paul Celan, *Selected Poems and Prose of Paul Celan*, trans. John Felstiner (New York: W.W. Norton & Company, 2001), 396.

[48] CP, 50.

[49] Grossman, "My Caedmon: Thinking About Poetic Vocation," 13.

[50] CP, 13.

CHAPTER 6

Making the Great *Tain*, 1951–1970

THOMAS KINSELLA, LIAM MILLER, AND LOUIS LE BROCQUY

THOMAS DILLON REDSHAW

The pertinence of the *Táin Bó Cúailnge* to the nationalist projects of Yeats's Literary Revival and Pearse's Rising has become a commonplace of Irish history—a commonplace reinforced by each glimpse of Oliver Shepard's 1914 bronze of the dying Cúchulainn in Dublin's General Post Office. Cúchulainn's stature as a hero as large in the imagination as any figure in the *Iliad* or the *Niebenlungenlied* is today tempered by the postmodern reader's awareness of Simone Weil's conviction—hard-won during the opening months of World War II—that heroism engages a necessary dehumanization. Even in the three monastic recensions of the Irish epic's portrayal of La Tène era, Ireland may be glimpsed as a world disordered by willful human appetites. In the telling, the tale foregrounds Medb's domineering ascendancy and Aillil's compliance, the unmanning of Fergus Mac Roich, the failure of the ethic of single combat to sort out competing *geassa* and avert slaughter, and the mortal exhaustion of that society's prepotency. Like all such tales, the *Táin* is a tale of troubled times.

For those reasons and more, the *Táin Bó Cúailnge* retains its status as a "world classic." Indeed, Oxford University Press keeps it in print under that rubric in Thomas Kinsella's 1969 English translation as *The Tain*. Had *The Tain* not been published at that historical moment, and not by Liam Miller's Dolmen Press, and not with Louis le Brocquy's illustrations, the epic's status may well have remained entirely a local, narrowly Irish matter. Kinsella, Miller, and le Brocquy worked most concertedly on *The Tain* from 1965 through 1970—from the Yeats Centenary and the fiftieth anniversary of the Easter Rising through the advent of the Northern "Troubles." On a broader scale, *The Tain* came into being in years when images of confrontation pervaded the world media—the Cultural Revolution in China, the Soviet suppression of the "Prague Spring," and student demonstrations in Mexico City, Paris, Berlin, and Chicago. Ireland made its own headlines in Dungannon, Derry, and Belfast as civil rights demonstrations gave rise to policing by the British Army and resistance in the North. Even the sleepy South had its share of ructions: for example, the three-year student occupation of Dublin's National College of Art and Design.[1] In the United States, the Civil Rights marches and killings in the South and urban rioting in the North through the anti-war demonstrations of 1968 to campus unrest after the 1970 shootings at Kent State University dominated both politics and the media. In 1965, Kinsella had become poet-in-residence at Southern Illinois University in Carbondale, Illinois. From there he sent Miller further corrections to the first Oxford printing of *The Tain*. In his letter Kinsella described Southern Illinois University as "a riot-torn, foreclosed University community," and Carbondale as "under the equivalent of martial law, with a curfew . . ., and tear gas on a hair trigger." Responding to the Kent

State shootings and the occupation of Columbia University, Kinsella closed his letter with a petition: "That some day we may have a floor under our feet that will not shift. . . ."[2]

The role that translating the *Táin Bó Cúailnge* played in the evolution of Kinsella's poetry has yet to receive sufficient commentary. Kinsella did hint to Miller, however, that the long experience of translating played a role in his shift of themes and styles from *Nightwalker and Other Poems* (1968) to his Cuala Press collection *Notes from the Land of the Dead* (1972).[3] Writing chiefly on the later Peppercanister poems, Derval Tubridy has helpfully linked Kinsella's practice of translation from the Irish to Miller's ambitions for his Dolmen Press. A product of deep friendship, the mutually nourishing artistries of Kinsella as a translator and Miller as a maker of books appear early in Dolmen's history. Kinsella's translation of one of the "pre-tales" to the *Táin*—a story known as *Longnes Mac n-Uisnigg*—was twice designed, set, and published by Miller—once in 1954 and again in 1960. One of Irish storytelling's ever popular "Three Sorrows," the tale of Deirdre and Naoisi was dramatized by both Yeats (1907) and Synge (1910). Indeed, recounting later the origin of his ambition to bring the *Táin* into English, Kinsella suggests that this tale's very popularity posed a problem. Writing in 1969, Kinsella observes:

> The making of this translation has been very much an aside to other things. It is fifteen years since I was first tempted to do it. I had just found the oldest version of the Deirdre story and been struck by its superiority over the usual one, and I thought I would look closer at the rest of the Ulster stories. There were plenty of 'retellings' in the bookshops, but actual translations were scarce. . . .[4]

Likewise, writing in *Dolmen XXV* (1976), Miller suggests that his production of *Longnes mac n-Uisnigg: Being the Death of the Sons of Usnech* (November

1954) exemplified a new stage of his own development as a maker of books. Kinsella's translation of this tale was the first title issued from 11 Silchester Park, Glenageary, where Miller and his family had recently moved. Miller housed the press in the garage, and there, as he notes, his "obsessions with typography and design . . . could be indulged."[5] *The Sons of Usnech* is a direct ancestor of *The Tain* in three ways. Most obviously, it represents Kinsella's first public offering in English of a whole Red Branch tale, his translation dating from 1953. Secondly, in the book's colophon, Miller records Kinsella's sense of the recalcitrance of the manuscript source as found in the Book of Leinster:

> The translation is not a literal one, but generally the deviations are slight. The basic material of the chant printed on pages 13 to 15 appears in prose in the original. The change to verse form is an attempt to overcome a notorious difficulty in the Irish text at this point.[6]

Similar concerns, especially about the *rosc* passages, mark Kinsella's translation a decade later of the whole *Táin Bó Cúailnge*. Third, in his colophon, Miller observes that *The Sons of Usnech* "is the twentieth book printed at the Dolmen Press." Crossing that threshold into the maturity of his press's output, Miller elected to make *The Sons of Usnech* a modest *livre d'artiste* embodying the design characteristics later so elegantly displayed in *The Tain* (1969).[7]

Just as Miller later featured le Brocquy's brush drawings as integrating complements to the text of the 1969 *Tain*, so here he selected the designs of an almost forgotten Irish artist to frame Kinsella's translation of *Longes Mac n-Uisnigg*. That artist was the jeweler and metal worker Mia Cranwill (1880–1972), who had provided decorations for Miller's edition of Ewart Milne's *Galion* (1953), a tale rendered from the Book of Leinster. After the Easter Rising in 1916, Cranwill returned to Dublin and opened a workshop in which she created ecclesiastical and civic ornaments, sacred goods, trophies for Gaelic League sports, and regimental flags for the Free State manufactured by Cuala Industries.[8] Her design vocabulary derived from the British arts-and-crafts movement and, particularly, the Celtic Revival. By the 1950s, however, both movements had become dated.[9]

By going back to such design conventions, Miller not only evokes the aesthetic of the Literary Revival, he also pays homage to nearly forgotten artists like Cranwill. Another sort of homage appears in Miller's use of red ink. In *The Sons of Usnech*, the color evokes both the passion of Deirdre and the blood spilled in the murder of Ainnle, Ardan, and Noisi. Here, as later in *The Tain*, Miller offers a nod to the red-letter conventions of Cuala Press printing. As produced by Miller, Kinsella's *The Sons of Usnech* alludes also to the very earliest Dolmen printings. Miller covered the boards of the book with brown paper printed with the repeated block showing Deirdre departing Ulster, her arms stretched out to the hills of the Mourne. The effect resembles that of the small-patterned wallpaper with which Miller had bound Dolmen's first, hand-sewn pamphlets.

Like Kinsella's other two translations from Old Irish—*Faeth Fiada: The Breastplate of Saint Patrick*, which Miller printed three times (1954, 1957, 1961), and his *Thirty-Three Triads* (1955, 1957)—*Longes Mac* n-*Uisnigg* received another printing and the title by which it is best known today: *The Sons of Usnech*. That printing displays a change in Miller's thinking about Kinsella's translation. For it he chose line drawings by Bridget Swinton (1926–2016) executed in a spare, abstracting style. Indeed Swinton's pictorial style resembles that of le Brocquy in the late 1940s, as in his painting *Travelling Woman with Newspaper* (1947).[10] Rather than evoking Celticism, Swinton's handling of the drawn line elides folkloric elements with European Moderne design. Such a choice hints at Miller's later selection of le Brocquy's now famous calligraphic drawings for the 1969 *Tain*.

From 1955 through to 1965, Miller's leading interest lay in presenting Irish writing past and present—from Spenser, Merriman, and Stanihurst to Marcus, Murphy, and Kinsella. Even so, he had strong interest in the artistic and technical challenge of printing drawings, linocuts, and wood engravings by such artists as Leslie MacWeeney (b. 1936) and the young Pauline Bewick (b. 1938). In 1965 Miller played a leading role in the founding of the Graphic Studio Dublin.[11] Indeed, Miller designed and printed a number of books whose prime content was visual rather than literary, among them suites of wood engravings by Robert Gibbons (1955), Elisabeth Rivers (1956), and Tate Adams (1958). Consequently, although it began with the printing of the literary text *Longes mac n-Uisnigg* (1954), Miller's making of *The Tain* may best be viewed as an imaginative effort to bring the whole of a national and literary classic into contemporary artistic focus. The influences at play on Miller's methods and aspirations differ, of course, from those at play on Kinsella's. Indeed, more may be observed directly about Kinsella's making of the text of his *Tain* than about Miller's making of his *Tain*. Only briefly does Miller discuss *The Tain* in *Dolmen XXV*, while Kinsella offers extensive commentary on his translation in the apparatus of the book itself (DXXV 10, 58–59).

Certainly the stimulation of studying Old Irish with John Kelleher at Harvard University in the fall of 1963 informed Kinsella's translation of the *Táin Bó Cúailnge*.[12] While he was working with the Department of Finance in Dublin, Kinsella had available to him within walking distance both a notable scholarly heritage and a trove of Old Irish texts.[13] In 1973, Kinsella recalled discovering "almost unreadable and diabolically expensive Celtic manuscripts, a morass of rare books and of translations, mostly out of print."[14] It was then he conceived the notion of producing "a cheap paperback, available to as many people as wanted it." Among these resources available to Kinsella during his time in the Department of Finance may be counted the holdings of Ireland's National Library, the Royal Irish Academy, and Trinity College. Available as well were scholarly editions dating from the time of Zimmer and Thurneysen in the 1880s and 1890s through to the contemporary researches of James Carney, Proinsias MacCana, and Cecile O'Rahilly. Indeed, though modestly designed to give a "minimum of information" (T 255), Kinsella's notes on the text suggest the rich depth of his own scholarship concerning the *Táin Bó Cúailnge*.[15]

The long project of translating the *Táin Bó Cúailnge* lies in the immediate background of Kinsella's poetry from *Poems* (1956) through *Nightwalker and Other Poems* (1968). During those fifteen years, Kinsella allowed his version of the Deirdre story to be published four times: twice in 1954, once in 1960, and again in *Poems and Translations* (1961). Kinsella discovered that Irish manuscript texts of any antiquity at all resisted "Englishing," and he responded to that resistance with a demanding theory of translation. In a note to an intermediate outline for *The Tain*, Kinsella disapproved of the "fanciful" and "adjectival" style of some of the tales, and observed that "they frequently introduce the supernatural, which appears ... only in some clumsy interpolations into the old texts."[16]

Kinsella's thinking about translating the *Táin Bó Cúailnge* also informs his 1966 lecture to the Modern Languages Association—a lecture at the heart of the foundation of Irish Studies in the United States. The challenge of translation leads him to conclude: "I am certain that a great part of the significance of my own past, as I try to write my poetry, is that the past is mutilated." Kinsella reaches this postcolonial moment having asserted that "every writer in the modern world ... is the inheritor of a gapped, discontinuous, polyglot tradition."[17] Kinsella gets there by reflecting in a self-deprecating way upon the translating he has already accomplished:

> I suppose that is the reason for my few laborious translations from the early Irish; the two or three that have been published and the *Táin Bó Cuailnge* which I have been translating for years, off and on. It is not one of the great things in world literature, perhaps; in its later form, which is complete, it has an overblown decadence; in its earlier form, which is good stylistically, it is unfinished and mutilated. But it seems extraordinary to me that, with all the fairy tale versions of the story, the romantic, the dramatised, and the bowdlerised, there has never been an acceptable translation of the better version—the earlier one—tidied a little and completed from other sources . . .

That paragraph from "The Irish Writer" wholly informs Kinsella's "Translator's Note" to *The Tain* as published in 1969. There Kinsella observes that he was "unprepared for the difficulties in the way of this mild curiosity" about, essentially, recovering the "superiority" of the oldest versions of the Red Branch tales. In turn, that note is informed both by Kinsella's admirable introduction and the wealth of his notes. All three taken together suggest the chief principles of his translation.

First, in the Modernist manner, Kinsella prefers to wrest the "primitive" or pre-Christian elements out from under the later monastic renderings in the Book of Leinster—from what he also refers to as "slackness and bombast" (T xv). This, of course, constitutes a means of preserving the otherness of the original—of attempting to respect the partly unknowable contexts of the oral originals. This is Kinsella's way of avoiding the production of a modern simulacrum in period English—like Lady Gregory's Kiltartan rendering in *Cuchulain of Muirthemne* (1902)—and of escaping the cultural and political demands of the Literary Revival. Instead of "refining away the coarse elements and rationalizing the monstrous and giantesque," Kinsella's tactics seek to reveal them. He proposes that the act of translation should strip away as many "obstacles as possible between the original and the reader," which entails a belief in and a fidelity to a knowable original.

Second, Kinsella thinks of the *Táin Bó Cúailnge* as a set of "Ulster stories," as a set of told narratives, and ultimately as the "nearest approach to a great epic that Ireland has produced" and which deserves embodiment in "a living version of the story." That is, the translator proposes a narrative unity and continuity in the succession of *Táin* stories, observing that "a reasonably coherent narrative extracted, with a little reorganisation" (T xi) and some "tidying" to free the story of "inconsistencies and repetitions." Indeed, he gives the reader this permission: "A reader who is anxious to know how the text actually runs should be able to restore the original disarray." Consequently, Kinsella grants that the ordering of the tales so as to approach continuous narrative is a function of the translator's imagination as informed by scholarship. Observing that his *Tain* is not "literal translation" but, rather, "a close compromise with one," Kinsella asserts that the "main purpose" of his work "is to give a readable and living version of the story" without attempting to replicate the "actual texture" of the narrative in the Old Irish (T xi).

In aiming to convey "the simple force of the story" (T xi)—rather than trying to engage "historical, mythological, symbolic, or other larger aspects" of the *Táin*—Kinsella hopes to preserve in contemporary English the spoken or told aspect of the narratives. Likewise, he hopes to represent the chanted or incanted force of the verse or *rosc* passages by matching "the original for length, ambiguity, and obscurity, and which carry the phrases and motifs and occasional short runs which are decipherable in Irish" (T xii). He also attempts to preserve other details of the recensions of the *Táin* that would normally be deemed narrative defects: "no unifying narrative tone"; "neutral realism" cheek-by-jowl with fantasy; storytelling cues and flourishes; traits betraying the "oral origin" of the stories; and above all the reliance of the tales upon topography, toponyms, and *dinnshenchas* (T xiii). By not taking these and other traits of the *Táin Bó Cúailnge* as flaws and by attempting to collect the whole of distant narratives in English, Kinsella aligns himself with the author of *Ulysses*. As Kinsella observes in *The Dual Tradition* (1995), Joyce stands for the Irish tradition as "healed—or healing—from its mutilation."[18]

Dating the manuscript record of Kinsella's drafting of *The Tain* (1969) poses more problems than dating the typescript record, for dates appear on the manuscripts only by association or happenstance. Even so, the archival record does reveal something of Kinsella's practice. He chose first to derive from the available recensions of the *Táin* comprehensive, forward-moving story. Consequently, several manuscript and typescript versions of the outline of the epic's episodes exist. The earliest manuscripts of Kinsella's narrative occur on Irish foolscap, or on blue foolscap cut into pocket-sized quarters, and are written out fluently in fountain pen in a small hand. Kinsella most likely wrote out these ms pages before 1963 at his desk in the National Library.[19] On National Library call slips in the file are listed sources for the pretales to the *Táin*. Some of these slips may date from before 1968–1969, Kinsella's Guggenheim year, and one lists *Scél Muicce Dathó* (*The Tale of Mac Datho's Pig*) as a "Separate Job."[20]

Kinsella went back to drafting the pretales after he had worked through the whole main narrative. The first whole ms of that narrative spans Irish and American letter-sized stationery and second sheets. The pages of this ms, which Kinsella finished at Southern Illinois University, suggest that he worked from a narrative already rendered into English. In order to arrive at a more refined translation, Kinsella had the habit of setting out in pen, usually ballpoint, seven-to-twelve lines of the narrative in English on the right-hand two-thirds of the page. On the left-hand third of the page appear problematic phrases and words in Old Irish, notes to the rest of the manuscript, and dictionary translations and definitions glossing specific lines. Kinsella then reworked the lines on the right, canceling and inserting phrases and words.[21]

Kinsella had the task of bringing the *Táin Bó Cúailnge* into memorable English well in hand at the start of 1965. In April of that year, Miller issued fifty copies of an episode or tale in the epic known as "Cúchulainn's Boyhood Deeds" as bound specimen pages for what Miller called *The Great Táin*.[22] This working title for Kinsella's translation suggests from the outset its high stature in Miller's artistic imagination and, consequently, its future importance in the Dolmen canon. Two aspects of these bound specimen pages are important. First, while this pamphlet lacks the decor of Cranwill's and Swinton's illustrations for *The Sons of Usnech*, it does make use of Miller's favored typeface for text—Pilgrim—as well as display capitals and colored type—blue rather red or green—and thus alludes to the aesthetic of Eric Gill, the dean of English letterpress printing and typography. Second, *The Great Táin* also represents, however, a design road not taken. Miller most likely would not have invested imagination, time, and effort in Kinsella's rendering of the *Táin* had not a substantial bulk of Kinsella's translation existed already. Indeed, in 1965 Miller was paying scant attention to literary publishing. He concentrated, rather, on scholarly publications connected to W. B. Yeats, the Yeats Summer School, and the Yeats Centenary.[23] In this context, it seems also that Miller's chaste design and choice of a blue card cover for *The Great Táin* alludes to Yeats, to Yeats's theatrical reworkings of the Red Branch tales, and to the craft of Cuala Press books.

Before Dolmen began to set *The Tain* early in 1969, Miller had the compositor's copy text of Kinsella's translation typed on foolscap with perhaps two carbon copies on onionskin. The clarity of impression of the original and its carbons suggests that they were professionally typed using the IBM Selectric in the Dolmen office.[24] These pages seem to constitute the third typescript of Kinsella's translation. Kinsella's very first typescript consists of some 209 pages on stationery having the Southern Illinois University watermark. This typescript features the central narrative of *The Tain* and lacks the pretales, some verse, and many *rosc* passages. Kinsella dictated this draft to a secretary at Southern Illinois University. His typist annotated the seventeenth page in red pencil: "Start here 2/3/66."[25] At this stage of composition the draft reveals Kinsella's apportioning of the narrative into episodes and the titling of these episodes. Kinsella left openings in this draft for further insertions of material, such as a nine-page passage taken from the *Lebor na hUidre*.[26] Most notably, dictating the stories of *The Tain* enabled Kinsella to take on the role of tale-teller and take the exploits of his Cúchulainn back to their oral roots.

From this draft eventually came a second and cleaner typescript of some 267 pages containing all fourteen episodes or chapters of the final 1969 narrative. This 1966 draft is likely the one that Kinsella alluded to in June 1967, when he described to Miller his plans for a summer trip to Dublin: "... [I] expect to be messing around Dublin mostly, trying to get Irish scholars to help me a bit with the finishing of the *rosc* passages of the Táin...."[27] Likewise, because numerous Xeroxed copies of this typescript exist, this is probably the draft on file at Dolmen that Miller mentioned a year later in August 1967: "The installment of the Tain arrived yesterday, and I think it is great. I have added [it] to the manuscript and eagerly await the early episodes." Miller then asked Kinsella, "Can you provide an outline scheme for the whole thing?"[28]

Kinsella copiously annotated and revised this second typescript. For instance, he often canceled and replaced the chapter titles: "The First deaths" became "death, death," or: "The Fight [cancelled] Combat with Fergus and others."[29] In this typescript, brackets indicate absent translations of verse, of *rosc* passages, and sometimes give episode titles, as in this case: "[Death of Forbaeth the Foolish]," later canceled. It may be that Kinsella thought of the episode titles at this point as marginal notes to be let into the text itself in Miller's signature red lettering. The product of two different stretches of typing, this draft served as the base text for the Dolmen typing.[30] That typing came from the IBM Selectric in Miller's editorial office in 8 Herbert Place, but exactly when that typing took place must remain a matter of speculation. Chapters I through VIII of Kinsella's *Tain* were ready for setting early in January, 1969, so the third typescript may well have been completed in the latter months of 1968, when Kinsella was in Dublin at the start of his 1968–69 Guggenheim Fellowship.

Missing from the second typed draft is "The Boyhood Deeds," later titled "Cúchulain's Boyhood Deeds," upon which Miller based a second specimen setting of Kinsella's *Tain*, which he had laid out and pasted up by January 31, 1968.[31] This specimen setting Miller designed was published privately in the same year that he was busy finishing Kinsella's *Nightwalker and Other Poems* (March, 1968). Back in 1965, when he laid out the specimen pages of *The Great Táin*, Miller had been preoccupied with Yeats scholarship and the Yeats Centenary. In 1968, however, Miller's attentions returned to contemporary Irish poetry and to new collections by Austin Clarke, Michael Hartnett, Donagh MacDonagh, John Montague, and Desmond O'Grady. Writing to Kinsella in February 1968, Miller confidently notes that he has decided on the main features of his typographic design for Kinsella's *Tain*: "The Boyhood deeds are fine—much better, if I may so say, and I have set these up to make what I will hope be the final and definitive specimen section and the type will be held for the [1969] book. A printed specimen will follow in a day or two."[32]

Titled *Cuchulainn's Boyhood Deeds*, that "printed specimen" bore little resemblance to the 1965 specimen setting titled *The Great Táin*. For one thing, Miller was now thinking in terms of a much larger or "epic" page size measuring 29 × 19.5 cm rather than 22.7 × 16 cm. For another, Miller discarded the blue wrap and blue-letter titling and display lettering, thus abandoning the design allusions to Yeats and the Cuala Press. He did consider red-letter titling, as his contemporary sketches for a slipcase suggest.[33] In another way, though, Miller did quietly allude to the Revival and Yeats, for the basic format of *Cuchulainn's Boyhood Deeds* echoes that of the Yeats Papers in whose mold he cast the 1969 *Tain* specimen.

While this setting still hints at Miller's admiration for Yeats, the very last phrase of its title—"with Drawings by Louis le Brocquy"—announces Miller's discovery of a different lexicon of design. Rather than choosing for *Cuchulainn's Boyhood Deeds* the antiquarianism of Celtic Revival design, Miller chose the anthropologically informed primitivism of Modernist art after World War II. The cover presents, in the lower right-hand corner, a wolfhound image drawn by le Brocquy and, on the interior, the frontispiece gives a one-page version of le Brocquy's sweeping, two-page image of massed hosts of Connacht and Ulster that appears at the end of *The Tain* (T 236–37).[34] Le Brocquy entered into the *Tain* project at Miller's invitation in December 1966, when Montague encouraged Miller to ask le Brocquy to join in making *The Tain*.[35]

Correspondence between Miller and Kinsella suggests that le Brocquy met twice with Miller early in the summer of 1967. On August 2, 1967, after asking Kinsella for a complete outline of *The Tain*, Miller commented: "Louis le Brocquy is excited and thinking away about the drawings."[36] Indeed, le Brocquy had completed a number of them by that date.[37] Sensing that both Miller and le Brocquy were moving quickly, Kinsella took pains to suggest on August 7, 1967, that his text of *The Tain* was unfinished: "For heaven's sake, please stress to le Brocquy + yourself that this is all still a draft only, and will undergo improvement over the next few months, alas. I think some of [the] improvement is going to come from getting further away from the original."[38]

Le Brocquy worked swiftly on the brush drawings. By September, 1967, Miller had the first set of blocks made and catalogued in a dummy binding for John Montague's Dolmen Edition *All Legendary Obstacles* (1966). Miller completed the final catalogue of blocks a little more than a year later, in December, 1968. "THE TAIN—List of Blocks" was then typed out in May, 1969, and initialed by Miller in June, 1969.[39] Anne Madden recalls that le Brocquy "made literally hundreds of drawings from which he retained the final eighty nine."[40] Miller's dating of the blocks he made from le Brocquy's ink drawings suggests the speed, excitement, and invention that Kinsella's text prompted in le Brocquy.[41] Le Brocquy's November 1968 note on the origin of the *Tain* brush drawings proposes that they resulted from his direct interaction with Kinsella's spare rendering of the narrative. In so doing, they take up Kinsella's notion of "getting further away from the original."

> . . . In particular [Celtic manuscript illuminations] suggest that graphic images, if any, should grow spontaneously and even physically from the matter of the printed text.

> If these images—these marks in printer's ink—form an extension to Kinsella's *Táin*, they are a humble one. It is as shadows thrown by the text that they derive their substance. (T viii)

Le Brocquy's letters to Miller from 1967 through 1969 contain details of his thinking not only about the nature of his brushwork images, but also about their use or placement of the images in Kinsella's text because: "Every page presents us with a new problem of composition. . . ."[42] Le Brocquy's views touched on many aspects of Miller's design of the Dolmen Edition *Tain*. For example, le Brocquy suggested that the two-page spread of the "battle" image be printed in reverse—white against black—on the volume's slip case. Le Brocquy emphatically disapproved of the *Tain* insert that Miller had persuaded *Ireland of the Welcomes* to publish world-wide.[43] While le Brocquy was creating these now famous drawings, and making portfolios of lithographs from them, Miller was approaching his final design for *The Tain* by way of setting *Cuchulainn's Boyhood Deeds*. At the same time, Kinsella was refining the epic's central narrative and setting to work on the pretales, the remaining verse exchanges, and the infamous *rosc* passages.

Resettled in Dublin for his 1968–69 Guggenheim year, Kinsella made good his ambition "to finalise" his translation "helped by the best circumstances, with necessary books to hand in the National Library." He was helped, as well, by having such scholars as James Carney, David Greene, Proinsias Mac Cana, and Breandán Ó Buachalla near to hand.[44] In his introduction to *The Tain*, Kinsella remarks on his debt to Mac Cana in respect, particularly, to rendering the archaic *rosc* passages, noting that Mac Cana's "suggestions were offered as starting points for the [translator's] imagination" (T vii). Observing that scholars have shied away from attempting these passages, Kinsella set them in "stepped form" and hoped to "match the original for length, ambiguity, and obscurity" so as to preserve something of their antique tone and weight of their premonitory interruptions of the narrative.

Likewise, Miller was beginning to settle on the final design for the Dolmen Edition *Tain*. Back in late 1966, Miller had already been thinking in very practical, craftsmanly terms about producing Kinsella's translation. An undistributed specimen setting for in-house use at Dolmen came between that of *The Great Táin* (April 1965) and *Cuchulainn's Boyhood Deeds* (February 1968). This is the opening page setting of the episode in *The Tain* titled "The Death of Froech," which Miller set in Pilgrim type. And Miller was still thinking in terms of *The Great Táin* when he sent Kinsella design specifications quite different from those he eventually adopted.[45] Miller proposes design elements that show he had in mind the presentation of Kinsella's *Tain* in a library edition suiting a classic—something resembling, perhaps, Joseph Dunn's translation published by David Nutt back in 1914.[46] Some aspects of this design did not survive: gold lettering, colored top, elephant hide slipcase. Other elements of the design did survive: headbands, Pilgrim type, text paper, and slipcase. In November and December 1966, Miller had put out inquiries about obtaining a German paper for the text: Zerkall 200 White Antique Finish sheets (30 × 25.5 inches). In December, Miller sought information of Felix and Dante Titling fonts from the Monotype Corporation, London.[47] At this point Miller envisioned issuing a limited, signed edition of 1,050 copies, some to be marketed by Oxford University Press in Britain and some by Dufour Editions in the United States.

Eventually Miller used Felix Titling, but only after briefly pondering an alternative. It struck Miller that *The Tain* deserved lettering from the calligrapher and Modernist poet David Jones.[48] Writing to Kinsella back in

1967, Miller proposed "I might write to that great celtic [*sic*] letterer, David Jones in hopes that he might letter the title—what do you think?"[49] That suggestion underscores Miller's continuing fidelity to Eric Gill's canon of design. On the other hand, it is likely that the handicraft of Jones's lettering would have competed with the artistry of le Brocquy's ink drawings for *The Tain*. Likewise, Miller's use in 1965 of blue titling and initials anticipated his use of red-letter printing in *The Tain* (1969). Dropping the adjective "Great," Miller arrived at a design for the title and half-title pages for *The Tain* that echo the conventions of the *Yeats Centenary Papers* (1965) and carry on from *Cuchulainn's Boyhood Deeds* (1968). Miller set the book's title high on the page in red and black capitals.

The third line of this 1969 design—"with Brush Drawings by Louis le Brocquy"—answers the question that Miller had raised for Kinsella in his December 1966 specimen sheet "The Death Fraoech." On that sheet, the third line of the title reads "With drawings by. . . ." Miller's ellipses pose the question that his summer 1967 meeting with le Brocquy answered. Clearly, Miller's response to the 1966 typescript of *The Tain* was that its narrative scope and strength of language required visual complements more sturdy and striking than colored titles and initials. He specified a frontispiece for the book and noted that the "Drawings required are head pieces to the various sections. . . ."[50] As *Dolmen XXV* amply suggests, Miller's visual responses to Kinsella's typescript were nurtured by his work with the Graphic Studio Dublin and with the printmaker Tate Adams (1958) on *The Soul Cages* (1958) and *Riders to the Sea* (1969) and with the painter Barrie Cooke and the American engraver Jack Coughlin on the second and third Dolmen Edition titles by Montague and Clarke. Using plates made previously for *Ireland of the Welcomes*, *Dolmen XXV* reproduces five *Tain* drawings that Miller selected from the Dolmen files beginning with a plate of Cuchulainn's Warp-Spasm (T

151). A page before the entry on the 1969 *Tain*, Miller offers the Raven image (T 99) full size. Just above the bibliographic entry itself he gives the drawing of Medb and Aillil's Procession (DXXV 57–59). Below that entry he gives the Irish wolfhound image that first appeared on the cover of *Cuchulainn's Boyhood Deeds* (1968). Facing that page, Miller reduces a whole page to show the dramatic relationship of le Brocquy's drawing to the text, to chapter titling, and to initial capitals.

As le Brocquy sent his brush drawings on to Dublin in the fall of 1967, Miller began setting out schemes for the book's binding, dust wrapper, and slipcase. He was also pasting up text on the grid of his page format, positioning illustrations, and laying out chapter heads. Such layout pages reveal some of his design decisions and their consequent effects of the presentation of Kinsella's text. For example, the very first page of Kinsella's narrative once bore the title "How The Tain Bo Cuailnge Was Found Again" in red-letter capitals. The first words of this pretale's opening sentence then followed in display capitals: "SENCHAN TORPEIST | gathered the poets of Ireland around him one day to see if | they could recall the 'Táin Bó Cuailnge' in its entirety."[51] As eventually printed in 1969, the page retains the red lettering but gives "the poets" in display capitals and revises the text: "THE POETS | of Ireland one day were gathered around Senchán Torpéist to see if they . . ." (TT 1). Moreover, on the layout page, Miller lettered in by hand the book's title so as to fill the whole column of print in Felix Titling capitals and take up the space that le Brocquy's *début-de-chapitre* drawing eventually occupied. Likewise, Miller's designs for the book's dust wrapper shifted to one adopted from an early design for the slipcase.[52] Miller then abandoned that for a white wrap with red and black titling and bearing, on the front, le Brocquy's image of Aillil and Medb in their chariots and, on the back, a portion of the Hosts drawing. During the summer of 1967, while le Brocquy was at work in France, Miller also drew up a design for the front face of the slipcase for *The Tain* that filled the rectangular space with letters in Felix Titling.[53]

This design displays some interesting features. Chief among them is that Miller was tempted to imitate the famous carpet pages of Irish monastic manuscripts: he filled the space allotted to print on the page, even though this led to an awkward division of Kinsella's name. Even Miller's spelling wavers sometimes, as when he gives "Cuailgne" for "Cuailnge." Miller held on to the long accent or *fada* in the generic term "Táin" and, indeed, retained the whole of his original 1965 title *The Great Táin*. Just how or why the fada in the title *Tain* disappeared in the 1969 Dolmen Edition printing remains a mystery. Design elements appear here in red, which Miller designates as "vermilion," including the initial decoration, which, being just a sketch, suggests that Miller had not received the first of le Brocquy's drawings at the time he worked up this design. When they began to arrive from France, le Brocquy's drawings encouraged Miller to be less antiquarian, more Modernist in his design of *The Tain*.

Paperback copies of Kinsella's *Tain* may easily be found in many used bookstores today because Oxford University Press co-published the Dolmen Edition as a World's Classic based upon the 1970 library edition, a reduced but nonetheless elegant version of the original Dolmen Edition. That cloth printing was designed by Miller, met le Brocquy's approval, and was widely marketed. The many paperback printings and reissues—some twenty by 1988—gradually abandon the distinguishing features of Miller's design and diminish the effect of le Brocquy's brush drawings. The 2002 reissue of *The Tain* replaces le Brocquy's images with a banal photograph of a charging bull. Miller supervised aspects of Susan Schaup's *Der Rinderraub: Altirisches Epos* (1976) and of the 1985 reduction of the original Dolmen

Edition for the University of Pennsylvania Press.[54] Both preserve the distinct features of Miller's Dolmen Edition.

Miller saw to it that Kinsella's *Tain* would catch the attention of Irish and British readers. Drawing on his long experience in the Lantern Theatre, and his connections to the Abbey Theatre, he arranged a reading of *The Tain* by Kinsella backed up by Paddy Moloney and the Chieftains. This took place at the Peacock Theatre on Sunday, August 31, 1969. He and Kinsella had worked at turning *The Tain* into scripts for performance. A May 1969 scenario of seventeen pages was designed for radio and featured two narrators, two male voices, and two female voices.[55] Miller and Kinsella also created a script for a theatre staging of *The Tain*. Theatrically Miller thought of *The Tain* in terms of Bertolt Brecht's "epic theatre" and sketched out stage set consisting of a ramp curving around a large playing space, a steep ramp leading up to it in the middle, and a raised lectern for a narrator—all backed up by a curved "cyclorama" on which, presumably, le Brocquy's brush drawings might be projected. Tomás Mac Ana of the Abbey and Hilton Edwards of the Gate received scripts for this ambitious staging. Raidió Telefís Éireann made plans for filming *The Tain* in June 1970, but these came to nothing. In the latter weeks of September 1970, after the Oxford University Press trade edition of *The Tain* had been published, Douglas Cleverdon at the British Broadcasting Company presented an hour-long dramatization of Kinsella's translation for BBC3. The large cast included Siobhán McKenna in the role of Medb. For this Seán Ó Riada composed the music and directed the orchestra. The BBC broadcast this performance on September 25, 1970, and again on November 6, 1970.[56] Claddagh Records had suggested that it might issue the BBC tapes as an LP recording.

The story of the creation of the Dolmen *Tain* derives much of its pertinence to Irish literary, artistic, and cultural history from the fact that Kinsella's translation, le Brocquy's brush drawings, and Miller's design of the book went immediately to the very center of Irish literary, artistic, and cultural life in the early 1970s. Kinsella's translation helped support the income and reputation of the Dolmen Press in the 1970s. Almost fifty years later, as an Oxford World's Classics paperback, *The Tain* offers to readers world-wide an informed and informative translation of the *Táin Bó Cuailgne*. It continues to give substance to the Celtic fantasies drawn by Jim Fitzpatrick, to the many children's versions of the Cuchulainn tales in English or Irish, fictions like Randy Lee Eickhoff's *The Raid* (1997), and even the wall murals in Derry and Belfast.

The Tain helped underscore Kinsella's rising reputation outside Dublin and London. Both the Dolmen and the Oxford Editions of *The Tain* eased Kinsella's transition from Southern Illinois University to Temple University in 1970 and, owing to the terms of his new appointment, brought Kinsella back to Dublin annually in the ensuing decades.[57] In the years that Kinsella was at work on *The Tain*, the notice that *Another September* (1958) and *Downstream* (1962) earned from London's Poetry Book Society was amplified by the New York publication of *Nightwalker and Other Poems* (1969) and *Notes from the Land of the Dead* (1973). Kinsella's slow composition of *The Tain* and its reception as a "classic"—an "accomplishment," to echo Yeats—certainly informed the evolution of manner and method in Kinsella's poetry. The success of Kinsella's translation of the *Táin Bó Cúailnge* also made certain the promise of Kinsella's other translation project *An Duanaire: Poems of the Dispossessed 1600–1900* (1981), which he dedicated to T. K. Whitaker "who gave the idea," and whom Kinsella had known since his days in the Department of Finance. From the 1980s on, *An Duanaire* has helped bring students to an appreciation of what Kinsella terms Ireland's "dual" tradition. For poets in both Irish and English, *An Duanaire* became a welcome source book.

The Dolmen *Tain* also confirmed le Brocquy's prominence in Dublin—as well as Paris, London, and New York—as Ireland's leading twentieth-century painter. The images that le Brocquy created for Kinsella's *Tain* and Miller's response to them helped shape, of course, the house style of the Dolmen Press. Le Brocquy made of his brush drawings or "ink marks," as he called them in 1967, several suites of lithographs that were shown not only at the Dawson Gallery in Dublin in 1969, but also at Gimpel Fils in London and Weitzenhoffer in New York. Miller helped le Brocquy obtain the paper for these lithographs, and he oversaw the making of their presentation boxes. Sold individually as well as in sets, le Brocquy's *Tain* lithographs came into many a home in the Dublin suburbs. Half a century on, they continue to sell well in galleries and at auction. Le Brocquy's *Tain* images also became a feature of the corporate art of Ireland for more than a decade. Le Brocquy translated his brush drawings into tapestries: *The Hosting of the Táin* once was displayed in the Modernist head offices of P. J. Carroll and Co.[58] Until late in 2018, an enlarged sheet metal cut-out of one of the *Tain* images dominated Dublin's Dawson Street from the corner of the Irish Life Assurance building, itself a Celtic Revival building with impressively polished bronze doors. Motifs from *The Tain* were translated into sterling silver in the 1970s by Sleator Limited and Royal Irish Silver. Le Brocquy's imagery clearly struck a sympathetic chord in educated popular taste. Other Irish artists took up themes from Kinsella's *Tain*: late in 1970 the young sculptor John Behan created the *Tain Suite* as décor for the remodeled bar in the Gresham Hotel.[59]

For the Dolmen Press and for Miller, *The Tain* established both as the leading proponents of Irish poetry, publishing, and fine printing. Long collected locally in Dublin, Dolmen printings of any sort acquired the prestige once accorded to the Yeats sisters' Cuala Press printings. The Dolmen *Tain* provided an elevated standard against which other examples of Irish fine presswork—like recent works from Dublin's Salvage Press—might be judged. Moreover, the international success of *The Tain* provided the Dolmen Press with an added degree of confidence—some of it financial—that a little later aided the production of Montague's *The Rough Field* (1972) and then Kinsella's own Peppercanister poems. In the 1970s, Liam Miller became a national spokesman for Irish writing, publishing, and graphic design. He came to serve, for instance, as the founding chairman of CLÉ, the Irish Book Publishers Association. Miller became the dean of Irish publishers. In respect to Irish poetry, Dolmen became the exemplar for Michael Smith's New Writer's Press, John F. Deane's Dedalus Press, and Peter Fallon's Gallery Press.

Notes

[1] See John Turpin, "Life Class. The Student Revolution at the National College of Art, Dublin, 1968–71," *Éire-Ireland*, 27, no. 3 (Fall 1992), 18–43.

[2] Thomas Kinsella to Liam Miller, 15 May 1970. Wake Forest University, Z. Smith Reynolds Library, Special Collections, Dolmen Collection, 12e. Writing two weeks later to Miller, Kinsella observed that Southern Illinois University was suffering from "a shambles of student riots, right-wing reaction, and impending political scrutiny (which would nose out very quickly any useless luxuries like myself)."

[3] Derval Tubridy, *Thomas Kinsella: The Peppercanister Poems* (Dublin: University College Dublin Press, 2001), 4–5.

[4] Thomas Kinsella, *The Tain, Translated from the Irish Epic Tain Bo Cuailnge* (London: Oxford UP, 1970), vii; hereafter cited parenthetically, thus (T vii).

[5] Liam Miller, *Dolmen XXV: An Illustrated Bibliography of the Dolmen Press 1951–1976*, Dolmen Editions 25 (Dublin: Dolmen Press, 1976), 20; hereafter cited parenthetically, thus: (DXXV 20).

[6] *Longes Mac n-Uisnigg: Being the Exile and Death of the Sons of Usnech*, trans. Thomas Kinsella (Dublin: Dolmen Press, November 1954), 35.

[7] See Ailbhe Ní Bhriain, "Le Livre d'Artiste: Louis le Brocquy and *The Tain* (1969)," *New Hibernia Review* 5, no. 1 (Spring 2001), 67–82.

[8] Theo Snoddy, *Dictionary of Irish Artists: Twentieth Century* (Dublin: Merlin Publishing, 2002), 120–21.

[9] Jeanne Sheehy, *The Rediscovery of Ireland's Past: The Celtic Revival, 1830–1930* (London: Thames and Hudson, 1980), 169–70.

[10] Dorothy Walker, *Louis le Brocquy* (Dublin: Ward River Press, 1981), 11, pl. 4.

[11] See Brian Lalor's chapter on Liam Miller in Lalor's *Ink-Stained Hands: Graphic Studio Dublin and the Origins of Fine-Art Printmaking in Ireland* (Dublin: Lilliput Press, 2011), 51–56.

[12] Kinsella acknowledges the Bórd Scoláireachtaí Cómalairte for a six-month fellowship in 1963 (T vii). Among the Irish poet-scholars who followed Kinsella to Harvard in the 1960s were Desmond O'Grady and Eamon Grennan.

[13] See George O'Brien, "Irish Civil Service Was the Biggest Patron of the Art since the Medici," Ticket, *Irish Times*, 3 February 2018, 25.

[14] Donal Musgrave, "Intellectually May . . . ," *Irish Times*, 29 August 1973, 13.

[15] Copies of scholarly articles in Kinsella's files sometimes bear evidence of his working methods. For example, while teaching at Southern Illinois University in the mid-1960s, Kinsella marked up a copy of Whitley Stokes's turn-of-the-century version one of the pretales. "Tidings of Conchobar Mac Ness," *Ériu* 4 (1908): 18–26. On page 24, Kinsella glosses *co-n-erbarthar* as "without a man," instead of following Stokes's "was 'unmarried,' literally 'in celibacy,'" thus preferring a wording free of connections to Latin, to Christianity, and to the conventional notions attached to the term "marriage." Kinsella Papers, MSS 774, 31.9.

[16] Kinsella Papers, MSS 774, 37.15.

[17] Thomas Kinsella, "The Irish Writer," in *Davis, Mangan Ferguson?: Tradition and the Irish Writer*, ed. Roger McHugh, The Tower Series of Anglo-Irish Studies II (Dublin: Dolmen Press, 1970), 66.

[18] Thomas Kinsella, *The Dual Tradition: An Essay on Poetry and Politics in Ireland*, Peppercanister 18 (Manchester: Carcanet Press, 1995), 91.

[19] Kinsella Papers, MSS 774, 31.24.

[20] Kinsella Papers, 774, 31.24. Even so, folder 32.26 contains an early ms draft on foolscap starting out: "The Tale of Mac Datho's Pig begins. . . ."

[21] Kinsella Papers, MSS 774, 32.1–2.

[22] Dolmen Collection, Box E. In an early ms and a later ts Kinsella gave this episode the title "Boyish Deeds." Kinsella Papers, MSS 774, 34.29; 31.30.

[23] Among those nine titles are: *A Memorial Sermon Preached at Drumcliffe on the Occasion of the Centenary of the Birth of W. B. Yeats* (June, 1965); *Thoor Ballylee—Home of William Butler Yeats* (June, 1965); and the first five of *The Dolmen Press Centenary Papers* (March–June, 1965). See DXXV, 41–43.

[24] Some evidence indicates that this copy text may be an early typing, for a carbon copy of the foolscap ts along with an outline of "The Tain Bo Cuailnge" bears the date December 12, 1966. Kinsella Papers, MSS 774, 37.1.

[25] Kinsella Papers, MSS 774, 32.7.

[26] Kinsella Papers, MSS 774, 32.11.

[27] Thomas Kinsella to Liam Miller, 12 June 1967. Dolmen Collection, 12E.

[28] Liam Miller to Thomas Kinsella, 2 August 1967. Dolmen Collection, 12E.

[29] Kinsella Papers, MSS 774, 332.2, Chapter 7.

[30] One clue that this ts consists of at least two typings is that the chapter numerals switch from Roman to Arabic after the fourth chapter. Kinsella Papers, MSS 774, 33.1.

[31] Dolmen Collection, 64b.

[32] Liam Miller to Thomas Kinsella, 6 Feabhra [February] 1968. Dolmen Collection, 12E.

[33] Dolmen Collection, Box E.

[34] Printed in reverse, this image appears on the Dolmen Edition and IUP slipcases and as the jacket and cover of the first Oxford University Press editions in cloth and paperback. In "The Táin: List of Blocks, Final" (June, 1969), this image is titled simply "battle."

[35] In her informal biography of le Brocquy, Anne Madden states that Miller approached le Brocquy about doing drawings for *The Tain*, but she gives no date for their meeting. Anne Madden le Brocquy, *Seeing His Way: Louis le Brocquy, A Painter* (Dublin: Gill and Macmillan, 1994), 178. Miller knew the le Brocquy family directly. In 1967 and 1968, he published three books by Sybil le Brocquy (1892–1973), Louis le Brocquy's mother.

[36] Sending copies of the ts for "The Boyhood Deeds," Kinsella acknowledged that

he had received copies of some of the le Brocquy drawings for *The Tain* from Miller. Thomas Kinsella to Liam Miller, 12 August 1967. Dolmen Collection, 12E.

[37] Liam Miller to Thomas Kinsella, 2 August 1967. Dolmen Collection, 12E.

[38] Thomas Kinsella to Liam Miller, 7 August 1967. Dolmen Collection, 12E.

[39] "The Tain: List of Blocks, Final," 6 pp. The catalog lists some 124 blocks and gives them such titles as "Raven" or "stepping on a lance in flight," as well as page and position in the printed text. Dolmen Collection, 64B.

[40] Madden, *Seeing His Way*, 179.

[41] The "List of Blocks" gives these dates: September 19, 1967 (T1–13); November 10, 1967 (T14–60); December 23, 1967 (T65–86); January 31, 1968 (Y87–119 and T12024), not including maps. Dolmen Collection, 64B. If Anne Madden's count of the final suite of drawings that le Brocquy sent to Miller is accurate, then it seems that Miller chose to reproduce some drawings, to divide the images in some drawings, and to enlarge, reduce, or reverse some images so as to arrive at 124 blocks for the *Tain.*

[42] Louis le Brocquy to Liam Miller, 8 May 1969, Dolmen Collection, 12E.

[43] Thomas Kinsella, "The Táin," *Ireland of the Welcomes* 16, no. 6 (March–April 1969), 21–28.

[44] Thomas Kinsella to Liam Miller, 9 April 1968. Dolmen Collection, 12E.

[45] Dolmen Collection, Box 114/16.

[46] See *The Ancient Irish Epic Tale Táin Bó Cúalnge*, trans. Joseph Dunn (London: David Nutt, 1914). An American scholar, Dunn keyed his translation to the commonly archived ms texts of the tales of and connected to the *Tain Bó Cúailnge*. The book that Nutt produced is an impressive example of scholarly printing and of Celtic Revival design.

[47] Dolmen Archive, Box E.

[48] Kinsella Papers, MSS 774, 37.7.

[49] Liam Miller to Thomas Kinsella, 3 August 1967. Dolmen Collection, 12E.

[50] Kinsella Papers, MSS 774, 37.1.

[51] Kinsella Papers, MSS 774, 37.17.

[52] Dolmen Collection, Box E.

[53] Liam Miller, Slip Case Design, Dolmen Collection, Box E.

[54] See Susan Schaupt, trans. *Der Rinderraub: Alterisches Epos* (Berlin: Rütten und Loe-

ning, 1976) and Thomas Kinsell, trans., *The Tain* (Philadelphia, University of Pennsylvania Press, 1985). The Schaupt translation was printed in Leipzig in the German Democratic Republic. The University of Pennsylvania Press edition was printed in Ireland at *The Leinster Leader*.

[55] Thomas Kinsella and Liam Miller, "Scenes from the Tain Bo Cuailgne," Dolmen Collection, Box 38.

[56] Production Schedule DEO57B, British Broadcasting Corporation, Dolmen Collection, Box E.

[57] Thomas Kinsella to Liam Miller, 30 May 1970. Kinsella Papers, MSS 774.38.22.

[58] Madden, *Seeing His Way*, 183–84.

[59] Adrian Frazier, *John Behan: The Bull from Sheriff Street* (Dublin: Lilliput Press, 2015), 61.

Figure 1. Sleíbthe Cuailgne.

CHAPTER 7

Story and Place in Thomas Kinsella's Poem "The Route of *The Táin*"

PAUL GOSLING

"The Route of *The Táin*" is a poem by Thomas Kinsella, first published in 1973 as part of the collection entitled *New Poems*.[1] It has been included in all the collected editions of his poetry and has featured in a number of recent anthologies of modern Irish verse.[2] Writing of the *New Poems* collection in 2006, Harry Clifton described it as "roughly a mid-point in the trajectory of Thomas Kinsella."[3] His long career spanned seven decades, during which he emerged as one of Ireland's most respected poets. Though the poem has been the subject of frequent comment by critics, the circumstances which prompted Kinsella to pen it have not been explored, nor has its topographic content been treated in any detail. The aim of this essay is to honor the poem and the poet by offering an analysis of these two aspects.[4]

As a professional archaeologist with an interest in the Táin, I was first drawn to the poem not by the prospect of lyric enlightenment but by the mundane possibility that it might offer insights into the topographic aspects of the story. Working as I have been on the placement of names mentioned in the *Táin*, I was at first puzzled by it.[5] Familiar places in County Louth—Omeath, Ravensdale—were juxtaposed with the names of real people—Gene Haley, a Harvard postgraduate student, Kinsella himself—whom I knew as renowned experts on the epic. Stranger still were the passages of terse reflection which seemed to focus on the frustrations and joys of researching the toponymic aspects of the story. Though I initially set the poem aside as a puzzling piece of ephemera about the *Táin*, I found myself being drawn back to it at intervals for no good reason. With each rereading, the articulation of the solitary joys and frustrations of the researcher brought a sort of comfort. Kinsella's vocalization of the silent epiphanies—"something reduced shivering suddenly / into meaning"—that accompany the identification of old toponyms is quite powerful, as is his rendering of the labor involved in research—"the whole tedious enabling ritual." Such passages temper the incongruities of devoting hundreds of hours to the study of a 2,000-year-old cattle raid that never took place.

The Story of the *Táin*

Táin Bó Cúailnge (cattle raid of Cooley), to give its full name, is the central story of what is known as the Ulster Cycle, a group of 50 or so tales of medieval date concerning the Ulaid (from whence Ulster), a tribal group who controlled the northeast of Ireland at the dawn of history. Though the antecedents of the *Táin* extend back to the seventh century AD, full-blown versions of the story only emerge in the early twelfth.[6] The *Táin* relates how the legendary Queen Medb of Crúachain Aí (Rathcroghan, County Roscommon) in a fit of pique, raises an army to capture a prize bull (Donn

Cúailnge) so she can match one-for-one the possessions of her husband, Ailill. Having initially demanded the loan of Donn Cúailnge, her request is refused, and thus she raises an army to capture it. Departing at Samhain (Halloween), her army traverses Ireland's north midlands to reach Cúailnge (Cooley, County Louth) where the bull is kept (Fig. 1). Their progress is hindered by a lone warrior, Cúchulainn, upon whom the defense of Ulster rests. Via a series of skirmishes and single combats, culminating in the fight with Ferdia at Ardee in Louth, Cúchulainn harries the Connacht army until the Ulstermen recover from a debilitating curse. Despite his efforts, Queen Medb captures Donn Cúailnge and retreats westwards through Ardee, Kells, and Mullingar towards the Shannon as spring begins. The Ulstermen, led by King Conchobhar (Conor), finally rouse themselves, pursue the Connacht army, and engage them in a tumultuous battle near Ballymore in County Westmeath. Though defeated, Medb succeeds in bringing Donn Cúailnge across the Shannon at Athlone, and back to Rathcroghan. Donn Cúailnge clashes with her husband's bull, Finnbennach, kills him, and returns to Ulster with the carcass of Finnbennach on his horns, only to die of his wounds. Connacht makes peace with Ulster. Supposedly set about the time of Christ, the story depicts an Ireland which is tribal, pagan, and rural, where heroic warriors battle each other to victory or death to satisfy the whims of haughty kings and queens, and where place and placenames are central to the storytelling.[7]

Place and Placenames in *Táin Bó Cúailnge*

In September 1969, The Dolmen Press published a new translation of *Táin Bó Cúailnge* under the full title *The Tain translated by Thomas Kinsella from the*

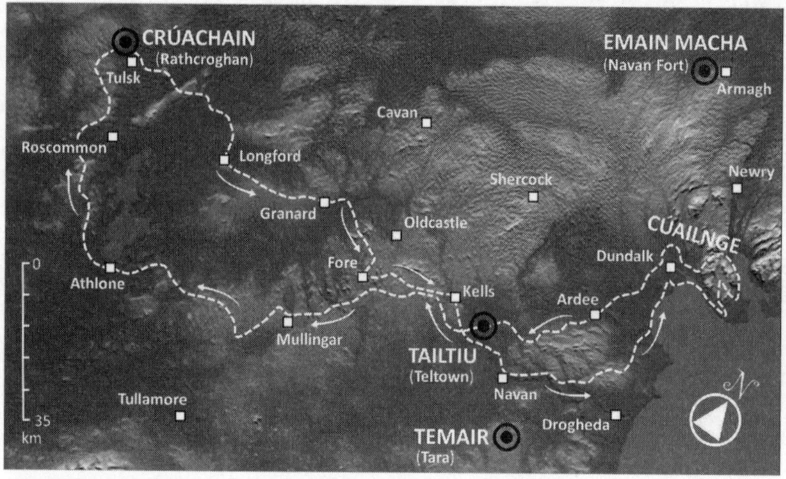

Figure 2. The full route of *Táin Bó Cúailnge* from Cruachan Aí.

Irish with brush drawings by Louis le Brocquy.[8] The book has been much celebrated, not least for Kinsella's treatment of the text but also for Louis le Brocquy's bold artwork and Liam Miller's distinctive book design.[9] What is often overlooked is a fourth innovative aspect: the inclusion of new topographic research on the placenames which feature in the text. This is most evident in the inclusion of maps tracing the route of Queen Medb's forces from Connacht to Ulster and back (Fig. 2). These had been prepared with the aid of Haley and were accompanied by a tabulated list of placenames with identifications.[10] Not since Eleanor Hull's *The Cuchullin Saga in Irish Literature* (1898) had the topographic aspects of the epic been afforded such primacy of place in a major edition of *Táin Bó Cúailnge*.

The success of the first limited edition led quickly to a second mass imprint, in hard and paperback formats, published in October 1970 by Oxford University Press.[11] While the first edition featured two maps of the overall route, the second was graced by an additional map focusing on Cooley,

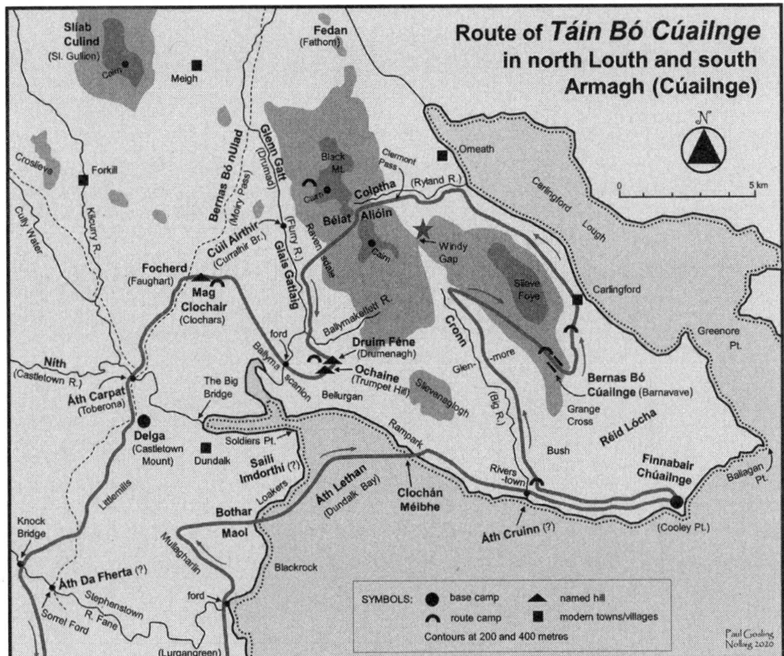

Figure 3. The route of Queen Medb's army.

County Louth (Fig. 3), and by comments on the placename identifications in an expanded "Notes on the Text" section. These were based on Haley's toponymic research; his D.Phil. thesis on the topography of *Táin Bó Cúailnge* had been completed in May, five months earlier.[12] Though little noticed then or now, a tantalizing statement in the introduction to the first edition (1969) was dropped in the second (1970). This read as follows:

> a full analysis of the route, including the detailed topography of the Cooley area, will be published soon in *The Route of the Táin*, a Dolmen Press book containing further maps and essays.[13]

It was to be penned by Haley and Kinsella but never saw print. Thus, the research on which the maps and toponymic identifications were based remained unpublished.[14]

The only crumb was a short article published in 1975 by Kinsella in the tourist magazine *Ireland of the Welcomes*.[15] In it, he outlined his indebtedness to the research of Dr. Gene Haley and his supervisor Professor John V. Kelleher of Harvard University. Though the article dealt with only 84 of the *c*.350 placenames mentioned in the *Táin*, it was a slickly presented full-color piece which was re-printed and retailed as a stand-alone brochure. As a result, it and the maps in the Oxford edition of *The Tain* inspired many subsequent re-tracings of the route in populist and tourist literature, including the Táin Trail cycling route (*c*.1998), the Táin Way walking route (2002), and the Táin March festival, which began in 2011 and continues to this day. In the new millennium, Haley made a welcome return to his placename research with a web-based project "Places in the Tain" (2012); via the latter, he has, in effect, published his doctoral research.[16] Though new translations of the story have been penned in the meantime by Eoin Neeson and Ciaran Carson, neither accords the same importance to the topographic aspects of the story.[17]

By highlighting the role of placenames, Kinsella's added substantially to his expressed aim of creating "a living version of the story."[18] Reflecting on this in 1975, he admitted that he "had reached a very late stage in the translation without taking much notice of them" [*i.e.* placenames], but via his contact with Kelleher and Haley, came to realize the "remarkable place" which they occupy in the *Táin*.[19] The exposition of placenames in medieval texts is known as *dinnshenchas* (literally: place lore) and is particularly characteristic of the Ulster Cycle stories, nowhere more so than in *Táin Bó Cúailnge*. Thus, the advance and retreat of Medb's forces across the north Irish midlands is related through a series of incidents at specific locations (Fig. 3). The explanations provided for individual toponyms often involve fanciful etymologies whose function is either incidental/additive, constituent, or creative.[20] The result is a literary tapestry in which the character of those involved are fleshed out, and an impression of reality is created. While most scholars agree that the people and events are purely fictional, many of the placenames are genuine, and the topographical settings appear to reflect an early medieval reality.[21] As Kinsella so aptly expressed it, "The strange events of the *Táin* may be pure fantasy . . . but even if they never happened, we know fairly accurately where they didn't."[22]

The Poem and the Book

As noted above, "The Route of *The Táin*" is frequently mentioned in commentaries on Kinsella's work. However, many of the citations are short, seeking only to position it in the wider contexts of Kinsella's oeuvre and modern Irish poetry in general. However, a few critics delve deep beneath the surface of its text, seeking the subliminal and symbolic.[23] Among these, Patrick Crotty's analysis is particularly important for present purposes. He identifies a recurrent theme of "peregrination across a landscape" in some of Kinsella's best known poems.[24] Categorizing these as "journey poems," Robert Garratt points out that "regardless of its form the external journey always involves an inner, psychological journey as well as an external one."[25] This is certainly the case in "The Route of *The Táin*" where the inner, psychological journey is best understood as a meditation on the project to re-publish the *Táin* in the later 1960s—witness the repetition of the phrases "our book" and "our map" in the first twenty lines. Though some of the published analyses of the poem do touch on this autobiographical aspect, none of them explore it in any detail.

The project to re-publish the *Táin* was unique in many respects, not least in its collaborative nature. Kinsella's partners were the publisher, Miller, the artist, le Brocquy, and the toponymic scholar, Haley. Miller was the instigator and manager, but the key ingredient was Kinsella's translation. As previously stated, the aim was the creation of a new "living version of the story"[26] via a fresh English translation, complemented by innovative artwork and mapwork, delivered in a bold book design.[27] The result was the Dolmen Press edition, published in September 1969 to instant acclaim in a limited run of 1,750 copies. That Kinsella derived much satisfaction from the collaborative nature of "our book" is evident from his evocation: "cheerfully as we made and remade it / through a waste of hours, content to 'enrich the present / honouring the past', each to his own just function."[28] Miller echoed these sentiments during a 1981 radio interview: "why our first edition came off magnificently was that Louis . . . was in Dublin, Tom had a sabbatical from his American university, and we were all able to work together . . . in a kind of ideal situation that very rarely happens" [in publishing].[29] In the essay he contributed to the *Dolmen Press: A Celebration*, Kinsella also recalls this period, writing of the

> . . . year [1968–9] spent in the peace of Raglan Road [Dublin] and in the assembly of the big Dolmen Press book . . . the text and Louis le Brocquy's illustrations, and the maps, coming together under Miller's guidance and control; the narrative and the drawings balanced between the baleful and the comic, never entirely settling for one or the other; yet with everything totally serious, each of us putting forth his best efforts, Miller exerting maximum pressure with the lightest of touches.[30]

This was obviously a vibrant period in the poet's life, and in one sense the poem is marking its closure. Though "The Route of *The Táin*" was first published in 1973, four years after the publication of the Dolmen Press book, the poem had evidently been finished more than a year before that.

The acknowledgments to the *New Poems* collection state that "many of these poems were written or begun in 1968–69."[31] And in re-presenting the poem as part of his essay celebrating the Dolmen Press, he specifically dates it "1971."[32]

The Participants and the Occasion

The literary commentaries on "The Route of *The Táin*" display little interest in the people mentioned in the poem or in the occasion of the re-tracing of the route. Yet the names of the participants are evident, as is the date of the events which led them to the uplands of Cooley. The journey took place in the late summer of 1969 as *The Tain* was being printed and bound by the Dolmen Press.[33] Kinsella alludes to this when referring to the group "who had set out [from Rathcroghan] / so cheerfully to celebrate our book."[34] In a 1981 radio interview, Miller recalled the occasion, relating that he, Kinsella, and le Brocquy found space to "take a few days off for the three of us . . . [to] go and visit all the scenes from the itinerary."[35] These few days also appear to have been of special significance for le Brocquy: an account of his career penned in 2008 by his son Pierre mentions that "the walkabout [of 1969] gives rise to a new bout of creativity in the realm of tapestry."[36]

They were joined on "the walkabout" by Haley.[37] His role in the project is flagged in the poem's opening line: "Gene sat on a rock, dangling our map." Symbolizing the cumulative results of research on the route of the Táin, the "map" was the product of Haley's toponymic and topographic work under the guidance of Kelleher. Haley has also recalled "the walkabout," again emphasizing the impact it had on all four men. In his account we learn that the core group were joined in Cooley by others:

> In August 1969, to celebrate the publication of Tom Kinsella's landmark translation, *The Tain*, a party of some dozen or more merry souls exited our vehicles a few meters within and at the top of the glen of Omeath and essayed the climb ahead. The poet translator [Thomas Kinsella]; the illustrator, Louis le Brocquy; the publisher, Dolmen's Liam Miller; friends and families, leading scholars (like my dear friend, the late professor Proinsias MacCana), and myself . . . all followed my route up and over . . . and down to Ravensdale on the far side.[38]

Though he became a champion of the placenames of the *Táin*, Kinsella has admitted that he "had reached a very late stage in the translation without taking much notice of them."[39] Haley's input appears to have transformed this viewpoint, and Kinsella's resulting enthusiasm is reflected in the evolving series of topographic maps which are a feature of the Dolmen and Oxford University Press editions of the book.[40] By late summer 1969, a decision had been taken to publish a separate "Dolmen Press book containing . . . a full analysis of the route."[41] This was to be penned by Haley and Kinsella; however, as noted above, it never saw print. As it turned out, the only publication to appear on the toponymic aspects was Kinsella's short essay published in 1975 in *Ireland of the Welcomes*.[42]

The poem speaks of the group being at Rathcroghan, in County Roscommon, in "the morning sunlight." While the physical distance from there to Cooley in County Louth is only about 150 miles, Miller's account suggests that they took "a few days [to] visit all the scenes from the itinerary."[43] The vividness of the journey is captured in Kinsella's description of the weather; contrast the phrases ". . . at Cruachan, where it began. / The morning sunlight pouring on us all" with "hills that seemed to grow / darker as we drove nearer" [to Cooley]. This invocation of the elements also establishes a mood of "irritation" which evidently affected the party as they sought to re-trace the path of Medb's army in the Cooley uplands (Fig. 2). That is, until the serendipitous "red fox" showed them the way.

The Text and the Placenames

The poem is printed here as it appears in the Wake Forest University Press edition of Kinsella's *Collected Poems*. While the wording is identical to that printed in *New Poems*,[44] the text is arranged in 62 lines rather than the original 63. From a topographic perspective, the poem enables one to determine the point on the landscape where Kinsella envisions himself: on the mountain slope above the by-road to Omeath just north of the Windy Gap (Fig. 3). This is possible because phrases and places mentioned in the epic are interleaved quite precisely with real places encountered during the re-tracing of the route. All in all, a total of 15 places are alluded to in the poem, including two placenames mentioned in the *Táin* itself. All bar one are in County Louth where the central scenes of the story were played out.

The rich toponymic detail gives the poem an opaque quality akin to a manuscript text which has to be studied and glossed to be fully understood. To explain the topographic content effectively, the text as presented below is provided with line enumeration in the manner of a diplomatic edition of a medieval document. The notes following the poem are thus offered in the spirit of marginal glosses. Consider them as a set of observations, many of which benefit from being read in conjunction with the maps which accompany Kinsella's translation[45] and Haley's "Places in the Tain" web project.[46]

Gene sat on a rock, dangling our map.
The others were gone over the next crest,
further astray. We ourselves, irritated,
were beginning to turn down toward the river
back to the car, the way we should have come.

We should have trusted our book.
After they tried a crossing, and this river too
'rose against them' and bore off
a hundred of their charioteers toward the sea
They had to move along the river Colptha
up to its source.
                    There:
Where the main branch sharpens away gloomily
to a gash in the hill opposite.

then to Bélat Ailiúin
                    by that pathway
climbing back and forth out of the valley
over to Ravensdale.

Scattering in irritation. Who had set out
so cheerfully to celebrate our book;
cheerfully as we made and remade it
through a waste of hours, content to 'enrich the present
honouring the past', each to his own just function.
Wandering off, ill-sorted,
like any beasts of the field,
one snout honking disconsolate,
another burrowing in its pleasures.

When not far above us a red fox
ran at full stretch out of the bracken
and panted across the hillside toward the next ridge.
Where he vanished – a faint savage sharpness
out of the earth – an inlet of the sea
shone in the distance at the mouth of the valley
beyond Omeath: grey waters crawled with light.

For a heartbeat, in alien certainty,
we exchanged looks. We should have known it by now
– the process, the whole tedious enabling ritual.
Flux brought to fullness; saturated;
the clouding over; dissatisfaction
spreading slowly like an ache;
something reduced shivering suddenly
into meaning along new boundaries;

through a forest,
by a salt-dark shore,
by a standing stone on a dark plain,
by a ford running blood,
and along this gloomy pass, with someone ahead
calling and waving on the crest
against a heaven of dismantling cloud,
transfixed by the same figure (stopped, pointing)
on the rampart at Cruachan, where it began.

The morning sunlight pouring on us all
as we scattered over the mounds
disputing over useless old books,

assembled in cheerful speculation
around a prone block, *Miosgán Medba*
– Queen Medb's *turd* . . . ? And rattled our maps,
joking together in growing illness
or age or fat. Before us
the route of *The Táin*, over men's dust,
toward these hills that seemed to grow
darker as we drove nearer.

Figure 4. Prehistoric monolith at Rathiddy, near Knockbridge, Co. Louth.

Commentary

Line 1: "Gene sat"—Gene Haley, whose doctoral research was on the placenames.

Line 4: "toward the river"—the Ryland River which outflows into Carlingford Lough at Omeath, Co. Louth (for its location, see Fig. 3).

Line 6: "our book"—the Dolmen Press edition of *The Tain* (1969).

Line 8: "rose against them"—quotation from page 102 of the Dolmen Press edition.

Line 10: Haley and Kinsella identified the "*Colptha*" as the Ryland River at Omeath (see Fig. 3).

Lines 10–11, 15: The passages in italics are quotations from page 102 of the Dolmen Press edition, stressed to emphasize "we should have trusted our book" (line 6).

Line 14: The "gash" is the deep cut in the mountainside above Clermont Pass Bridge, west of Omeath (see Fig. 3).

Lines 15–18: "*then to Bélat Ailiúin* / by that pathway"—the pathway is the Cadger's Pad which connects Omeath with Ravensdale on the west side of the mountain (see Fig. 3).

Line 21: "as we made and re-made it" *i.e.* the Dolmen Press edition.

Lines 22–3: "'enrich the present honouring the past.'" The source has not been identified—John Greening writes of the many "unattributed quotations" which feature in Kinsella's later work.[47]

Line 23: "each to his own just function"—Kinsella to his translation; le Brocquy to his art; Miller to his book design; Haley to his placenames.

Line 26: "one snout honking disconsolate"—this is best understood as a reference to the poet himself; a culmination of the mood conveyed in previous lines through the repeated use of "irritate" (lines 3 and 19).

Line 27: "another burrowing in its pleasures"—this is most likely to be Gene Haley, lost in his maps. Along with Kinsella, they had become separated from "the others" (line 2), *i.e.* Louis le Brocquy and Liam Miller.

Line 28: The darting run of the fox symbolizes the frequently sudden nature of inspiration—"something reduced shivering suddenly into meaning" (lines 41–2).

Lines 32: "an inlet of the sea"—this is Carlingford Lough on the shores of which Omeath is situated (see Fig. 3).

Line 43: "through a forest"—this and the following five lines are referencing places which feature in the *Táin* or related stories from the Ulster Cycle. The "forest" is possibly "an Fid Mór" whose name is preserved in the name "Fews," an area of south Armagh.

Line 44: "by a salt-dark shore"—Kinsella's interpretation of "saili imdorchi" a placename mentioned in the *Táin*. He and Haley equate it with the Loakers, a section of coastline on the outskirts of Dundalk which was formerly an extensive salt marsh (see Fig. 3).

Line 45: "by a standing stone on a dark plain"—this is "Cloghafarmore" (stone of the big man), an impressive Standing Stone at Rathiddy, near Knockbridge, Co. Louth, where Cúchulainn is reputed to have died (Fig. 4).

Line 46: "by a ford running blood"—this is probably a reference to Áth Fhir Diad' (Ardee, Co. Louth) where Cúchulainn fought and killed Ferdia (Fig. 5).

Line 47: "along this gloomy pass"—this is the Windy Gap at the top (north end) of Glenmore in Cooley. Kinsella and Haley equate this saddle-point with the "Bernas Bó Cúailnge" of the *Táin*, but recent scholarship locates the pass at Barnavave mountain, four miles to the southeast.

Line 51: "at Cruachan, where it began"—now Rathcroghan, near Tulsk, Co.

Roscommon. The *Táin* commenced from here, as did Kinsella, le Brocquy, and Miller when re-tracing the route (Fig. 6).

Line 53: "we scattered over the mounds"—these are the numerous earthworks in the landscape around Rathcroghan.

Line 54: "useless old books"—best understood in conjunction with lines 56–57 as an example of Kinsella's sardonic wit: the wry comic image of middle-aged men mulling over obscure manuscript texts while standing around the fossilized turd of a mythical queen.[48]

Line 56: "*Miosgán Medba*"—this is a prone block of limestone which lies north of Rathcroghan mound (Fig. 6).

Line 57: "our maps"—drafts of the topographic maps by Haley and Kinsella that were included in the Dolmen and Oxford University Press editions.

Line 61: "toward these hills"—the hills of south Ulster, *i.e.* Cooley and south Armagh (Fig. 2).

Figure 5. Cúchulainn carrying the body of his foster-brother Ferdia.

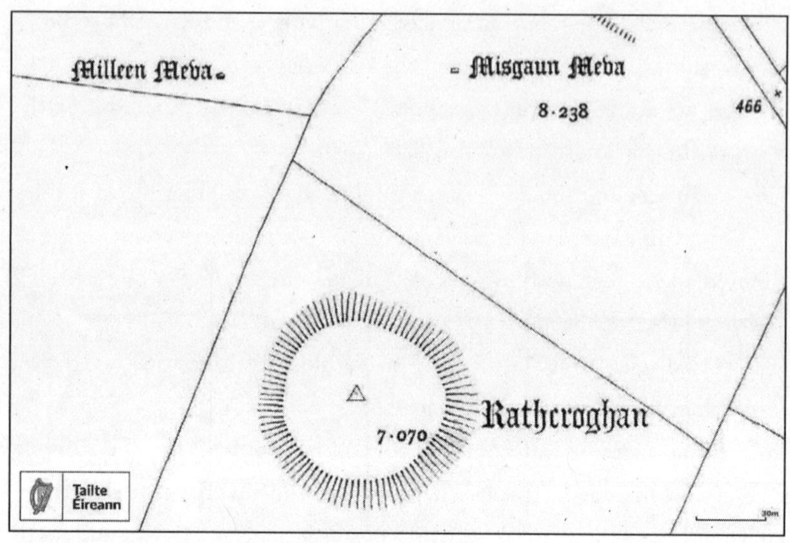

Figure 6. From the Ordnance Survey of Ireland map of Co. Roscommon.

Conclusion

The *Dictionary of the Irish Language* defines the word "táin" as: "driving out, off; cattle-raid, plundering expedition; driven cattle, herd, flock."[49] The Dolmen Press project to republish the *Táin* can also be perceived as a kind of expedition, in this case to translate and revive the epic. As such, it has a parallel in medieval literature where the poet Seanchán Torpéist recovered the story of the *Táin* which had been lost. Set about AD 600, the story recounts how Seanchán—"chief poet of Ireland"—initially thought that the text had been taken abroad but actually recovers it in Roscommon.[50] The modern expedition by Kinsella—a chief poet of his age—and his colleagues echoes this in the quest to recast the same epic in a new form. Kinsella's poem is a sort of mnemonic of that project in the guise of a journey of rediscovery from County Roscommon to Cooley in County Louth in 1969. The Dolmen Press edition of *The Táin* was of course part of a much larger cultural venture to recast and popularize Gaelic literature through translation.[51] It began in the last decades of the nineteenth century and, fueled by nationalism, flowered in the first years of the twentieth. Though it faltered in the decades after independence, Kinsella and his collaborators brought one aspect of it—*Táin Bó Cúailnge*—to full fruition in the late 1960s with the publication of the Dolmen Press edition—a true "livre d'artiste"[52] which has yet to be surpassed.

Notes on Figures

Figure 1: "Sleíbthe Cuailgne" (mountains of Cooley) is a pencil sketch of the Cooley Peninsula in Co. Louth from the southwest. Drawn by Peadar Ó Dubhda (1881–1971), an Irish language scholar, on the title page of a copy of Mary Hutton's *The Táin* (Maunsel, Dublin 1907). The viewer looks across Dundalk Bay, affirmed in Kinsella's translation as the site of Áth Lethan (the broad ford) where Cúchulainn killed a warrior named Lethan. The pinpointing of Áth Lethan was a key breakthrough in toponymic research, and opened up a whole raft of placename identifications on the Cooley Peninsula: "Cúailnge" in the Táin. This included "Ochaine," the hill where Cúchulainn defeated the warrior Nadcranntail. This is the wooded hill shown on the left, which is known today as Trumpet Hill, but was still remembered in Ó Dubhda's youth as "an Fathán": a voicing of Ochaine, both of which stem from "foithin," meaning "a shelter, covert" (eDIL s.v. foithin: see endnote 49) (Photo: P. Gosling).

Figure 2: The full route of *Táin Bó Cúailnge* from Cruachan Aí (Rathcroghan, Co. Roscommon) to Cúailnge (Cooley, Co. Louth) and back again as reconstructed by Gene Haley and Thomas Kinsella (Map: P. Gosling, 2021).

Figure 3: Map showing the route of Queen Medb's army through north Louth and south Armagh. This map first appeared in the 1970 edition of Kinsella's *The Tain* (Map III). It was based on research conducted by Gene Haley for his doctoral thesis, "The Topography of the *Táin Bó Cúailnge*" (1970). This version of the map includes amendments and additional detail based on field research by the present author. All of the placenames mentioned in this paper are indicated. The star indicates the point on the landscape where Kinsella envisions himself in the poem (Map: P. Gosling, 2021).

Figure 4: "by a standing stone on a dark plain" (line 45). The impressive prehistoric monolith (height 9½ft) at Rathiddy, near Knockbridge, Co. Louth, where Cúchulainn is reputed to have died. Slieve Gullion, in south Armagh, is visible in the background (Photo: P. Gosling, 2021).

Figure 5: "by a ford running blood" (line 46). Cast bronze sculpture by Ann Meldon Hugh (1998) on the banks of the River Dee at Ardee, Co. Louth. It depicts Cúchulainn carrying the body of his foster-brother Ferdia, who he has just slain at the ford (Photo: P. Lynch 2015).

Figure 6: "at Cruachan, where it began" (line 51). Extract from the Ordnance Survey of Ireland 25-inch (1:2500 scale) map of Co. Roscommon, edition of 1914. It shows "Rathcroghan" mound, "Milleen Meva" and "Misgaun Meva," the latter being the prone limestone block mentioned in line 56. The Irish words "millín" and "meascán" both have similar meanings—"small lump or ball" and "mass, lump" (*Foclóir Gaeilge-Béarla*, Dublin 1977)—but in this instance, the latter may well denote "turd" as Kinsella suggests (line 57). The map is reproduced with permission of Tailte Éireann (Copyright Permit No. MP 005124).

Notes

[1] The Dolmen Press, Dublin (1973). All quotations from "The Route of *The Táin*" are taken from the Wake Forest UP edition of Kinsella's *Collected Poems*, henceforth CP. The line numbers cited are those of the poem as printed in this essay.

[2] Thomas Kinsella, *Collected Poems 1956–1994* (Oxford: Oxford UP, 1996); Thomas

Kinsella, *Collected Poems 1956–2001* (Manchester: Carcanet Press, 2001); Thomas Kinsella, *Selected Poems* (Manchester: Carcanet Press, 2007); Peter Fallon and Derek Mahon, eds. *The Penguin Book of Contemporary Irish Poetry* (Harmondsworth: Penguin Books, 1990), 22; Wes Davis, ed. *An Anthology of Modern Irish Poetry* (Harvard: Harvard UP, 2010), 250.

[3] Harry Clifton, "Crucial Collection: Thomas Kinsella, *New Poems 1973*," *The Poetry Ireland Review* 86 (May 2006), 6.

[4] I would like to dedicate this essay to Mel O'Loan, friend and *Táin* companion since the late 1970s when we first re-enacted pieces from Kinsella's translation at Doolargy overlooking Dundalk Bay.

[5] See the trio of *Archaeology Ireland* Heritage Guides entitled "The Route of *Táin Bó Cúailnge* in . . .": County Louth (2015), counties Roscommon and Longford (2016), and counties Westmeath and Meath (2019).

[6] See Brent Miles, *Heroic Saga and Classical Epic in Medieval Ireland* (Woodbridge: D. S. Brewer, 2011) for a discussion of the origins and development of the texts of *Táin Bó Cúailnge*.

[7] For an excellent summary, see Dáithí Ó hOgáin, *The Lore of Ireland: An Encyclopaedia of Myth, Legend and Romance* (Cork: Collins Press, 2006), 488–92.

[8] Dolmen Editions IX, The Dolmen Press, Dublin (1969). The full title is notably different from the cover title.

[9] Ailbhe Ní Bhriain, "*Le Livre d'Artiste*: Louis le Brocquy and *The Tain* (1969)," *New Hibernia Review* 5 (Spring 2001), 68–82.

[10] Thomas Kinsella, *The Tain* (Dublin: Dolmen Press, 1969), 272–77.

[11] Thomas Kinsella, *The Tain* (Oxford: Oxford UP, 1970).

[12] Gene Haley, "The Topography of the *Táin Bó Cúailnge*," unpublished D.Phil. thesis, Harvard University, 1970.

[13] Kinsella, *The Tain* (1969), 272–73.

[14] This has, in part, been redressed by my own work: see Paul Gosling, "The Route of *Táin Bó Cúailnge* Revisited," *Emania: Bulletin of the Navan Research Group* 22 (2014), 145–67.

[15] Thomas Kinsella, "The Táin," *Ireland of the Welcomes* 24, no. 6 (November–December 1975), 19–30.

[16] Gene Haley, "Places in the Tain: the Topography of the Táin Bó Cúailnge mapped and globally positioned," website dated 2012. Available at https://genehaleytbc.wordpress.com.

[17] Eoin Neeson, *The Imperishable Celtic Epic An Táin* (Dublin: Prestige Books, 2004); Ciaran Carson, *An Táin* (London: Penguin, 2008).

[18] Kinsella, *The Tain* (1969), 255.

[19] Kinsella, "The Táin" (1975), 20.

[20] Rolf Baumgarten, "Etymological Aetiology in Irish Tradition," *Ériu* XLI (1990), 116.

[21] Gosling, "The Route of *Táin Bó Cúailnge* in counties Roscommon and Longford" (2016), 2.

[22] Kinsella, "The Táin" (1975), 20.

[23] Ian Flanagan, "'Tissues of Order': Kinsella and the Enlightenment Ethos," Special Issue: Thomas Kinsella, *Irish University Review* 31, no. 1 (Spring/Summer 2001): 65–66; Derval Tubridy, "Difficult Migrations: the 'Dinnseanchas' of Thomas Kinsella's Later Poetry," *Irish University Review* 31, no. 1 (Spring/Summer, 2001), 177–79.

[24] Patrick Crotty, "Stunning Places: Thomas Kinsella's Locations," *Poetry Ireland Review* 87 (August 2006), 36.

[25] Robert F. Garratt, *Modern Irish Poetry: Tradition and Continuity from Yeats to Heaney*, first edition (Berkeley: University of California Press, 1986), 36.

[26] Kinsella, *The Tain* (1969), 255.

[27] Ní Bhriain, "*Le Livre d'Artiste.*"

[28] CP, 120, lines 21–3.

[29] Kevin Casey and Andy O'Mahony, "Two Interviews with Liam Miller" in Maurice Harmon, ed. *The Dolmen Press: A Celebration* (Dublin: Lilliput Press, 2001), 34.

[30] Thomas Kinsella, "The Dolmen Press," in Harmon, *Dolmen Press: A Celebration*, 148.

[31] Thomas Kinsella, *New Poems* (Dublin: Dolmen Press, 1973), 6.

[32] Kinsella, "The Dolmen Press," 150.

[33] Casey and O'Mahony, "Two Interviews with Liam Miller," 35; Pierre le Brocquy, "Chronology of a life," sub-section of the Louis le Brocquy web pages on the Anne Madden website (dated 2006). Available at https://www.anne-madden.com/LeBPages/lebrocquy.html.

[34] CP, 120, lines 19–20.

[35] Casey and O'Mahony, "Two Interviews with Liam Miller," 35.

[36] le Brocquy, "Chronology of a life."

[37] Haley, "Topography of the Táin," (1970).

[38] Haley, "Places in the Tain."

[39] Kinsella, "The Táin" (1975), 20.

[40] Kinsella, *The Tain* (1969), Maps I–II; Kinsella, *The Tain* (1970), Maps I–III.

[41] Kinsella, *The Tain* (1969), 273.

[42] Kinsella, "The Táin" (1975).

[43] Casey and O'Mahony, "Two Interviews with Liam Miller," 5.

[44] Kinsella, *New Poems*, 57–58.

[45] Kinsella, *The Tain* (1969), Maps I–II; Kinsella, *The Tain* (1970), Maps I–III.

[46] Haley, "Places in the Tain."

[47] John Greening, "Jibes at the Jibers," *Times Literary Supplement*, 5188, 6th September 2002, 24.

[48] Cf. Dennis O'Driscoll, *Troubled Thoughts, Majestic Dreams: Selected Prose Writings* (Oldcastle: Gallery Press, 2001), 116, 129.

[49] eDIL s.v. táin. Electronic Dictionary of the Irish Language: online database at https://dil.ie.

[50] Ó hOgáin, *Lore of Ireland*, 450–53.

[51] See Maria Tymoczko, *Translation in a Postcolonial Context: Early Irish Literature in English Translation* (Manchester: St. Jerome Publishing, 1999).

[52] Ní Bhriain, "*Le Livre d'Artiste*."

CHAPTER 8

"A meaningful drama / Beginning in the grey mists of antiquity"

THOMAS KINSELLA AS ANTHOLOGIST, CONSERVATOR, EDITOR, TRANSLATOR, AND RENEWER OF TRADITIONS

BRIAN G. CARAHER

The quotation featured in the title of this chapter comes from the fourth section of one of Thomas Kinsella's most well-known and highly regarded poems, "Nightwalker" (1968). This flaneurial and existential tour-de-force —strongly indebted to the modernist poetry of T. S. Eliot and W. H. Auden, as well as the experimental prose of James Joyce—peaks in its penultimate movement with a recognition that the pains and travails of the self-reflexive, auto-focused, poetic voice are situated in a much larger, trans-individual tradition or socio-cultural context:

> From time to time it seems that everything
> Is breaking down. But we must never despair.

There are times it is all part of a meaningful drama
Beginning in the grey mists of antiquity
And reaching through the years to unknown goals
In the consciousness of man, which makes it less gloomy.[1]

These six prosaic lines of blank verse occur in the middle of a poetic movement which stages a stylized and visionary dialogue between the "Moon of my dismay, Virgin most pure," and the poet "stand[ing] at the ocean's edge." The lines present, perhaps even argue, a philosophical dilemma which the "mask" of the moon "reads" from the bookish "brain" of the poet, but which comes across as though spoken by the moon. The section ends with the poet's "head fallen back heavy with your [the moon's] control, / And oppressed," but with the message and its burden delivered. The poet, the "Nightwalker," must rise from his slough of personal and social despair and attend to "a meaningful drama" running across numerous generations commencing "in the grey mists of antiquity" and straining toward "unknown goals" of which the poet appears a single, though crucial, actor. Such awareness, such "consciousness of man," lends trans-generational meaning, social significance and personal resurgence to the existential crisis the "Nightwalker" has mapped evocatively through the opening three movements of the poem.

Section five of "Nightwalker" tantalizingly *tastes* this ambitious historical project through the medium of "massed human wills"—that is, through the material evidence of human presence and cultural effort from "the grey mists of antiquity" onward. It will be my argument that Kinsella's subsequent and heroically sustained work as anthologist, conservator of other poets' work, editor of neglected poetry, and translator and renewer of distinctly Irish poetic traditions cumulatively and collectively lends detail and historical substance to this sensed "human taste" of "massed human wills" from the climactic sections of "Nightwalker."[2]

Perhaps to start lending sense to this notion of "massed human wills" we need to turn to some of the more perceptive commentators on the work of Kinsella. Denis Donoghue, one of the finest Irish interpreters of modern Anglophone poetry, has argued:

> If there is a distinctive Irish experience, it is one of division, exacerbated by the fact that division in a country so small seems perverse. But the scale doesn't matter. At various times, the division has taken these forms: Catholic and Protestant, Nationalist and Unionist, Ireland and England, North and South, the country and the one bloated city of Dublin, Gaelic Ireland and Anglo-Ireland, the comfortable and the poor, farmers and P.A.Y.E. workers, pro-Treaty and anti-Treaty, child and parents, the Irish and the English languages, the visible Ireland and the hidden Ireland, landlord and tenant, the Big House and the hovel. To which it is now necessary to add: a defensive Church and an increasingly secular State, Irish law and European law.[3]

Donoghue goes on to single out and praise the work of Kinsella as being able not only to engage the nature and implications of this "distinctive Irish experience" but to do so in an exemplary fashion for his own time and generation as well as for modern Irish poetry in general. Indeed, as Andrew Fitzsimons argues, "the range and reach of Kinsella's work is among the most extraordinary in contemporary poetry."[4] Kinsella tastes the divisions, the faultlines, of Irish experience. He does so by questioning and then superannuating the deeply self-serving poetics and partisan poetry of W. B. Yeats, for one thing, and attending respectfully to the tenor and ramifications "of virtually the whole available range of Irish literary, religious, and historical experience":

> Among the poets who have engaged such division, Thomas Kinsella is the one who has turned the experience into the most formidable poetry. At the beginning of his career he tried to circumvent Yeats's high-horse rhetoric by recourse to Auden. More recently he has taken possession of virtually the whole available range of Irish literary, religious, and historical experience and, in his translation of the Táin, found for himself an unYeatsian resonance. There are more accessible poets; Kinsella has set his chisel to some very hard stone. But he has become an Irish poet by taking full responsibility for everything that phrase entails.[5]

W. J. McCormack has praised Kinsella in terms not dissimilar from Denis Donoghue. For one thing, McCormack notes that Kinsella's "critical writing has been slight in bulk though weighty in implication."[6] That is to say, Kinsella has been a significant exception to the dismal norm of much "critical" and journalistic discussion of Irish literature, culture, and politics, especially during the 1970s and 1980s: "Irish book reviews were, and are, opportunities for banality, dishonesty and lachrymose idiocy."[7] Kinsella rises above the frequently unhistorical, tribalist, and sectarian debates which McCormack charts alarmingly and with historical precision in *The Battle of the Books: Two Decades of Irish Cultural Debate*. Moreover, Kinsella's poetry "avoids the identification of community and *polis* so fatally active in these disputes" that tend to reflect various entrenched ideological or sectarian or tribalist positions.[8] Kinsella reads, works, thinks, and writes across sectarian divisions and with a deeper, stronger, thoroughly historized sense of the Irish divisions Denis Donoghue has articulated. Moreover, Kinsella enacts a modern, modernist, and transnational sense of Irish social and political contexts and their points of critical connection.

In a feature article for *The Irish Times* on the occasion of Kinsella's 90th birthday, the poet Harry Clifton notes that his mentor and model for an urban Irish poetry and poetics is significantly "a force of cultural retrieval who has brought back *The Táin* and *Poems of the Dispossessed* to contemporary understanding."[9] Clifton's seminal praise for "that elegant wordsmith Thomas Kinsella" subtly notes the latter's skill and energy in respecting urban modernity and ancient to early modern Irish traditions. Kinsella is actually the man for the project that Yeats botched. He is the "force of cultural retrieval" who recollects the full range of Irish poetic traditions while delivering them in a form alive "to contemporary understanding" and burdened with the knowledge of antiquity, urbanity, and the complete range of divisions and dualities that Denis Donoghue has itemized as "distinctive Irish experience"—namely, the "massed human wills" of Ireland, ancient and modern, north and south, east and west, hidden and visible, dead and living.

Kinsella's most sustained critical performance and cultural commentary, *The Dual Tradition: An Essay on Poetry and Politics in Ireland* (1995), is the best guidebook to mapping his ambitious cultural task of identifying and recuperating the divided traditions of the island and its literatures. Kinsella's work—before and after this masterful study—as an anthologist, a conservator, an editor, and a translator comes into coherent perspective once we take the time to understand the historical and critical project of renewal occurring in this pivotal text. *The Dual Tradition* demonstrates Kinsella's coherent, long-range, literary-historical and socio-cultural strategies in recovering, documenting, and rendering accessible "the dual tradition" of writing in Ireland from its earliest traces in the fifth and sixth centuries AD through early modern and modern dimensions of its twinned tongues of Irish and English, Gaelic and Anglophone, literatures. The text as a whole renders clearly the strategies Kinsella followed in his landmark edition of *The New Oxford Book of Irish Verse* (1986). Kinsella's capacious and stunningly balanced anthology supplants W. B. Yeats's rather partisan and highly selective anthology of fifty years earlier, *The Oxford Book of Modern Verse*, as well as Yeats's notorious and highly partisan *A Book of Irish Verse* from 1895.[10]

"Strangers," the first chapter of *The Dual Tradition*, samples what survives from the indigenous or "native oral literature" from the fifth through the seventeenth centuries, counterposing it with medieval texts in Latin and Norman French as well as English texts from Waterford and Dublin from the fifteenth century onward.[11] This chapter selectively samples and socio-historically contextualizes verse collected in the first 155 pages of Kinsella's *The New Oxford Book of Irish Verse*. *The Táin* (*Táin Bó Cúailnge*) is also glossed succinctly in this initial chapter of *The Dual Tradition*. In brief, the chapter maps the social counterposing and interweaving of oral Irish remnants, literate and clerical Latin texts, and Norman and English importations into Ireland over the course of a millennium and then some. It leaves off short of the cataclysmic disruptions that the years 1601 (Battle of Kinsale) through 1607 (Flight of the Earls) brought to the diverse literary and cultural traditions of early to late medieval Ireland. Indeed, an excursus on Kinsella's magnificent translation and powerful modern edition of *The Táin* will serve to illustrate this highly significant point.

The Tain (1969)—translated, edited, and commented upon at length in relation to both textual annotations and socio-historical contextualization—is one thoroughly deserving of its strong international reputation. Ciaran Carson has produced a more recent translation of this Irish epic but one utterly in the shadow of Kinsella's masterwork:

> The present translation would not have been possible without Kinsella's ground-breaking text. Had Kinsella not undertaken his translation, there would have been no public consciousness of *Táin Bó Cúailnge*. As I write, my

original copy of the Oxford paperback edition of 1970 is on my desk, as it has been throughout the process of my translation.[12]

In disclosing his indebtedness to Kinsella, Carson also succinctly summarizes the massive impact of Kinsella's "ground-breaking text":

> In 1969 Dolmen Press published *The Táin*, translated from the Irish by Thomas Kinsella, with brush drawings by Louis le Brocquy, in an edition of 1,750 copies. It was immediately hailed as a classic for the vibrancy of the translation and the magnificence of its graphic accompaniment. A mass market edition was published by Oxford University Press a year later. Its cultural impact was immense. No easily accessible translation of the work had existed until then.[13]

Carson's own 2007 trade edition is a very good, highly readable version of *The Táin*; yet it does not project the scholarly circumspect, graphically magnificent, and critically innovative edition that Kinsella produced in 1969 with the collaboration of one of Ireland's outstanding modern visual artists, Louis le Brocquy. Carson renders only thirteen chapters of the core narrative derived from two of the medieval textual sources of the tale. He also omits some fifty pages of pre-*Táin* narrative fragments which prepare the social contexts, the significant origins of the characters, and the range of motives at stake in prompting the actions of the main narrative. Carson dwells on the principal actors from Connacht and Ulster who engage in combat over the Brown Bull of Cooley Peninsula and delivers a compelling tale of envy, ambition, and broken rules of hospitality and royal prerogatives. He also forges ingenious ways to render the lyrical passages of the narrative. However, Carson's text will always be over-shadowed by its powerful progenitor.

Kinsella's translation exhaustively mines the full range of textual resources that comprise the fragmentary remains of a "text" which Kinsella himself pieces together in order to create a modern, living, and Anglophone *Táin*. This *Táin* derives its fresh, modern texture through active conservatorship of ancient Irish textual materials as well as from an ingenious sense for translating and dovetailing various stages and dialects of Irish Gaelic into a complete Hiberno-English epic. Part of this brilliant conservatorship is the way in which a series of eight "pre-*Táin*" narratives are recovered from a stunning variety of ancient sources and redacted by Kinsella to produce the opening fifty pages of his translation.[14]

The first such narrative poses the putative origin of the tale, yet one which is potent with ancient social and cultural motives as well as a deeply self-referential gloss on Kinsella's own project of recuperation and redaction:

> The poets of Ireland were one day gathered around Senchán Torpéist to see if they could recall the "Táin Bó Cúailnge" in its entirety. But they all said they knew only parts of it.[15]

Senchán Torpéist (circa 560–647) was Chief Poet of Connacht and, from 598 until his death 49 years later, was Ollam of Ireland—a highly prestigious post as head poet, reciter, and rhetorician of the entire island. So it is the Ollam of Ireland himself who seeks a solution to the early medieval loss of narrative fullness and cohesion of one of the crucial epics of the Ulster cycle. Senchán sends his son Muirgen in search of a reputed missing version of the epic; but Muirgen finds instead the grave of Fergus mac Roich, one of the key actors of the tale, a former King of Ulster who has sided with Queen Medb of Connacht against his fellow Ulstermen. Fergus, thus, knew both sides of the conflict and knew personally all the key actors, though he himself was compromised by both sides, as well as by his own actions. Fergus may be seen as one of the earliest Irishmen marked by "division," what Denis Donoghue has characterized as "the distinctive Irish experience." Muirgen, the son of Senchán, separates himself from his traveling companions and sits before the gravestone of Fergus mac Roich:

> Muirgen chanted a poem to the gravestone as though it were Fergus himself. He said to it:
>
> 'If this your royal rock
> were your own self mac Roich
> halted here with sages
> searching for a roof
> *Cúailnge* we'd recover
> plain and perfect Fergus.'
>
> A great mist suddenly formed around him—for the space of three days and nights he could not be found. And the figure of Fergus approached him in fierce majesty, with a head of brown hair, in a green cloak and a red-embroidered hooded tunic, with gold-hilted sword and bronze blunt sandals. Fergus recited him the whole Táin, how everything had happened, from start to finish. Then they went back to Senchán with their story, and he rejoiced over it.[16]

Over "three days and nights," "plain and perfect Fergus" returns from the dead to remember and recite "the whole Táin." Muirgen has invoked and received the full narrative he seeks for his father from one of the key actors of the epic, and one who had access to the complete *dramatis personae*, their speeches, and complicated motives. Kinsella annotates his ninth-century source for this astounding anecdote.[17] However, the reader of Kinsella's *Tain* may also sense that Muirgen, son of Senchán, is an early medieval prototype or avatar of Kinsella, the modern editor and translator striving to resuscitate the dead, broken fragments of an Irish tale of dispute, division, and discord and make it new and make it live once again but now for a contemporary Hiberno-English audience.

Experience of division, moreover, maps deeply onto the eighth and final fragmentary narrative that Kinsella recovers for the opening section of *The Táin*, "The Quarrel of the Two Pig-Keepers, and How the Bulls Were Begotten."[18] Kinsella's careful annotations record the ninth-century source of this fragment, and they itemize his translator's departures from certain troublesome words and phrases as well as his editorial rearrangement of sentences to enhance narrative cohesion.[19] The "quarrel" charted here exhibits the spread of "bad blood" between the kings of Connacht and Munster to their otherwise friendly, cooperative, and mutually supportive royal "pig-keepers," Friuch and Rucht—names which Kinsella prefers over defective ones in the original text because they emphasize in Gaelic strong links to traits of boars or wild pigs.[20] The two friends are tricked into contests and games of brinksmanship by partisans of the two provinces they represent such that envy, jealousy, and ongoing "quarreling" become the pig-keepers' second nature. Envy and quarrels spread to infect the birds of prey, the salmon, the maggots, and the cows of Connacht and Munster. Indeed, the two pig-keepers have been so denatured of their cooperative natures by their deceitful competitions that they metamorphically inhabit for two years the bodies of birds of prey, salmon, maggots, and cows until they are reborn from the last in the sequence as the two bulls, the White Bull of Connacht and the Brown Bull of Cooley.[21] A wildly fanciful narrative fragment, for sure, yet it provides an astounding origin for the two bulls who occasion the envy and combative competition between Queen Medb and the Ulstermen to come in the main body of the epic narrative. The previous six fragments of "Before *The Táin*" offer origin and "begotten" narratives for Conchobor and Cúchulainn and the beginnings of personal envy and social division among their progeny and fellow Ulstermen.[22] Thus, the narrative of the two friendly pig-keepers who metamorphose—not unlike the metamorphoses of Ovid's tales—into the two highly-prized bulls dramatizes emphatically the motif of the subversion of social cooperation and the engendering of divisiveness across the ancient Irish landscape, especially its animate life from humans to maggots, salmon, birds of prey, pigs, and cattle. In Kinsella's hands *The Táin* emerges as a stunning achievement. Moreover, strong awareness of the socio-cultural contexts which underwrite the retrieved, reconstructed, and renewed text helps to situate this landmark edition and translation as best-selling critical and scholarly work virtually without peer in contemporary Ireland.[23]

The second chapter of *The Dual Tradition*, "Colonials and Dispossessed," charts the poetry and politics of Ireland in the seventeenth and eighteenth centuries, following "the catastrophe" of the collapse of the old Gaelic order in the wake of the Battle of Kinsale and the Flight of the Earls.[24] This chapter strongly draws upon the verse collected on pages 156 to 263 of Kinsella's *New Oxford Book of Irish Verse* as well as his numerous translations of the material collected and edited by Seán Ó Tuama for their 1981 collaborative anthology, *An Duanaire 1600–1900: Poems of the Dispossessed*. The "dual tradition" of verse in Irish and verse in English comes into its own in this chapter. The "Colonials" of the title are the Anglophone conquerors and overlords, and the "Dispossessed" are the indigenous speakers of Gaelic pushed largely into the hinterlands of Connacht, following not only the Flight of the Earls but also the Cromwellian wars of the 1640s and 1650s and the Battles of the Boyne and Aughrim in 1690 and 1691. As Kinsella notes: "Any of the dispossessed found east of the Shannon after 1 May 1654 might be killed by anyone who chose."[25] Indeed, from the middle of the seventeenth century onward, "poetry in Irish was the poetry of a subject people,"[26] the dispossessed voices exhumed and evoked so conscientiously in *An Duanaire*.

Kinsella's analysis in *The Dual Tradition* comes to dwell on the careers, poetry, and politics of Aogán Ó Rathaille of Kerry and Jonathan Swift of Dublin.[27] By doing so, Kinsella draws out the lineaments of "the dual tradition" as it crystallizes in the wake of these two brilliant writers, one from each tradition:

> By the second half of the eighteenth century the essential forms of the modern scene were established. There was an Anglo-Irish literature in English, dealing in a limited range of subject and reference and presenting these to a limited audience, primarily English but with an important element in English-speaking Ireland. Another literature existed in Irish, quite separate and involving a different people, who were sometimes part of the Anglo-Irish subject matter.[28]

An Duanaire collects and preserves surviving documents of that other literature, those displaced Irish-speaking voices, though significantly and poignantly in the two tongues of "the dual tradition." The poetry collected is significantly "neglected," yet the anthology itself can and should be viewed as an exercise in documenting, or providing a documentary record, of the final stages of an audience-centered poetry in the Irish language.[29] Declan Kiberd's single sentence on Kinsella in *After Ireland: Writing the Nation from Beckett to the Present*, though, undermines the latter writer's substantial achievement in "writing the nation" through its historical record of the experience of division and duality:

> Even a poet as sympathetic to Gaelic tradition as Thomas Kinsella remained convinced that Irish as a fully expressive community language had died in the mid-nineteenth century: those who now composed in it were like medieval church leaders sending documents to one another in Latin.[30]

Kiberd seems dismissive and neglectful of Kinsella, it could be said, especially in coming to terms with the social and historical dimensions of charting the dynamics of the dual tradition and modernity.

Kinsella's powerful second chapter of *The Dual Tradition*, moreover, concludes with attention paid to two of the most astounding documents of the Gaelic tradition and ones prominently collected and displayed in *The New Oxford Book of Irish Verse*—namely, Eibhlín Dhubh Ní Chonaill's "The Lament for Art Ó Laoghaire" and Brian Merriman's "The Midnight Court." The first poem is a highly inventive and lyrically extended "keen" (*caoineadh*), "one of the great love-laments in Irish," and is significantly by a woman author, one of the first recorded in Gaelic literature.[31] The second poem is by far the most substantial inclusion in the 1986 anthology of Irish verse, an extraordinary twenty-five pages in length. Merriman's "The Midnight Court" (1780) is arguably the finest expression of Gaelic literary culture, an *aisling* or dream-vision narrative, "a long poem of conscious art, full of social, literary and historical reference, with all the problems dissolved in parody" at the end with the awakening of the poet-dreamer, Merriman himself.[32] Kinsella claims Merriman's poem is "a powerful curiosity," "a lucky combination of impulse and occasion" but also "where a literature in Irish can be experienced fully functioning for the last time, before the language of the majority of the people changed to English and the Irish language disappeared, with the dispossessed, into the remoter parts of the country."[33] The latter socio-cultural and socio-historical assessment may seem harsh, and far too harsh for Declan Kiberd to stomach. Writing in Irish continues into the twenty-first century, but the issue of a "fully functioning" literary culture and fully receptive audience for Gaelic are moot and hotly debated matters. What is at stake for Kinsella comes to the fore in the next two chapters of *The Dual Tradition*.

"The Nineteenth Century," the third chapter of *The Dual Tradition* examines the shift in the cultural politics of the English language as it comes into the possession of the dispossessed, and not merely the overlords, of the island. This chapter draws heavily upon the poetry collected on pages 267 to 308 of *The New Oxford Book of Irish Verse* and features discussion of Thomas Moore, James Clarence Mangan, Thomas Davis, Samuel Ferguson, and briefly the prose writer William Carleton. The issue explored in these Irish writers writing across the breadth of the nineteenth century is their adaptation of English as the means to reach a dual audience: the increasingly Anglophone Irish middle and working classes as well as readers in Britain:

> Writers wrote and published for the 'dominant' neighbouring audience, marketing their Irish matter with an explanatory air. And the same air was beginning to be appropriate in Ireland, where the change of vernacular from Irish to English was leaving a majority audience divided from its past.[34]

These Georgian and Victorian era writers wrote of Irish matters, images, struggles, grievances, both old and new, in the appropriated language of the conqueror in order to address both literate Irish and British audiences and to air, plead, and justify the merits and strengths of the Irish peasantry and the largely Anglophone Irish middle-class. Moore's *Irish Melodies*, Mangan's "versions" or "translations" of Gaelic laments, and Ferguson's "verse retellings of ancient Irish tales" are crucial, highly-popular documents in this socio-cultural and socio-linguistic watershed.[35]

The fourth chapter of *The Dual Tradition* carries the argument and the exposition of the third chapter forward into a discussion of major modern writers of the twentieth century. "Yeats and Joyce" is the longest chapter in Kinsella's critical history of poetry and politics in Ireland, and with good reason. Both writers continue the socio-linguistic project of Moore, Mangan, and Ferguson, addressing both an Anglophone Irish audience and a larger audience of English speakers outside Ireland. Both writers are keenly aware of their dual audiences, yet the socio-cultural and historical burden of their writings differ profoundly.

Kinsella explores Yeats's commitment to the governing class and the landlords of Ireland, "the colonial view" of how the Irish should be governed by a privileged elite.[36] Kinsella's expansive argument takes in many examples of Yeats's writing, early through late, though the volumes from the 1920s and 1930s and some of Yeats's commentary get the greater attention. For instance, in the discussion of "Blood and the Moon" from *The Winding Stair and Other Poems* (1933), Kinsella argues that Yeats places himself in alignment "with the individual ignominies and oddities of Swift, Goldsmith, Berkeley, and Burke set in the unity of an Anglo-Irish tradition as a model of the real."[37] Violence and blood-sacrifice are rationalized within this ruling-class, colonial, and aristocratic mindset. Indeed, the notorious concluding lines from "The Statues" in *Last Poems* (1938–39) encapsulate the issue that bedevils Yeats's elitist perspective on his "ancient sect" of Anglo-Irish rulers:

When Pearse summoned Cuchulain to his side,
What stalked through the Post Office? What intellect,

What calculation, number, measurement, replied?
We Irish, born into that ancient sect
But thrown upon this filthy modern tide
And by its formless, spawning, fury wrecked,
Climb to our proper dark, that we may trace
The lineaments of a plummet-measured face.[38]

"The Statues" was occasioned by the 1937 erection of a commemorative statue, featuring the dying Cuchulain from the last episode of *Táin Bó Cúailnge*. The statue was in honor of the dead and martyred rebels of the Easter 1916 Uprising who had taken the General Post Office as one of the key battle sites in the rebellion against British overlordship. Yeats claims real Irishness ("We Irish") for "that ancient sect" he would speak for and who are the implied audience for this poem. Implicitly Yeats includes Cuchulain in that company, and that ancient hero of the Ulster Cycle stands as an avatar and model of Yeats's chosen company and not "this filthy mod ern tide" of the "formless, spawning" rebels lead by Padraic Pearse. Such rebels cannot take the true measure of Cuchulain and his "ancient sect," in Yeats's purview. They are working and middle-class Irish upstarts who seek control of their own affairs; they seek to decolonize and democratize Ireland and to found a republic, regardless of their poor planning and potentially misguided self-sacrifice. Yeats's "filthy modern tide" would seem the most recent instalment of the "massed human wills" of the long, troubled history of Ireland whom Kinsella invokes as his subject matter, socio-cultural context, and audience—ancient and modern—in the final segment of "Nightwalker."

And what of the poetry and politics of James Joyce, the culture-hero of Kinsella's fourth chapter? Joyce's prose—especially *A Portrait of the Artist as a Young Man* and *Ulysses*—garners sole attention, largely in terms of the deep understanding of Irish history, social and cultural divisions, and the keen measure of "healing" to be found therein. Kinsella traces what Joyce learns from Thomas Moore, from "official Protestantism" and "Catholicism and unthinking nationalism," from "English culture in Ireland," from examining closely the stereotypes of the Ulsterman and the "comic Irishman," and from his "search" for an enduring art and "the enabling feminine."[39] For Kinsella, Joyce is the exemplary modern Irish artist, cognizant of the dualities and divisions he inherits, but finding a way forward into modernity and a post-colonial and post-traumatic sense of Irishness:

> Joyce, with a greatness like Yeats's, was able to accept the tradition as he found it, still recovering from the death-blow to the Irish language. Joyce's isolation is a mask. His relationship with the modern world is direct and intimate. He knew the filthy modern tide, and immersed himself in it.[40]

Joyce stands forth as "the first major Irish voice to speak for Irish reality since the death-blow to the Irish language," yet he does so in a manner which "simultaneously revives the Irish tradition and admits the modern world."[41] Hiberno-English is Joyce's principal, chosen, socio-linguistic medium; yet he speaks for the subordinated tradition of the dispossessed and "the filthy modern tide" of an Ireland striving to move beyond colonialism and the stranglehold of an Anglo-Irish culture for which Yeats speaks and propagandizes. For Kinsella, "an Irish writer in the twentieth century who cares who he [or she] is and where he [or she] comes from might find that Yeats stands for the Irish tradition as broken, and Joyce stands for it as healed—or healing—from its mutilation."[42] That is a massive claim, as well as the conclusion of the chapter, "Yeats and Joyce." The "dual tradition" stands ruptured and counter-posed in Yeats, but Joyce seeks to heal Irish dualities and the experience of division through fastidiously suturing Irish culture from "the grey mists of antiquity" to the "filthy modern tide" of a democratic republic struggling to be born. The "dual tradition" now lives in and through the appropriated and remade tongue of Hiberno-English. However, there is nothing to prevent the "healing" and repurposing of Irish Gaelic within this Joycean effort to recuperate from social and historical "mutilation." The contemporary Irish tongue, after all, is itself a recuperating medium, one replete with substantial importations of Latin, French, and English vocabulary.

The fifth chapter of *The Dual Tradition*, "Modern Irish Poetry," explores the state of poetry in the wake of Yeats and Joyce and carries Kinsella's literary history up to the 1980s. The chapter draws substantially upon the poetry collected on pages 320 to 391, the final part, of *The New Oxford Book of Irish Verse*. Kinsella's quick, capacious survey finds a clear social grain and telling patterns in writers such as Austin Clarke, Patrick Kavanagh, and Samuel Beckett. In general, these poets measure themselves often against Yeats and Joyce and seem to have difficulty superseding them. For Kinsella, "there are obsolete attitudes surviving, where the old colonial element is still strong."[43] However, Kinsella declines to explore the poetry of Louis MacNeice, Richard Murphy, Seamus Heaney, and Michael Hartnett, who are all generously represented in his 1986 anthology. These poets push beyond Yeats and collectively, in a more Joycean and post-colonial manner,[44] try to explore versions of what Denis Donoghue calls "the distinctive Irish experience" of division and duality, past and present.

The sixth and final chapter, "The Politics of the Dual Tradition," yields not so much a summary of Kinsella's argument as further exemplification of it across three telling instances: 1) Seamus Heaney's poetry and politics, 2) the battleground of "Northern Irish Poetry" or "Ulster Poetry," and 3)

George Moore's social and political duality. In certain respects, Kinsella now seeks to map his social and historical exposition of "the distinctive Irish experience" of division and the evolving dynamics of "the dual tradition" onto the terrain of contemporary post-colonial study:

> Ireland was the closest of England's colonies, and the most thoroughly civilized. The mechanics of colonialism were tested in Ireland and the stages recorded in Irish literature, in both languages. It is one of the findings of Ireland's dual tradition that an empire is a passing thing, but that a colony is not.[45]

For one, Kinsella notes "the post-colonial confusions" and social contradictions marking the furor over the color of Seamus Heaney's passport and whether to anthologize him as an "English," a "British," an "Ulster," or an "Irish" poet.[46] This vexed issue leads directly into an extended analysis of Northern Irish poetry, the segregation and national classification of which Kinsella regards as "a journalistic entity rather than a literary one, and with features of propaganda more than journalism."[47] The journalistic effort to forge a separate and distinctive "tradition" of poetry in the "province" of Northern Ireland—with Louis MacNeice chosen "as patron of an Ulster branch of modern British verse"—strikes Kinsella as an ill-guided, "truculent" and distinctively "colonial" project:

> Apart from Heaney and Mahon the poetry in Northern Ireland, and especially the commentary, has a minority air, isolated and truculent: the air of a colony that has been left to look after itself and of the colonial at home nowhere.[48]

Such analysis, of course, does not consider the emergent work of Ciaran Carson, Medbh McGuckian, Paul Muldoon, and Sinead Morrissey. It is, however, keenly directed toward the divisiveness and the duality strongly instanced in the poetry and politics of John Hewitt. Kinsella reads Hewitt's verse as thoroughly expressive of "the colonial mentality," at home neither in Ireland nor in Britain, yet also keenly aware of "the principal injustice, dispossession" that has been inflicted upon the Irish at home.[49] Indeed, "Hewitt's colonists see that the days of empire are numbered and there is an element of worry," yet they cannot cope with or confront a future that requires "acceptance of guilt with its obligations":

> It is the dual state of things: the sullen Irish, dispossessed but refusing to disappear; and the self-righteous colonist, high and dry. They would both like things to be different: the dispossessed back in possession, the invader really at home. Facing the facts, they are left with one another. Whatever their differences, they are left with a shared reality.[50]

Kinsella confronts the facts and gestures in the direction of "a shared reality" in his controversial yet incredibly prescient poem, "Butcher's Dozen" (1972).

"Butcher's Dozen" is an immediate, powerful response to the now discredited Widgery Tribunal of Inquiry report of April 1972 which whitewashed the facts, concealed the guilt, and obscured the civil obligations of the British government regarding the Bloody Sunday Massacre, when thirteen unarmed civil-rights demonstrators were shot dead by the British Army in Derry City on January 30, 1972.[51] "Butcher's Dozen" follows the *aisling* tradition of Irish poetry, a tradition Kinsella's knows well, especially with regard to his brilliant translation of Brian Merriman's "The Midnight Court," often seen as the final great achievement of the Gaelic poetic tradition, in *The New Oxford Book of Irish Verse*. The first of The Peppercanister Series, "Butcher's Dozen" potently embodies "the dual tradition"—Anglophone and Gaelic—Kinsella historicizes so adeptly. It also memorably embodies the most arresting of Kinsella's interventions in the distinctive Irish experience of division and duality. The speaker of the poem is transported to Derry's "Bogside of the bitter zeal" a month after the thirteen murders and then listens in turn to the ghosts of the thirteen dead come to speak to him. The ghosts invoke a range of Irish Nationalist and Republican attitudes and perceptions of the crimes for which they are the pitiful victims. However, the thirteenth ghost strikes an unusual note: "'Yet pity is akin to love.'"[52] This ghost counsels understanding of the other and the other's tradition:

> Love our changeling! Guard and mind it.
> Doomed from birth, a cursed heir,
> Theirs is the hardest lot to bear,
> Yet not impossible, I swear,
> If England would but clear the air
> And brood at home on her disgrace . . .
> (CP, 137)

Kinsella's analysis of John Hewitt's "colonial mentality" and the duality of the homeless colonial and the dispossessed native hits home here. The dispossessed must "pity" and "love" their fellow countrymen, collectively the "cursed heir" of England's imperial failures and colonial mindset. They must seek to "[p]urge the filth and do not stir it" and help those bedevilled by colonialism "mix themselves in the common blood":

> We are all what we are, and that
> Is mongrel pure. What nation's not

Where any stranger hung his hat
And seized a lover where she sat?
(CP, 137)

Kinsella strikes a Joycean note regarding the mixed, "mongrel pure" salad of ethnicities and gene pools that characteristically combine to comprise "a nation." The playful echoes of the twelfth chapter of *Ulysses* ("Cyclops") are unmistakeable: a Bloomean ethic of love and acceptance regarding division, duality, and the composition of nationhood wins the day against the hatred, the unhistorical nonsense, and the racism of The Citizen in Kiernan's Bar on Little Britain Street. In certain respects, "Butcher's Dozen" dramatizes the current, ongoing act of Kinsella's "meaningful drama" begun "in the grey mists of antiquity" yet still seeking a way to resolve its ongoing clash and intimate conflict of dual traditions.

There have been a number of sustained studies of Kinsella's poetry and the arc of his poetics from early work to late.[53] This chapter has striven to bring Kinsella's own critical work to the fore and highlight its centrality to his major, masterful task as Ireland's pre-eminent conservator, critic, renewer and modernizer of poetic traditions—a peerless Ollam of Ireland today.

Coda

I first met Thomas Kinsella at the pondside cupola in St. Stephen's Green, Dublin in July 1973. I was about to commence graduate studies in poetry and poetics in New York, yet then traveling by bicycle in Ireland, May through August that summer, visiting cousins in Tipperary, Donegal, and Dublin. I had studied Kinsella's early work as an undergraduate and had been utterly taken with "Baggot Street Deserta" and "Nightwalker." I had a copy of *Ulysses* (a dog-eared version of the textually dodgy 1961 paperback) but happened to be reading W. S. Merwin's newest collection, *The Carrier of Ladders*, when Tom took up a seat on the other side of the cupola one July morning. Within minutes two children, a boy about four or five and a girl two or three years older, started larking about the outer edge of the cupola. The boy got his head stuck between two of the wooden slats of the railing facing the pond, and the girl (perhaps his sister) went into hysterics about what might happen. Kinsella and I responded, almost as one, to the situation, with Tom taking the lead to calm and speak soothingly to the boy, while holding his head to prevent any self-injury. Eventually I went outside the cupola to steady the boy's flailing legs and waist and try to assure the girl we would free her (presumed) brother. Kinsella coaxed the boy's head slowly back through the wooden slats, and I lowered him down to the lawn, only for the boy and girl to scamper away toward the northeast (Shelbourne Hotel/ Baggot Street) exit from the Green without a word, though presumably full of relief. Kinsella and I exchanged mannered pleasantries, and I thought about mentioning how I admired his poetry, especially the *Nightwalker and Other Poems* volume, but checked myself, thinking it would spoil the rather Bloomean Good Samaritan and his student-helper moment in the Green. Instead, we went back to our readings—he in Irish and I in English, the dual traditions of the place.

Notes

[1] Thomas Kinsella, "Nightwalker" in *Collected Poems* (Winston-Salem, NC: Wake Forest UP, 2006), 83.

[2] All quotations taken from "Nightwalker" may be found in Thomas Kinsella, *Collected Poems* (Winston-Salem, NC: Wake Forest UP, 2006), 83–4.

[3] Denis Donoghue, *We Irish: Essays on Irish Literature and Society* (Berkeley and London: University of California Press, 1986), 16.

[4] Andrew Fitzsimons, "Thomas Kinsella," in *The Cambridge Companion to Irish Poets*, ed. Gerald Dawe (Cambridge: Cambridge UP, 2018), 227.

[5] Donoghue, *We Irish*, 16.

[6] W. J. McCormack, *The Battle of the Books* (Mullingar: Lilliput Press, 1986), 31.

[7] McCormack, *Battle of the Books*, 9.

[8] McCormack, *Battle of the Books*, 84.

[9] Harry Clifton, "In Praise of That Elegant Wordsmith Thomas Kinsella," The Ticket, *The Irish Times*, Saturday, May 5, 2018, 28.

[10] See Brian G. Caraher, "When Thomas Moore Was the Headline Act," in *The Reputations of Thomas Moore: Poetry, Music, Politics*, eds. Sarah McCleave and Tríona O'Hanlon (London and New York: Routledge, 2020), 91–2.

[11] Thomas Kinsella, *The Dual Tradition: An Essay on Poetry and Politics in Ireland* (Manchester: Carcanet Press, 1995), 7–20.

[12] Ciaran Carson, "A Note on the Translation," in *The Táin: A New Translation of Táin Bó Cúailnge* (London: Penguin Classics, 2007), xxiv–xxv.

[13]Carson, "A Note on the Translation," xxiv.

[14] *The Tain*, edited and translated by Thomas Kinsella from the Irish epic *Táin Bó Cúailnge* (Dublin: Dolmen Press, 1969), with brush drawings by Louis le Brocquy. Reissued Oxford: Oxford University Press, 1970, ix–xi, 1–50, 255–61.

[15] Kinsella, *The Tain*, 1.

[16] Kinsella, *The Tain*, 1–2.

[17] Kinsella, *The Tain*, 255.

[18] Kinsella, *The Tain*, 46–50.

[19] Kinsella, *The Tain*, 260–61.

[20] Kinsella, *The Tain*, 46, 260.

[21] Kinsella, *The Tain*, 47–50.

[22] Kinsella, *The Tain*, 3–45, 255–60.

[23] See also two essays of mine which explore much further this line of socio-culturally and socio-linguistically informed inquiry into *Táin Bó Cúailnge*: Brian G. Caraher, "Genre Theory: Cultural and Historical Motives Engendering Literary Genre," in *Genre Matters: Essays in Theory and Criticism*, eds. Garin Dowd, Lesley Stevenson and Jeremy Strong (Bristol: Intellect Books, 2006), 34–5; and Brian G. Caraher, "Genre Theory: A Sociolinguistic Approach to the Aesthetics of Literary Form," in *Inspiration and Technique: Ancient to Modern Views on Beauty and Art*, eds. John Roe and Michele Stanco (Bern and Oxford: Peter Lang, 2007), 301–2.

[24] Kinsella, *The Dual Tradition*, 21, 21–42.

[25] Kinsella, *The Dual Tradition*, 29.

[26] Kinsella, *The Dual Tradition*, 30.

[27] Kinsella, *The Dual Tradition*, 31–7.

[28] Kinsella, *The Dual Tradition*, 37.

[29] For validation of this point, see "Thomas Kinsella in Conversation with Adrienne Leavy" in *Reading Ireland* 11 (Winter 2019) and *New Hibernia Review* 24, no. 1 (Spring 2020).

[30] Declan Kiberd, *After Ireland: Writing the Nation from Beckett to the Present* (London: Head of Zeus, 2017), 295.

[31] Kinsella, *The Dual Tradition*, 38-9; *The New Oxford Book of Irish Verse*, 218–21, 404.

[32] Kinsella, *The Dual Tradition*, 40; *The New Oxford Book of Irish Verse*, 222–47, 404.

[33] Kinsella, *The Dual Tradition*, 41.

[34] Kinsella, *The Dual Tradition*, 47.

[35] Kinsella, *The Dual Tradition*, 48, 53, 58–9.

[36] Kinsella, *The Dual Tradition*, 66, and 64–82 more broadly.

[37] Kinsella, *The Dual Tradition*, 77.

[38] W. B. Yeats, *The Poems: A New Edition*, ed. Richard J. Finneran (New York: Macmillan, 1983), 337.

[39] Kinsella, *The Dual Tradition*, 82–7.

[40] Kinsella, *The Dual Tradition*, 90.

[41] Kinsella, *The Dual Tradition*, 90–91.

[42] Kinsella, *The Dual Tradition*, 91.

[43] Kinsella, *The Dual Tradition*, 107.

[44] See Dillon Johnston, *Irish Poetry after Joyce*, second edition (New York: Syracuse UP, 1997).

[45] Kinsella, *The Dual Tradition*, 111.

[46] Kinsella, *The Dual Tradition*, 112–13.

[47] Kinsella, *The Dual Tradition*, 114, and 113–22 more broadly.

[48] Kinsella, *The Dual Tradition*, 117, and 113–17.

[49] Kinsella, *The Dual Tradition*, 118–19.

[50] Kinsella, *The Dual Tradition*, 119–20.

[51] Kinsella, *Collected Poems*, 133–37, 365. The Saville Report of June 2010 completely overturned the conclusions of the Widgery Tribunal, and 14 March 2019 saw the first and only indictment to date of a member of the British Army ('Soldier F') for the murders staged on the 30th of January 1972.

[52] Kinsella, *Collected Poems*, 137.

[53] See Donatella Abbate Badin's, Thomas Jackson's, and Brian John's introductory studies in the mid-1990s through Maurice Harmon's and Andrew Fitzsimons's more detailed studies in 2008 to David Lynch's more politicized study in 2015. The critical focus of these various studies has principally been on Kinsella's poetry.

CHAPTER 9

"Let us see how the whole thing / works"

VIOLENCE AND SELFHOOD IN THOMAS KINSELLA'S *A TECHNICAL SUPPLEMENT* (1976)

LUCY COLLINS

The poetry of Thomas Kinsella engages in a process of relentless self-scrutiny. As human subject, and as artist, the poet interrogates the role of embodied experience in the journey towards knowledge, exploring how the speaking subject tests intellect and emotion and is, in turn, shaped by this activity. Kinsella, who began publishing in the 1950s, is a poet of process—reflection on the act of writing has become, for him, integral to the larger search for meaning that drives his creative work and is depicted directly within it. The figure of the poet is at once a constant and disruptive presence in the text, offering intellectual coherence in principle, yet continually questioning assumed certainties. Kinsella's elaborate processes of writing and revision, his close attention to the circumstances of publication, and his alteration of printed poems all contribute to this sense of textual instability. These practices also reveal the writing self to be vigilant of all aspects of the creative process. In this essay, I will focus on the representation of violence in the 1976 collection *A Technical Supplement*, a work that exemplifies Kinsella's use of the physical to interrogate the act of writing itself, and one that displays the complexity of his approach to the subject position in his poetry.

The Peppercanister Poems: New Directions in Poetry Publishing

To establish meaning as contingent, as provisional, even as potentially contradictory, has been a significant part of Kinsella's poetic project. The Peppercanister series, starting with *Butcher's Dozen* in 1972, expresses this conviction in the form of publication itself, not only indicating the aesthetic trajectory of Kinsella's work but also determining the ways in which the poetry would be received and read. The series marked a turning point both in the poet's art and his publishing practice, clearly indicating the aesthetic continuities that he felt were necessary to the fullest realization of his ideas. The origins of the project were somewhat circumstantial, however. In response to the Widgery Tribunal's exoneration of the British Army's involvement in Bloody Sunday in Derry, Kinsella composed "Butcher's Dozen"—a bitter satirical poem that demanded, in the poet's view, a new mode of publication. Though his earlier work had been published by Liam Miller's Dolmen Press and latterly by Oxford University Press, Kinsella determined to publish "Butcher's Dozen" himself, calling his new venture after the "Peppercanister" church, an eighteenth-century building visible from Kinsella's Dublin home.

This publishing project allowed Kinsella to bring out work comparatively frequently and to maintain high levels of aesthetic control over the presentation of poems. The sense of continuity built by the sequence positions each publication as a stage rather than as an end point in an unbroken act of poetic inquiry. Even as this decision was being made, however—a decision at once aesthetic and ideological—Kinsella was already thinking about the book as printed object. The publication of different versions of the same text then became the pattern for Kinsella, emphasizing the cumulative nature of poetic practice, as one that might pass through a number of phases that were not susceptible to neat categorization in book form. Around this time Kinsella began to subject his printed work to further revision, both in order to strengthen its links to his larger pattern of thought and to streamline its formal effects.[1] Sometimes these revisions involved the rearrangement of groups of poems to facilitate particular resonances and to suggest new priorities. Of particular significance is the way in which the search for meaning becomes integral to the revision process, and re-writing becomes a means of re-thinking for the poet:

> When you have done your best and put it aside, giving it time to "digest," it is extraordinary how clear things get. Stroke out the bad material and the work that won't fit and bring the rest closer to the final phase. The good work survives.[2]

Revision Practices: Kinsella and the Process of Composition

This process of reflection, followed by the refinement of the poetic text, exemplifies what Dirk Van Hulle would term a "progressive" model of textual revision—one which leads to a decisive improvement in the work.[3] This assumption also shapes the transition from notes to established poetic form, though it applies with less certainty to revisions that occur later in the life of the text, especially after it has been in print for some time.[4] The recognition that a text may register "loss as well as gain as a consequence of organic growth" brings manuscript materials to new prominence in the analysis of thematic development.[5] Textual revisions can extend from small adjustments, such as the changing of individual words, to significant alterations in form and meaning. This distinction can be closely observed in Kinsella's practice not only at the level of the individual poem but also of the entire volume, where selective changes applied across the gathering may have a cumulative impact not felt in the text of a single poem. Wim Van Mierlo calls attention to the questions of definition that are generated by these possibilities, and especially to how we understand the terms "text," "work," and "book."[6] Given the cumulative process that shapes Kinsella's writing from this point onwards, these distinctions are especially pertinent. His unfolding body of work moves through a number of distinct phases and takes a variety of forms: the material that forms the Peppercanister "books" also constitutes the "text" that readers will later encounter in the volumes of selected and collected poems. In terms of print history alone, Kinsella's work offers a rich scope for the exploration of revision processes and metatextual elements. Furthermore, the inferences that may be drawn from his manuscript and draft materials are different from those supported by the published texts, and access to these deepens our understanding of the relationship between the poet's thought processes and aesthetic choices.

Siegfried Schiebe's division of writers into "mindworkers," who map out the work prior to writing, and "paperworkers," who use the process of writing to generate and arrange ideas, is difficult to apply with certainty in Kinsella's case.[7] His repeated use of the figure of the poet as a walker, who tests and arranges his ideas against the backdrop of a familiar and stimulating landscape, suggests the activity of a mindworker. His creation of numerological schema is just one instance of this act of conceptual mapping. In practice, however, Kinsella's manuscripts display the kind of cumulative work and spatial configuration that reveal extensive development and movement of ideas across boundaries of stanza and poem. This, together with his persistent depiction of the practice of writing in the text of his poems, suggests that he is essentially a paperworker. However, a spatial rather than a chronological model of revision may be helpful in considering the ways in which Kinsella moves between the microcomposition of individual lines and the macrocomposition of entire volumes of poems. This practice sees lines of verse being tested against the progression of the whole and often discarded or left aside, only to be returned to in a later compositional phase. Indeed, the refining of abstract meaning through its material expression in language is an important means by which Kinsella seems to generate inspiration, leading to a deepening intellectual engagement.

The rise of genetic criticism has altered our understanding of the role of the creative process in determining the meaning of a printed work of literature. Kinsella's archive at Emory University reveals not only his meticulous practices of revision but also the complex ways in which his thinking developed during key phases of his writing life.[8] These archival materials trace the movement from notes and short poetry passages to extended sections that may be expanded or refined and moved to new locations within the structure of the publication as a whole. Yet it is also possible to read some of the poetic composition as preceding the overall conception of a volume, as incomplete drafts from an earlier phase may determine the development of a new project. For example, phrases and ideas from a single page of notes may later reappear in several different publications across perhaps a five-year period, suggesting that these constitute foundational ideas for an entire creative phase. Once these materials have undergone initial development, it is very often their ordering that will be key to their impact in the published version. Kinsella's organic approach to the development of ideas across his extensive body of work, together with the fact that his published poems may yet be subject to further revisions, makes the chronological arrangement of material difficult. Kinsella's return to earlier ideas and images in order to deepen his understanding of particular concepts, and to reinforce their evolving position in his work, becomes especially pronounced from 1970 onward.

Reading *A Technical Supplement*

A Technical Supplement is the sixth of the Peppercanister Series and was published in 1976, both in paperback and hardback. As in so much of Kinsella's work, the final order of the twenty-four poems that make up the sequence, and their relationship to the individual illustrations included, is important. The paperback edition bears a drawing of a scalpel on its cover and the image of the blade, with its capacity to divide—to create multiplicity out of singularity—speaks both to Kinsella's numerological scheme and to the diverse forms of creative origin with which genetic criticism is itself concerned. The volume as a whole explores energies that are at once creative and destructive: they give rise to language and, at the same time, threaten to consume it. As Maurice Harmon has observed, "The poems are at times

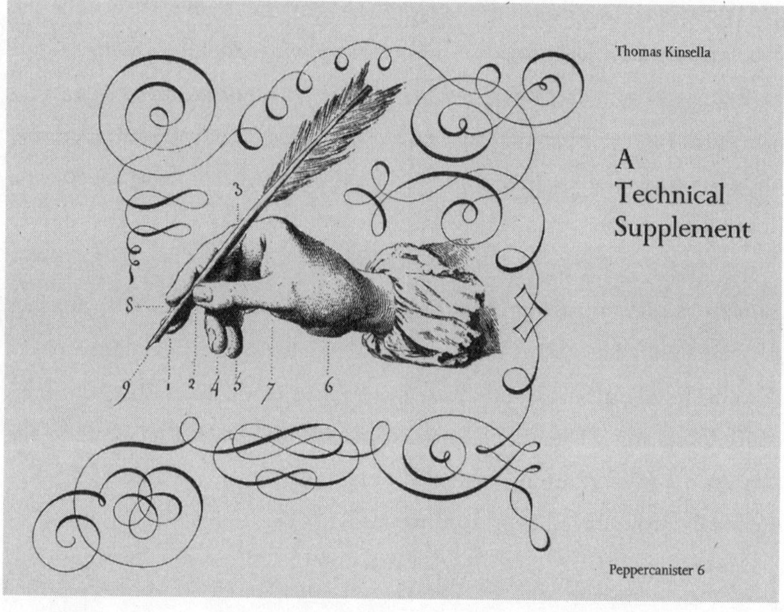

Figure 1. Thomas Kinsella, *A Technical Supplement*, title page.

stunningly alive; the circuit of energy between language and subject is short to the point of immediate ignition."[9] The title page illustration of the hand holding a quill exemplifies this nexus of bodily and representational elements.

This tension between unity in division, between the part and the whole, informs the structure of the work in significant ways: its fragmented nature allows the accumulation of diverse details in the interests of complete understanding, of seeing "how the whole thing / works."[10] The sequence reflects, or suggests, that the shape of meaning needs to be apprehended in its entirety, that to break it up into parts is to render it ultimately unknowable. The precise meaning of individual poems may be difficult to grasp, but the accumulated details of language reinforce larger frameworks of understanding and provide a connective tissue between texts that are varied in form and image. Motifs of the suffering body predominate, from the classical Laocoön to images of human dissection and animal slaughter. Experiences of abjection connect the depicted processes of evisceration with those of ingestion, breaking the boundary between self and world and raising ethical questions concerning the articulation of human needs. Such destabilization also functions on a textual level in the Peppercanister series in which the individual poem is complete yet leaves its meaning open to clarification and revision in later texts. Ian Flanagan has identified this phase of Kinsella's work as a "categoric renunciation . . . of the various attempts to categorize and contain his narrator."[11] This departure from established structures marks a new commitment to an aesthetics of incompletion. The poet himself described this mode of publication as "a plunge of a different kind into the nature of things . . . without being committed to any particular point of view except that of dynamic response to what happens."[12] Such an observation emphasizes the responsiveness of this work, but it is the complex relationship between sensation and its representation which is often the subject of scrutiny here. The body, as the physical manifestation of the life force, is both the site of creation—the writing self who sits down with pen and paper—and the focus of Kinsella's investigation into human motive and intellect, thus occupying simultaneously the position of subject and object in the poetry. The anatomization of selfhood entails the repeated penetration of corporeal and mental boundaries, an unflinching analysis of our concealed natures and their impact on our being in the world. It is significant, then, that the philosophical inquiry is pursued in the twenty-four poems of *A Technical Supplement*, both by means of the extremity of bodily experience and of the testing of intellectual and emotional realities; indeed, the recreation of the visceral is embedded so deeply in this philosophical process that it becomes inseparable from inquiries made about and through language.

That this sequence should be termed a "supplement"—something that completes or qualifies another—prompts us to read this work in relation to earlier texts. In its original edition, the poems are accompanied by a number of illustrations from Diderot's *Encyclopédie*,[13] an eighteenth-century work that represented diverse areas of knowledge without seeking to synthesize them within a particular philosophical scheme. This linguistic and visual intertext emphasizes Kinsella's own attraction to various forms of influence and inspiration, as well as his interest in systematic elements that would facilitate rather than limit his range of inquiry. As Derval Tubridy has pointed out, the relationship between the illustrations and the poems is an important one. Kinsella makes his source explicit in the opening sequence with a quotation from a letter from Diderot to Voltaire: "there comes a time when all ashes are mingled, then what will it boot me to have been Voltaire or Diderot or whether it is your three syllables or my three syllables that survive."[14] Yet, as we see elsewhere in Kinsella's work, endurance is all: the drive to create overcomes this "attack of spleen" as Diderot terms it, and he returns to his encyclopedia. To question, to come close to despair yet to persist—all become hallmarks of Kinsella's construction of the subject position in his poetry, applying equally to human evolution to the smallest action of the individual.

A Technical Supplement: Preparatory Writing

The archival materials relating to *A Technical Supplement* may be roughly divided into three parts: preliminary notes and preparatory writings; draft

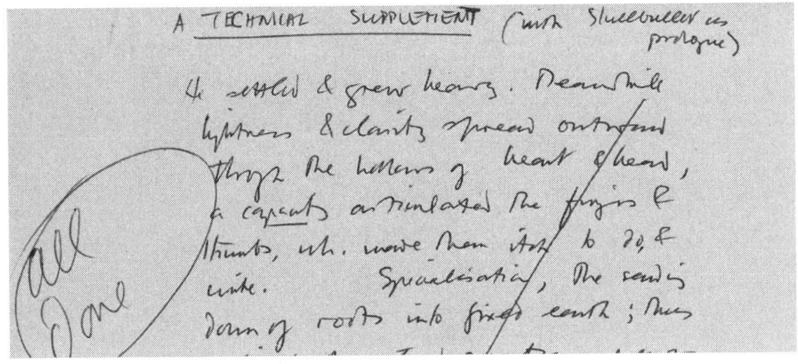
A TECHNICAL SUPPLEMENT (with Skullbullet as prologue)

He settled & grew heavy. Meanwhile lightness & clarity spread outward through the hollows of heart & head, a capacity articulated the fingers & thumbs, wh. move them itself to do & write. Specialisation, the sending down of roots into fixed earth; thus

All Done

Figure 2. Thomas Kinsella, *A Technical Supplement*, prose sheets.

poems; and fair copy, with small amendments only. The preparatory writings are all in manuscript while the majority of the draft poems are in typescript with revisions in ink. All are on plain loose sheets with the order in which poems are to be printed occasionally signaled by phases of numbered pages. The early prose sheets, headed "A Technical Supplement" and including the side note "with Skullbullet as prologue," suggest that the concept and title for the volume were conceived long before publication, perhaps growing from an existing piece of writing that would now function as a prologue.[15]

The first phase of the writing begins with an embodied male figure whose "heart & head" are not just emblematic of emotion and intellect but are part of an anatomical schema that includes "fingers & thumbs" (Fig. 2), and later "eyes," "neck," "brows," "lips," "mouth," "tongue" and "teeth." These physical features are described here in relation to their particular capacities (to convey "lightness and clarity," for example) and to "inner functions"—a manifestation of energies that create and sustain the human form. From the start of these prose writings the context for the body is vividly material: the poet reflects on "the sending down of roots into fixed earth" (Fig. 2);

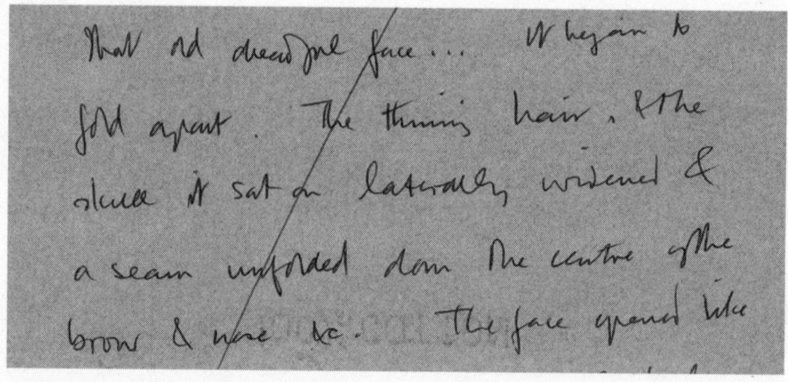
That old dreadful face . . . It began to
fold apart. The thinning hair, & the
skull it sat on laterally widened &
a seam unfolded down the centre of the
brow & nose &c. The face opened like

Figure 3. Thomas Kinsella, *A Technical Supplement*, prose sheets.

later in this passage, references to "mountaintops" and "the sea-bed," to "buildings," "pillars," and "ships" juxtapose primal landscapes with built environments from different eras. These ambitious transitions can be traced too in some of Kinsella's earlier Peppercanister publications. *One* (1974) constitutes a meditation on singularity that is a deliberate development of the zero trope of *Notes from the Land of the Dead* (1972), a sequence concerned with life in its embryonic form. In these prose notes, then, the continuity of Kinsella's creative project is made clear.[16] Its movement, however, is towards anatomization: it is here that the relentless self-scrutiny that had been evident in Kinsella's earlier poetry is given literal representation:[17] "Look in the mirror & stare. That old dreadful face. It began to fold apart. The thinning hair, & the skull it sat on laterally widened & a seam unfolded down the center of the brow and nose" (Fig. 3).[18]

Here the capacity of the reflection to distort the face and multiply its features is indicated; only later in these sheets does the presence of violence indicate that Kinsella is going to develop this image of self-division. On

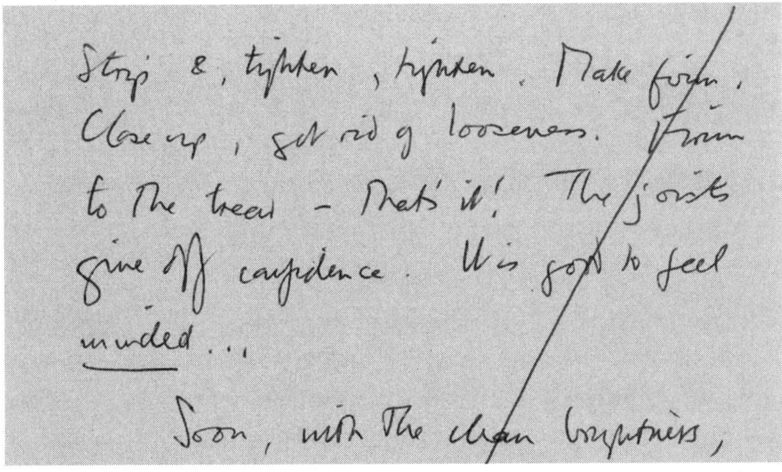

Strip &, tighten, tighten. Make firm.
Close up, get rid of looseness. Firm
to the heart – that's it! The joints
give off confidence. It is good to feel
minded . . .

Soon, with the clean brightness,

Figure 4. Thomas Kinsella, *A Technical Supplement*, prose sheets.

page five of these preparatory writings, a guillotine "speaks" and "jets of blood respond, with dignity, suddenness, a pleasing effusion."[19] The following sheet sees the violence move closer to the speaking subject—"a simple knife-slash. . . ."[20] In all these cases, however, the violation of wholeness creates rather than destroys potential, changing the relationship between the part and the whole: "for each mutilation, there is a new healing."[21] Like the process of drafting itself, multiplicity initiates energies that are both the theme and the driving force of Kinsella's poetic project.

Dialogue is perhaps the natural outcome of these meditations but the specific address, when it comes, is in the form of a monologue. This passage also seems to reflect directly on the act of writing itself. The earlier phrase "play with this voice for a while" is self-reflexive, conscious of what might emerge as a result of the creative process. It is followed by further admonitions to "strip and tighten, tighten" (Fig. 4), yet it is hard at this stage to determine whether these energies are to be part of the subject of the writing or a comment on the process itself. On the next sheet of these prose writings the demands become organic: "Dig down & destroy. Sieve, filter, scour, cleanse, prepare, refresh, roughen with clean chemicals, health and freshness [. . .] Rake & level, roll & seed, water & protect,"[22] indicating how processes of growth move beyond the space of the text. Yet the context of writing is never far from the poet's mind, as he goes on to articulate: "I have opened my mind to a few poems, and though I haven't 'understood' them yet fully, feel relieved that, being by someone I have always. . . . avoided, they seem surprisingly good." These remarks, which in this context may appear to be a separate comment on his reading at the time, are later incorporated into the text of a poem in the print version of *A Technical Supplement*.[23]

"I wonder if I might": Towards Draft Poems

The chronological dimension of the genetic process is important in tracing creative development but often difficult to establish with certainty in the Kinsella archive. The group of poems in typescript is likely to represent a much later stage in the composition process, indicating a missing interim phase of manuscript poems. While a cluster of handwritten poem drafts is included among the papers, these texts reveal extensive reworking of one segment of preparatory writing only—the "monologue" section featuring repeated iterations of the phrase "excuse me, I wonder if I might. . . ."[24] Since this passage later appears in a typed page where earlier inked revisions have been incorporated, it seems likely that other handwritten drafts working with different sections of the earlier prose passages once existed, though these are not retained in the archive. Thus, the typescript poems may be judged to represent a stabilized form of hand drafting, showing a stage after the prose material has been shaped into poetic form but before the poems have become a clear sequence. For example, one poetic fragment—consisting of five stanzas of four lines each—returns to images from the first page of preparatory writing. Now the embodied male is represented as "it" and is buried, in Beckettian mode, "up to the knees" in earth, much as the root image in the prose passage suggested. The foremost identifying feature in this poem extract is the stare, continuous in the opening stanza yet ceasing in the fifth—"the eyeballs stopped staring / they grew quiet, and then passive"[25] refining the earlier description "his eyes ... no longer looked outward; went passive, giving easy transit to light, in either direction."[26]

The image of the splitting face remains prominent, and largely unchanged, in the transition to poetic form:

> Where is everybody?
> Look
> in the mirror, into that face.
>
> It began to separate, the head
> opening like a rubbery fan ...
>
> The thin hair blurred and crept apart
> widening from a deepening seam
> as the forehead opened down the centre.[27]

With the exception of one word—"into", which becomes "at"—this passage will remain intact in the first printed edition of the poem. What is even more remarkable, given Kinsella's elaborate craft, is that the image of the mirrored face with its thinning hair and seamed brow endures across the entire drafting process. This poem is without a number in its typescript version and uniquely contains two footnotes that interpolate the thinking at key points, suggesting that this may be considered a pivotal moment in the thinking of the sequence as a whole.

What does appear among the poems in this phase is a scene entirely absent from the preparatory notes—that of the abattoir which will become an important trope of the volume. The routine killing of animals takes the graphic division of the face to a new realism and places human suffering within a wider context. The thinking of the poem and its form is fully developed at this stage: six-line stanzas situate the speaker as a witness to the "dripping groves / in Swift's slaughterhouse"—a reworking of benign landscape into a nightmare scene that ironically conflates the name of the famous author of *A Modest Proposal* with the enormous American meat processing firm, Swift's.[28] This reference shows the ways in which Kinsella's persistent treatment of inner city Dublin as a space of personal and political contemplation became layered with references to American cultural landscapes following his move there. Established in typescript, the abattoir poem undergoes some small but key revisions in ink: it is allocated number VI in the sequence, and the "smiling veteran" who first appeared at the end of Stanza 1 of the first typed draft of the poem is now moved to the opening line (Fig. 5), emphasizing human stewardship of the violence this poem describes.

The human dimensions of this text have other connotations too. Kinsella chooses to reverse the order of the two phrases "on the concrete, before their faces" (Fig. 5), giving more prominence to the face, a feature that human and non-human participants share. The spatial aspect of the poem is important too. Kinsella adjusts the description to emphasize the point of entry that the live animals make to the scene ("They come in behind a

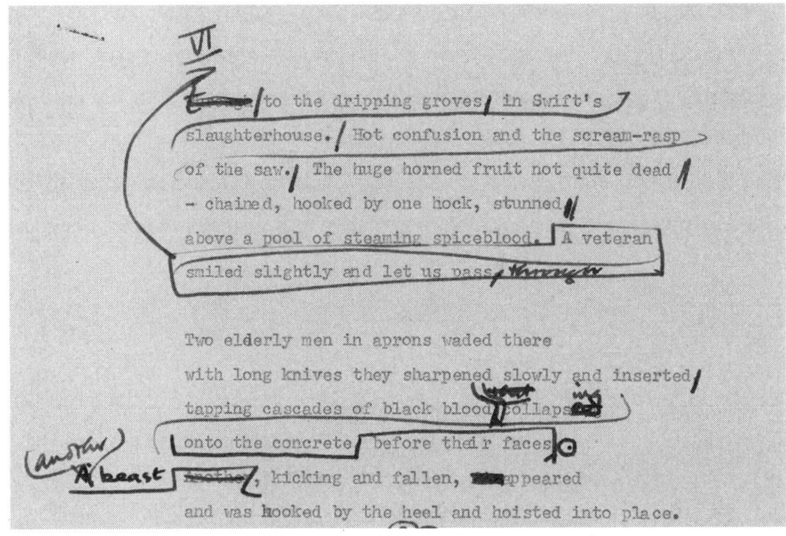

VI

to the dripping groves in Swift's
slaughterhouse. Hot confusion and the scream-rasp
of the saw. The huge horned fruit not quite dead
- chained, hooked by one hock, stunned
above a pool of steaming spiceblood. A veteran
smiled slightly and let us pass, through

Two elderly men in aprons waded there
with long knives they sharpened slowly and inserted
tapping cascades of black blood collaps
onto the concrete before their faces
(another) A beast another, kicking and fallen, appeared
and was hooked by the heel and hoisted into place.

Figure 5. Thomas Kinsella, *A Technical Supplement*, typescript draft.

plank barrier *on an upper level*") and where they are held in order to position the animals themselves as witnesses to the deaths of others.[29] The poet also changes many of the pronouns from singular to plural, emphasizing the collective nature of this experience and the vast numbers of animals that are killed in this way. In the course of the poem, the living creatures become "merely meat" but in their inert state are yet capable of energy. "In a clean room" a chemical liquid "transfuses" the animal part—now described as a "ham"—suggesting the movement of energy between living and dead.

The condition of self-division is an important symbol for Kinsella by this stage in the drafting process. The reworked version of the draft that begins "Where is everybody?" signals clearly that this should be placed before the text starting "That day, when I woke" in the sequence. The latter poem is the most significant expression of self-division thus far in *A Tech-*

nical Supplement: "That day, when I woke, a great private dream-blade / was planted in me from bowels to brain."[30] This transition also suggests that the preceding poem, with its ghastly imagery of the opening head, occurs in the moments before sleep. Yet even when the poet is awake, the threat to bodily integrity cannot be shaken off—"I knew it was not going to go away"—and creates a simultaneous presence and absence of sensation:

> From that day forth I knew
> what it was to taste reality
> and not to; to suffer tedium or pain
> and not to; to eat, swallowing with pleasure,
> and not to;[31]

Kinsella's desire to allow both experience and the failure to experience a balanced place in his creation offers an inherent contradiction in perception—how can the absence of sensation be "known" in any perceptible sense? The contemplation of two mutually exclusive states sheds interesting light on Kinsella's textual practice too: his archive allows us to see all possible versions of these poems simultaneously, before exclusion and arrangement refines interpretation.

A Technical Supplement in Print

Since Kinsella himself was the publisher of the Peppercanister series, he could control every aspect of the publication of these texts. The first printed edition of *A Technical Supplement* as Peppercanister 6 refines and rearranges the poems in the archived drafts and introduces texts not found there. In particular, it demonstrates an important relationship between word and image that played no role in the verbal drafting process. The hand holding a quill, which appears on the title page, is at once the signifier of the writer and the part of the anatomy associated with deliberate action. As prologue, Kinsella includes an extract from Diderot's letter to Voltaire, dated 1758: lamenting his age, Diderot professes himself "*tired out with tricks and shufflings.*" Kinsella himself, nearing fifty in 1976, may have identified with Diderot's expression of unappreciated labor but also with his intellectual determination: "*and back to the Encyclopaedia I go.*" This book thus addresses the notion of creative labor itself, the difficulty of the precise acts of anatomization and documentation. Printed on unnumbered pages, its centerfold depicts the dissection of an eye, drawing attention to the creative and moral importance of observation. The three other illustrations embedded within the text are of Laocoön, with proportions sketched, a severed head with the circulatory system and spinal cord visible, and a demonstration of trepanning. Here artistic representation, anatomical knowledge and direct bodily intervention are each invoked. Suffering is placed in a narrative context, as the killing of Laocoön's sons by snakes sent in divine retribution emphasizes the grief of loss, where later images highlight physical pain specifically. The presence of these images is an important dimension in the ordering of material which now begins with what had previously been envisaged as a six-line prologue ending with "let us see how the whole thing / works." The anatomical detail in *A Technical Supplement* simultaneously brings the body into stark relief and objectifies it in the eyes of the reader. The second poem in this series dissociated the speaker from the abject body, so that the voice is that of a lecturer, scientist, or demonstrator: "You will note firstly that there is no containing skin / as we understand it, but 'contained' muscles / – separate entities, interwound and overlaid."[32] This would seem an apt metaphor for the sequence as a whole—the poems are "separate entities" that are yet proximate to, and dependent upon, one another. By integrating this into the sequence, Kinsella brings intention and action together, continuing with a poem on dissection, its "dry staring buttons of muscle" drawn from the early notes.

The act of dissection, realized directly here, bears obliquely on Kinsella's painstaking and observant examination of creativity later in the sequence. It is also an analogue of the reading process and is indicative of the level of attention to subtleties of form and detail required by much of the work, as well as the need to constantly qualify our responses to it. The power of visual interpretation is also implicit in this dissection process; to be meaningful it must be witnessed, and also named and described, so that the interior of the body—that which is normally hidden or secret—is exposed twice, once physically and once in language. The muscular structure that is laid bare in this instance is both vulnerable and strong, each fiber dependent on the other, a unified whole. That the skeleton seems fragile beneath this shows a fear of the disintegration of the body, its ultimate resistance to further classification. Kinsella therefore acknowledges, both in this and in later poems from the sequence, that the impulse to probe deeply can also be a dangerous one with potentially overwhelming implications: "a blade licks out and acts / with one tongue. / Jets of blood respond / in diverse tongues."[33]

This image of bodily incursion encompasses a precise yet forceful breaking of the boundaries of self, which are graphically represented in the fate of the "other" in Poem 6. Here, in the "dripping groves" of the slaughterhouse, Kinsella relies on gruesome sensory detail—"the scream-rasp of the saw," the "pool of steaming spice-blood"—to assault the reader with the sound, smell, and sight of the crowded scene.[34] The violence is abrupt and economical: we witnessed creatures divested of their skin: "a man [. . .] loosens the skin around their tails / with deep cuts in unexpected directions; / the tail springs back; the hide pulls down to the jaws."[35] Yet in this poem human response to these events is withheld. In the following poem the speaker asks:

> Is it all right to do this?
> Is it an offense against justice
> when someone stumbles away helplessly
> and has to sit down
> until her sobbing stops?[36]

As in Rembrandt's painting *Slaughtered* Ox, where a hanging carcass is observed by a young woman, here the introduction of the female witness places the instincts of human and animal in close proximity. However, by separating the response from the dynamic scene of slaughter, Kinsella ensures that it acquires, if anything, a greater significance in recording human despair at excesses of violence. Yet the tears of his female figure do not exonerate the poet from identification with both the creature and the slaughterers here: the artist or writer, in gazing into the object and penetrating beneath its surface, performs an analogous act of incision. This is rendered powerfully in the fourth poem of the series which also echoes Kinsella's use of the imagery of cells and microscopic observation to approach the most minute alteration of the living organism. Depth becomes a significant aspect of this poem: the "deepening damage" after the first rupture and the blood that wells up, "bathing the point as it went deeper." The instrument of incision takes on the life-force of this body:

Persist.

        Beyond a certain depth
it stands upright by itself
and quivers with borrowed life.

Persist.

        And you may find
the buried well. And take on
the stillness of a root.[37]

From his earliest work, Kinsella has been preoccupied with the interrelationship between the speaking voice within the poem and the man who is the object of its scrutiny. For him, the split self is both a testament to a complex and often contradictory response to human desire and suffering and a result of the inevitable self-consciousness of representation—the deliberate nature of language. It seems that, for Kinsella, language is both a powerful instrument for the expression of isolation and pain, and the means by which those experiences are brought into conscious being. Seeing ourselves at second-hand, through another's eyes or through a mirror or static image, splits the self into observer and observed and causes "otherness" to be associated with the observing mind: "the beginning / must be inward. Turn inward. Divide."[38] The disintegration that marks this severance of self from self is destructive of any clear sense of identity and affirms the pain and disorientation of the speaker. When, in Poem 22, the face divides and becomes two faces—each whole yet neither quite itself—the acknowledgment of the impossibility of definition, or even unified meaning, deepens: "(But then the original could not / have been called 'itself' either. / What but some uneasiness made it divide?)."[39] What changes fundamentally is the relationship between the staring figure, the self-gazing into the mirror, and the object of the gaze, the self-gazing back. The moment represents doubleness being discerned and the relationship between the two selves—ostensibly the bifurcating image yet also the living face and the representation of the face—being acknowledged. The uneasiness here belongs to the speaker who cannot properly maintain the gaze. To see in such circumstances is also to be aware of the questionable nature of the act of witnessing and of its subjective cast. The surgical illustration of an eye operation, scalpel poised before the eyeball, suggests the unique aspect of visual representation—that imperfections of the eye determine our view of the world. Roland Barthes has commented upon the role of sight in the representation, on the gap that exists between the self's apprehension of the body, and how that same body is viewed by another:

> Where is your authentic body? You are the only one who can never see yourself except as an image; you never see your eyes unless they are dulled by the gaze they rest upon the mirror or the lens . . . even and especially for your own body, you are condemned to the repertoire of its images.[40]

Interestingly here, the "you" Barthes addresses is in fact the "I," and this objectification of the self is clearly in keeping with the inquiry into its presentation and reception. In representing himself as an image, he is also insisting that the reader views him as such: if the self can never be witnessed directly, neither can the author be apprehended without the mediating presence of the text. The notion that we see ourselves only second-hand is a formative one, which draws attention to the mode of representation and to the writer who is on both sides of any such act, at once creating it and participating in its retrieval.

This self-division, realized in Kinsella's sequence by the "great private blade," creates a tyranny of multiple sensation. At the boundaries of A Tech-

nical Supplement is always the infliction of pain in the search for knowledge, and it is clear also that language and form must undergo the same rigorous process to achieve the poet's most precise ends. From this point onward, Kinsella's approach to language becomes even more rigorous, his insistence on measuring and qualifying, on seeking the most precise meaning possible, results in the endlessly shifting form and tone we see in this sequence, from the explanatory, to the insistent, to the conversational. It is through the dexterity of tone, through the constant shifts and surprises of form, that Kinsella ensures that the speaking subject of his poem, as well as puzzling over physical and psychic aspects, constantly reinvents himself in the face of these to issue new challenges to the reader.

The collection as a whole is framed by the poems of self-investigation in which images of violence predominate; those recording the pleasures of everyday life (eating, reading) are placed towards the center of the volume. The text beginning "No one did anything at first," in spite of being put through multiple drafts in manuscript and typescript, does not appear at all in the first printing of *A Technical Supplement*; instead it reappears as a prologue to the printing of the poems in the *Collected Poems* (2001) and is used there to form an important connection with the image patterns of *Notes from the Land of the Dead* (1972) and *One* (1974). This demonstrates the long reach of Kinsella's creative process, during which developed material is often withheld from publication because its place in the scheme of a volume is uncertain. Though there were no substantive changes to individual poems from *A Technical Supplement* at the time of the 2001 publication, this inclusion serves to reposition the poems in relation to earlier texts, now that the Diderot illustrations have been removed.

In spite of the incomplete nature of the archive materials relating to Kinsella's *A Technical Supplement*, this work provides a rich source for genetic critics. Like so many of the objects in Kinsella's archive, it provides interesting evidence of the poet's writing practices: we gain insight into the organic nature of his artistic project since the early 1970s and the complex philosophical, psychological, and historical materials that help to shape his thinking. The exploration of this work also benefits from knowledge of key debates and issues formative of the field of genetic criticism itself and helps to open Kinsella's poetic achievement to new critical approaches.

Notes

[1] Though Kinsella often made extensive changes to printed poems between their first appearance and their re-publication in *Collected Poems* (2006), I am concerned here with manuscript genetics rather than textual genetics. This is because *A Technical Supplement* underwent few changes after the initial print stage but offers good evidence of Kinsella's composition process.

[2] Dennis O'Driscoll, "Interview with Thomas Kinsella," *Poetry Ireland Review* 25 (Spring 1989), 63.

[3] Dirk Van Hulle, *Manuscript Genetics, Joyce's Know-How, Beckett's Nohow* (Gainsville, FL: UP of Florida, 2008), 10.

[4] Most critics writing since 2001 use the text of the *Collected Poems 1956–2001* (Manchester: Carcanet Press, 2001) or *Collected Poems 1956–2001* (Winston-Salem, NC: Wake Forest UP, 2006). Derval Tubridy's *Thomas Kinsella: The Peppercanister Poems* (Dublin: University College Dublin Press, 2000) addresses the genesis and development of the work from draft to most recent print version up to 1999. Andrew Fitzsimons also makes extensive use of archival materials in *The Sea of Disappointment: Thomas Kinsella's Pursuit of the Real* (Dublin: University College Dublin Press, 2008).

[5] Van Hulle, *Manuscript Genetics*, 10.

[6] Wim Van Mierlo, "Reflections on Textual Editing in the Time of the History of the Book," *Variants: the Journal of the European Society for Textual Scholarship* 10 (2013), n.pag.

Louis Hay, one of the founding fathers of French genetic criticism, considers the "work" to have many potential manifestations, of which the printed text is only one. Louis Hay, "Does 'Text' Exist?" *Studies in Bibliography* 41 (1988), 64–76.

[7] Van Hulle, *Manuscript Genetics*, 47.

[8] Thomas Kinsella Papers, Special Collections and Archives Division, Robert W. Woodruff Library, Emory University, Atlanta, Georgia, USA.

[9] Maurice Harmon, "'Move, if you move, like water': The Poetry of Thomas Kinsella 1972–88," in *Contemporary Irish Poetry: A Collection of Critical Essays*, ed. Elmer Andrews (Basingstoke: Palgrave Macmillan, 1992), 201.

[10]CP, 177, Poem I in *A Technical Supplement* (Dublin: Peppercanister Press, 1976).

[11] Ian Flanagan, "'Tissues of Order': Thomas Kinsella and the Enlightenment Ethos," Special Issue: Thomas Kinsella, *Irish University Review* 31, no. 1 (Spring/Summer 2001): 55.

[12] John Haffenden, "Thomas Kinsella," in *Viewpoints: Poets in Conversation with John Haffenden* (London: Faber and Faber, 1981), 111.

[13] The 1976 text includes five illustrations from Diderot's *Encyclopédie*, and incorporates a sixth in the cover design.

[14] Kinsella, *A Technical Supplement* (Dublin: Peppercanister Press, 1976), n.pag; Kinsella, "A Technical Supplement," *Collected Poems* (Wake Forest UP, 2006), 175. Subsequent references to the printed text refer to the Wake Forest UP edition, abbreviated as CP.

[15] Kinsella Papers, box 15, folder 24.

[16] Edgar Allan Poe's likening of composition to scientific process is relevant to Kinsella's practice in this early phase of the Peppercanister project (Peppercanister 5–9 especially): "the work proceeded ... to its completion with the precision and rigid consequence of a mathematical problem." Quoted in Van Hulle, *Manuscript Genetics*, 13.

[17] Kinsella's "Mirror in February," published in book form in *Downstream* (1962), is the first of his poems to deal directly with the reflected image of the self. The trope of the mirror appears frequently in later poems, especially in *Songs of the Psyche* (Peppercanister 9) in 1985.

[18] Kinsella Papers, box 15, folder 24, page 2 of a sequence of 6.

[19] Kinsella Papers, box 15, folder 24, page 2.

[20] Kinsella Papers, box 15, folder 24, page 2.

[21] Kinsella Papers, box 15, folder 24, page 2..

[22] Kinsella Papers, box 15, folder 24, page 2.

[23] "I have been opening my mind to some new poems / by a neglected 'colleague' of mine / —with some relief. One or two / of a certain quality" (Poem XI, *A Technical Supplement*).

[24] Kinsella Papers, box 15, folder 25.

[25] Kinsella Papers, box 15, folder 25.

[26] Kinsella Papers, box 15, folder 25.

[27] Kinsella Papers, box 15, folder 25.

[28] Brian John plays on the term "shambles" to denote both Jonathan's Swift's mental disarray and an alternative term for the slaughterhouse. Brian John, *Reading the Ground: The Poetry of Thomas Kinsella*. (Washington DC: The Catholic University of America Press, 1996), 179–180.

[29] Kinsella Papers, box 15, folder 25.

[30] Kinsella Papers, box 15, folder 25.

[31] Kinsella Papers, box 15, folder 25.

[32] CP, 177, Poem II in *A Technical Supplement*.

[33] CP, 180

[34] CP, 180

[35] CP, 180

[36] CP, 181, Poem VII in *A Technical Supplement*.

[37] CP, 179, Poem IV in *A Technical Supplement*.

[38] CP, 187.

[39] CP, 192.

[40] Roland Barthes, *Roland Barthes by Roland Barthes* (London: Vintage, 2020), n.pag.

CHAPTER 10

"Lone Artificer"

LATE POEMS AND *READINGS IN POETRY*, PEPPERCANISTERS 24–29 (2006–2011)

ALEX DAVIS

Late Poems collects work in the Peppercanister series: chapbooks 24, 26, 27, 28 and 29, with some of the contents of the individual volumes revised or omitted. Its title might be contrasted with that chosen by A. E. Housman for the volume that belatedly succeeded *A Shropshire Lad*—*Last Poems*, the studied finality of which indicates not the chronological lateness of its contents (which are in fact drawn from throughout Housman's mature poetic career), but its author's determination that, with his avocation as he believed expiring, any subsequent collections would be posthumous.[1] If Kinsella's title refuses to sound the last post in the manner of Housman, it also differentiates itself from that of Austin Clarke's *Later Poems*, a work that, like *Late Poems*, succeeded a *Collected Poems*. In 1964, in a review of Clarke's subsequent collection *Flight to Africa*, Kinsella drew attention to the "oddly unbalanced" quality of *Later Poems*, the contents of which extend from *Pilgrimage* (1929) to *The Horse-Eaters* (1960) (PO, 212).[2] What equilibrium Clarke's collection possesses is signaled by the comparative form of the adjective in its title: these are poems *superseding*, stylistically and thematically, the mythological narrative poems central to Clarke's previous phase.

Late Poems represents continuation and self-reflection upon earlier preoccupations rather than, as in the case of Clarke's volume, their overcoming. Clarke was in his early thirties when *Pilgrimage* first appeared; he was in his mid-sixties when Dolmen and Oxford University Press issued *Later Poems*. *Late Poems* covers a far shorter period of creativity: *Marginal Economy* —the earliest Peppercanister included—was published in February 2006, when Kinsella was seventy-seven; *Fat Master* and *Love Joy Peace*—the most recent Peppercanisters—in 2011. Andrew Fitzsimons has described *Late Poems* as "a book of culmination, of last things, and of first things looked at again in the light of age;"[3] and certainly senectitude is a strong motif in these collections. It is sounded in "Legendary Figures, in Old Age," the first poem in the title sequence of *Belief and Unbelief* (2007), in the context of the need for continued albeit dwindling vitality. The "elders" are "old shapes without shame," whose senescence is imbued with passion's afterburn:

> And I heard one of them saying
> to those around her:
> "We cannot renew the Gift
>
> but we can drain it to the last drop." (LP, 57)[4]

That final line recalls *Notes from the Land of the Dead*: this is the final distillate of the "last drop" that the male speaker's "[l]ips and tongue / wrestle" from the woman's body in "A Hand of Solo."[5] Such terminal ardor stands in marked contrast to the enervation of the "others" of "Lost Cause," the following poem in "Belief and Unbelief": "grey-featured and slow-moving," their condition, "wasting of their eternity," is owing to an inability to find "the causes of their complaints"; "failing to bring the process of understanding . . . to its conclusion," as Maurice Harmon glosses the poem,[6] they would appear ignorant of "the current / of understanding" articulated in the sequence's penultimate poem, "Prayer II":

> That the rough course
>   of the way forward
> may keep us alert
>   for the while remaining.
> (LP, 63)

Late Poems includes a fair number of poems of this petitionary kind. Their heterodox creed is adroitly captured by Catriona Clutterbuck as the expression of "faith through scepticism and . . . scepticism through faith," in the service of "the task of sustaining idealism in the context of its inevitable debunking."[7] This requires, in the words of "Prayer I,"

>   a turning away
> from regard beyond proper merit,
> or reward beyond real need,
> toward the essence and the source.
> (LP, 62)

The presence of two prayer-poems in "Belief and Unbelief" may well bring to the reader's mind George Herbert's identically titled pair in *The Temple*. Herbert's "Prayer II" claims "an easie quick accesse" to the divine decidedly different from the existential "rough course" advocated by Kinsella.[8] Herbert's (Anglican) orthodoxy might be said to find a "heretical" counterpart in the title poem to *Love Joy Peace* (the last of *Late Poems*). Whereas Herbert, in "Prayer II," takes succor in his belief that "these three wait on thy throne, / *Ease*, *Power*, and *Love*," Kinsella's trinity—a graffito from "[m]any years ago, in our first neighbourhood"—is recalled in the context of a meditation on the history of the church that foregrounds its growing veniality:

> —the hierarchies; councils of elders;
> elaborate, self-admiring men
> embracing each other, dressed up like old women,
> in a frankincense odour of property.
> The Temple clattering with worldly goods.
> (LP, 87, 88)

Yet the charitology central to Herbert's *The Temple* ("O let grace / Drop from above!"[9]) is equally a key theme in "Love Joy Peace," which, having adduced "[a] house swept bare by Martin Luther" in his theological emphasis on "[t]he gift of grace," turns to reflect on Augustine's awareness of the "human creature, imperfect," which, "exercising the fleshly appetite, / is redeemed by enabling grace" (LP, 88, 89). This is the corporeality Augustine recognizes in his *Confessions*, that we are "flesh and blood, no better than a breath of wind" (*Confessions* 1.13), the saint's acknowledgement of which Derval Tubridy identified in the earlier sequence "Godhead," whose dualistic concerns are not unrelated to "Love Joy Peace."[10] The "wind that passes" in "Spirit," which concludes *Godhead* is that same "breath of wind / that has passed" in "Foetus of Saint Augustine," in *Belief and Unbelief*, the future bishop's "little shape" imagined as "examining the carnal basis / for issues of such spiritual complexity" (CP, 339; LP, 60).

In the one Peppercanister of the 24–29 series not reprinted in *Late Poems*, although published simultaneously with *Marginal Economy*, the literary critical *Readings in Poetry*, Kinsella includes interpretations of Shakespeare's Sonnets 29 and 30. It is a revealing choice in the light of some of the concerns of the accompanying Peppercanisters. The speaker of these closely linked sonnets is one who, as Colin Burrow notes, employs the conventions of early modern complaint.[11] Kinsella's speaker in *Late Poems* often shares the isolation of Shakespeare's persona, who, "in disgrace with Fortune and mens eyes" (Sonnet 29) is faced, as Kinsella observes, not only with the downturn of his material fortunes but also "the actual deprivation of grace" (RP, 20).[12] "Love Joy Peace" concludes by invoking the restorative power of "[g]race as desire," much as Shakespeare's two sonnets reach a resolution, however transient, through thoughts of the "sweet love" (29) of the "deare friend" (30) with whom grace (in various forms) is repeatedly linked in the sonnets. Kinsella concludes his reading of Sonnet 29 by matter-of-factly stating: "the problem solved" (RP, 13–14). That the solution is as much aesthetic as amatory is implied in Kinsella's preface to *Readings in Poetry*, in which he excoriates the "poetic chaos" of a poem that, like Shakespeare's Sonnets 29 and 30, seeks consolation in friendship. The romantic solitary of Thoreau's "Great Friend" "miss[es] the grace / Of an intelligent and kindred face" that will enable him to shed himself of his feelings of solipsistic withdrawal from the natural world through being "the expression of her [i.e., nature's] meaning." In Kinsella's interpretation, Thoreau's "problem" remains unsolved precisely to the extent that the poem fails *qua* poem. "Great Friend" degenerates, he writes, into "disorder or emptiness," largely through its author's formal ineptitude: it wholly fails to establish "the order that the poem itself is trying to establish."

By way of contrast, Kinsella's "Love Joy Peace," like many of Shakespeare's sonnets, constitutes a self-reflexive interrogation of the relevance of art itself in the existential pursuit of order. This is what the poem calls "[g]race as routine":

The lone artificer loosening the charged facts
from an imagination arguing with itself
until the ache is eased
(LP, 90)

As Donatella Badin comments, such ease is "like the grace that comes by producing a carefully crafted object."[13] And the final section of "Love Joy Peace" segues sardonically to one form of "grace" provided by artifice by means of a striking parallel between the religious concept of unconditional grace or predestination (those who "enter effortless into the Kingdom") and the "[d]ivine afflatus" of the artistic "spontaneity" ascribed to the likes of "the stage-Shakespeare, not blotting a single line; / Mozart and his deathless simplicities, / noted down while he conversed." Against this mythology of the romantic improvisatore, Kinsella proffers faith in the "earthly genius, / the day labourer": Bach, for example, whose artistry is explored at length in "Fat Master," a poem that, in its depiction of the virtuoso organist, complements the vignette of Mahler as both composer and conductor in *Her Vertical Smile* (and Seán Ó Riada in *A Selected Life*).

In a shared phrase, "Fat Master" (as revised in *Late Poems*) and "Love Joy Peace" envisage Bach as essaying "into the heart of matter" (LP, 77, 90). It is an expression that, in its substance and diction, is indicative of *Late Poems*. The absence of the expected second definite article reinvigorates a cliché, which now strongly foregrounds the physical denotations of the second noun, providing a characteristic instance of a developed style that Harry Clifton perceptively describes as only an "apparent flatness": a "dry, careful annotating" that is "one of the few instantly recognisable tones in the English-language poetry of the past 50 years."[14] Clifton's poetic scrivener is the "day labourer" Ben Jonson portrays in his elegy for the real-Shakespeare, a text half-quoted in "Love Joy Peace," "... *that must sweat to write a living line*" (LP, 90, author's italics). For Jonson, "the poet's matter, nature be," and art is the product of the poet "strik[ing] the second heat / Upon the muses' anvil."[15] Kinsella has always been fond of taking the Jonsonian dictum that the "matter" of poetry is nature to voracious extremes. "Art Object," from *Belief and Unbelief*, for instance, begins with a carnivore's teeth "buried in the live neck" of "[h]er young prey" and ends with scavengers coming "for the remains" (LP, 57). ("Flesh Eater," in *Love Joy Peace* offers the extraordinary image of a "great Mouth" that, on uttering the word "Truth," quite literally "swallowed Its own word" [LP, 84]). Yet the opening lines of "Art Object" are in fact an instance of ekphrasis: a verbal rendering of a fourth century *opus sectile* artwork from the Basilica of Junius Bassus on the Esquiline Hill, which vividly renders a tigress attacking a calf, a detail of which is reproduced on the cover of Peppercanister 27. The poem's dependence on a preexisting *objet d'art* throws into relief the metaphorical or, to use a favored term of Kinsella, allegorical quality of the poem. The tigress's slaughter of the calf is comparable to the creation of the artwork in that both constitute "[a] need fulfilled." In this respect, in the penumbra of "Art Object" lies the imagery of ingestion mapped in *Nightwalker and Other Poems*—from "Our Mother," in which the eponymous figure's "eyes feed, / / As mine on her," as both family members wait at the hospital bedside of a girl "[w]ith bowels burning and disarrayed" (CP, 55), to the grub in "Leaf-Eater," groping "back on itself ... / To eat its own leaf" (CP, 76). The significance of both of the earlier poems is buttressed by "Ballydavid Pier," from the same collection, in which the stillborn "[f]oetus of goat or sheep" glimpsed in the water becomes the premise for the reflection that

Allegory forms of itself:
The line of life creeps upward
Replacing one world with another
(CP, 57)

Such is the movement of "Art Object," in which the initial ekphrasis does *not*, in Murray Krieger's well-known formulation, "crave . . . the spatial fix."[16] Rather, ekphrasis secedes to the temporal flow of allegory, as the literal "scene" of carnage prompted by the *opus sectile* becomes a narrative highly suggestive of the necessity of creative sustenance, the adjectives describing the scavengers, "moderate / and methodical," picked up in the account of the "daily, methodical" Bach in "Love Joy Peace."

Nevertheless, in "Fat Master" Bach's performance at the organ, his "orderly offering," is depicted as possessing its own tigerish ferocity: "waves of new matter" rise "in growl of the bass and torque of the treble" and the music's "essentials" finally "disengage, grateful in the roar of release." Significantly, "Fat Master" emphasizes the audience's reception of Bach's recital: among them, "[s]tunned on our benches," is the speaker, whose experience is one of gratitude for the "lasting forms" the performance provides (LP, 76–78). Reception is also at the center of another poem in *Fat Master*, "The Last Round: an allegory," in which Kinsella's recurrent rhetorical trope explores, by means of the boxing ring, audience participation. In this case, "[w]e howled down off our benches" while the spectacle "echoed up into the dark spaces around us" (LP, 69–70), much as, in "Fat Master," the music was "echoing among the columned dark arches." The two poems comprise an intriguing and disturbing diptych that has an analogue, perhaps, in the weight Kinsella places, in *Readings in Poetry*, on the auditor's or reader's response to the artwork. Reviewing this Peppercanister alongside *Marginal Economy*, Peter Denman objected that the critical volume "disrupts rather than contributes to the Peppercanister project."[17] Its omission from *Late Poems*, which was doubtless made for generic reasons, leaves it now at a tangent to that project: an indirect but sometimes suggestive commentary, as here, on the poetic Peppercanisters. For the preface to *Readings in Poetry* dwells on poetry as a communicative act "where each reader's unique experience is brought to bear" on the text (RP, 16), a reciprocity explored in the auditor's reaction to the performative "offerings" of Bach in "Fat Master, as the music "descend[s] upon us / to where I lift my face in thanks." Kinsella's claim that "with adequate readings of a good poem the differences [between interpretations] should be marginal" might appear to bring his stated aim in *Readings in Poetry*—viz., to provide, by means of his close readings of poems by Shakespeare, Yeats, and Eliot "a re-enactment in each case of a response to the poem, taking account of the textual detail of content, method and structure" (RP, 14)—into closer alignment with the reader-response theory of Wolfgang Iser than that of Stanley Fish. Yet, the epigraphs to the volume, taken from Coleridge's *Biographia Literaria*, perhaps suggest a nearer kinship to I. A. Richards's conception of the enabling role the reader's projective imagination plays in establishing poetic unity.[18]

Be that as it may, Bach's performance no less than the boxers' is, in the words of "Fat Master," "raw with the rhythms of the real." This is a line that looks back to what is arguably *the* crucial poem in *Another September*—that *ars poetica* of frustration, "Baggot Street Deserta," in which Kinsella's speaker, gazing from the window of his flat, yearns for imaginative "contact" with the "border-marches / Of the Real" (CP, 13). The 1950s milieu of the early poem is evoked in "First Night," from *Marginal Economy*: "a naked room / up under the roof," the poet's "brain at the window, / absorbing a new view of the world" (LP, 14). In the later poem, however, the demotic rhythms and negligible imagery stand in marked contrast to the octosyllabics and lush metaphorical language of "Baggot Street Deserta." Such is one of the meanings of the "economy" of the chapbook's title: the almost parsimonious poetic that Clifton observed in *Fat Master* and *Love Joy Peace*, a late pressing of the more astringent style ushered in by "that Red-Sea dividing collection" (in W. J. McCormack's arresting, and mildly misleading, rhetorical flourish) *Nightwalker and Other Poems*.[19]

"First Night" also introduces a further meaning of "marginal economy." In his contemporaneous interpretation of Sonnet 30 in *Readings in Poetry*, Kinsella lays emphasis on Shakespeare's extended deployment of legal and economic imagery, specifically that of "judicial assembly" and "accountancy and wealth" (RP, 23, 24). In "First Night" the bar-room bore's tedious reminiscences, which eventually terminate in a "legalistic close," extend to the "major figures" in twentieth-century Irish history, although he pointedly refuses "to take in / the realities of the past forty years." He is a willfully marginal figure within the marginal economy of Ireland at this date, the ideology of which Kinsella traversed decades before in "A Country Walk," from *Downstream*: a distinctly anti-pastoral poem that portrays a country in which "[o]ur watchful elders . . . / / have exchanged / A trenchcoat playground for a gombeen jungle," a republic unforgettably excoriated in the jeremiad directed at "THE NEW IRELAND" in "Nightwalker" (CP, 46, 81). While *Late Poems*, as one reviewer noted, contains relatively few direct references to Irish history and culture, "First Night" and the succeeding poem in *Marginal Economy*, "The Affair," are exceptions.[20] The latter poem details Kinsella's strained relationship with Conor Cruise O'Brien, and employs, like Sonnet 30, the figure of anamnesis, though to very different ends from Shakespeare.[21] Kinsella had targeted O'Brien before, in *One Fond Embrace*, over the issue of Anglo-Irish political relations.[22] Here his disagreement centers on O'Brien's strident views on Yeats and fascism, as articulated in his controversial 1965 essay "Passion and Cunning," and O'Brien's "acid review," as the poem describes it, of Kinsella's *The New Oxford Book of Irish Verse* (LP, 16). (In the Peppercanister publication of this poem, the review is described as "murderous").[23] The poem's topicality, reminiscent of certain of Clarke's satires of the 1950s and 1960s, is in the service of a more general observation about Irish culture. O'Brien's review took issue, *inter alia*, with the anthology's introduction's restatement of the argument of Kinsella's essay "The Divided Mind" (an argument later expanded in *The Dual Tradition*) that the Irish literary tradition is riven by the impact of the language of the colonizers on an established indigenous vernacular. This is the "main thesis" the poem claims O'Brien failed to understand, his review raising a quizzical critical eyebrow at the "one single thing called 'Irish poetry' which has 'two bodies.'"[24] The occasion for the poem is especially fitting: "Standing, watching, on opposite sides of the grave," the two men face-off at the funeral of Valentin Iremonger, civil servant, poet, and anthologist of Irish poetry.[25] With his "three-piece colonial accent," the speaker's graveside adversary, himself an Irish diplomat and author, becomes oddly representative of the anglicization that brought about the cultural rupture Kinsella speaks of in his 1973 essay: "I recognise that I stand on one side of a great rift, and can feel the discontinuity in myself" (PO, 32).

Kinsella's career within the civil service surprisingly informs his interest in the Stoic Roman Emperor Marcus Aurelius. In his acceptance address given on the award of an honorary degree at the University of Turin, Kinsella said, prior to reading an extract from "Marcus Aurelius" from *Marginal Economy*: "Needing an uncommitted and marginal voice, but one that had access to the bureaucratic world as well as the sensual, a figure that was alienated and involved at the same time, I found these modern qualities in ancient Rome, in the person of Marcus Aurelius. The world as viewed and recorded by him, threatened by outer and inner forces hard to define, seemed familiar . . ." (PO, 128). A century and a half earlier, Matthew Arnold had also been struck by the emperor's and his world's seeming modernity: "one of the best of men . . . he lived and acted in a state of society modern by its essential characteristics, in an epoch akin to our own. . . . Marcus Aurelius thus becomes for us a man like ourselves, a man in all things tempted as we are."[26] Granting Marcus Virgilian pathos, Arnold's 1863 review-essay attempts to humanize the Stoic ideal, as expressed in the *Meditations*, for his mid-Victorian readers. Like Arnold, Kinsella presents the Roman as both statesman and philosopher:

> he kept a private journal, in Greek, for which
> he is best remembered. Almost certainly
> because it engaged so much of the baffled humane
> in him, in his Imperial predicament
> (LP, 23)

If, as his Turin address surely implies, Kinsella sees some sort of shadowy reflection of himself in Marcus, the Roman's divided mind in Kinsella's representation markedly differs from the all-too-human vacillations observed in Arnold's. In "The Divided Mind" Arnold is perceived as central to "the mainstream of a [English-language] tradition," the homogeneity of which is absent for the Irish poet (PO, 32). As construed by Kinsella, Marcus can be seen as obliquely contributing to Kinsella's argument on the dual tradition of the Irish writer: an "observer" conscious of "violent forces," including those on the *limes* or border, Marcus's "conditions," as Fitzsimons argues, "echo the poet's own situation."[27] Marcus's *Meditations*—intended, as Kinsella notes, as "a private journal," unremarked upon until centuries after its composition—was written in part against the backdrop of his campaigns against the Germanic tribes and was the product of his later years. Although familiar to modern readers as comprising twelve books, it is structurally inchoate, blending its famed Stoicism with Epicureanism and other elements, its reiterated preoccupations aptly summarized by Kinsella as

> accepting established notions of a cosmos
> created and governed by a divine intelligence
> – while not believing in an afterlife;
>
> proposing exacting moral goals, with man
> an element in that divine intelligence
> – while pausing frequently to contemplate
>
> the transient brutishness of earthly life, (LP, 23–24)

In its mélange of skepticism and faith, the *Meditations* (the older recorded title for which is "To Himself") shares much with the frequently ruminative quality of *Late Poems* as a whole. (The work is quite possibly one model for the "private journal" or *Adagia* of another poet of skeptical faith, Wallace Stevens, whom Kinsella labeled a "philosopher" in an early review [PO, 163]). Kinsella's three-part division of "Marcus Aurelius" reflects the threefold division that Marcus discusses in *Meditations* 2.2, an aperçu closely approximated in the final couplet of the poem's first part, "On the Ego"—"A little flesh. A little breath. / And the mind governing"—a part itself divided into three sections as laid out on the page in both Peppercanister 24 and *Late Poems*. (Kinsella's declaration, in *Readings in Poetry*, that "there are no absolute readings—especially in modern poetry," invites the reader to speculate further: that the structuration of the ancient text into its later divisions just possibly conditions the presence of twelve lines in this part).

The multivalence, as here, of many of the works in *Late Poems*, at both formal and thematic levels, mobilizes their reader to engage in the ongoing Kinsellan project of the need to elicit pattern and order from the matter at hand. Yet, equally, there is the need to acknowledge the disorder that, in "Songs of Understanding" in *Marginal Economy*, is said to constitute "a fundamental inadequacy / in the structure as a whole," albeit essential to the "ongoing dynamic." The dialectic of order and chaos is driven home, in the third section of "Marcus Aurelius," in the often violent and pointless contingencies of existence, both personal and communal. Drawing on salacious material in the *Historia Augusta*, the poem concludes with the "passion" of Faustina the Younger, Marcus's wife, for rough trade, including a gladiator in whose blood she is said to have conceived Marcus's successor, the hubristic and deranged Commodus, whose assassination, "succeeded by chaos and civil war," Kinsella identifies, after the fashion and in something of the tone of Gibbon's *The Decline and Fall*, as having "ended one of the Empire's longest periods / of civic affluence and stability."

Man of War (2007) take as its subject humanity's propensity for belligerence, the "brutal basis in the human species" (LP, 33). The sequence is among the most intriguingly structured in *Late Poems*. A three-part main text, "Argument," "Retrospect, and "A Proposal," is followed by five "Notes" (reduced from seven in Peppercanister 26). As in the notes to Eliot's *The Waste Land*, the paratexts to *Man of War* counterpoint the main text: in Harmon's adroit description, they "disrupt and arrest" the reading process, creating a "dynamic" between the two sections of the work.[28] For example, the claim in the "Argument" that some "theorists" find "a meaningful connection" between the human capacity for warfare and "animal, or natural, behaviour" is picked up in the first note, "*An Insect Analogue*," which finds a "semblance" of human rapacity in the inexorable and destructive march of "[c]olumns of ants" (LP, 34, 41). The effect on the reader of flicking from text to paratext is cumulative, and bleak: the violence endemic to humanity is viewed, in "Argument," to permeate all spheres of existence, including the "principles of science, art and law." Note 5, "*Instances from the Greek*," includes a snippet from the thirteenth book of the *Iliad*, in which Ajax the Greater and Ajax the Lesser confront the attacking Trojans, led by Hector. This fragment works in an almost synecdochical manner, standing in for a book in the epic that is particularly bloody, in which Homer repeatedly focuses on the maimed bodies of the warriors, while showing that the war has dragged to a standstill: neither Zeus nor Poseidon has the upper hand, and the consequences for the mortal Greeks and Trojans is unspeakable carnage. That the extract Kinsella chooses refers to the Lesser Ajax's Locrian soldiers' "slings and bows of the twisted wool" (LP, 45) conjoins *Man of War*'s panorama with Adorno's grim remark, in *Negative Dialectics*, that "no universal history leads from savagery to humanization, but there is one leading from the slingshot to the megaton bomb."[29]

Man of War offers no panacea for its somber diagnosis: the rueful "proposals" made at the end of the main text are, as critics have observed, ameliorative after the fashion of Swift's.[30] If war, as further "*Instances from the Greek*" adumbrate, exemplifies the human "use of order," where does this leave the poet at this late stage? In "Elderly Craftsman at his Bench," in *Fat Master*, Kinsella revisits an important poem from *New Poems 1973*, "Worker in Mirror, at his Bench." The worker in the earlier poem sought "structure" in "simplicities":

> I tinker with the things that dominate me
> as they describe their random persistent coherences.
> Clean surfaces shift and glitter among themselves.
> (CP, 124)

The elderly craftsman acknowledges art's provisional order and the importance of that which Kinsella termed decades before, in an interview with John Haffenden, "a kind of creative relaxation in the face of complex reality."[31] The craftsman says that he has "learned to put my work to one side; / to relax," precisely *because* "there is no peace here" (LP, 67). It may well be the case that in *Late Poems*, especially in *Fat Master* and *Love Joy Peace*, there is a greater acceptance of the ultimately inexplicable condition of that "complex reality," and that no single theory or artwork will carve nature at the joints.[32] And this raises the issue with which this chapter concludes: that of the "late style" (*Spätstil*) of *Late Poems*. As works written in (relative) old age are these products of what Barbara Herrnstein Smith non-pejoratively termed the "senile sublime," a phrase Eve Kosofsky Sedgwick unpacks as indicating "the bare outlines of a creative idiom seen finally to emerge from what had been the obscuring puppy fat of personableness, timeliness, or sometimes even of coherent sense."[33] Yet there is simply too much connective tissue between the individual Peppercanisters to see *Late Poems* as stripped down in the manner Sedgwick is describing, and the "puppy fat" of Auden, the Movement, and others was shed by Kinsella many years ago. Edward Said's own late study, *On Late Style*, uses Adorno's hugely influential analyses of Beethoven's final compositions to argue for an "artistic lateness," seen, for example, in Ibsen's final plays, that eschews the kind of "harmony and resolution" often perceived in Shakespeare's *The Winter's Tale* and *The Tempest* (which Said adduces) to embrace "intransigence, difficulty and unresolved contradiction."[34] However, as Gordon McMullan and Sam Smiles warn, identifying late style with old-age style (*Altersstil*) courts the facile equation of aesthetic and biological lateness: "not every elderly practitioner can be presumed to have old-age style merely from the fact of being old."[35] If the criterion for a late style is "aesthetic achievement," the appellation might equally be bestowed on the final works of a prematurely deceased writer such as Keats or Jules Laforgue, in their *The Fall of Hyperion: A Dream* and *Dernier Vers*, respectively. And it follows, *mutatis mutandis*, that what we might dub, employing a Shakespearean adjective, a "lated" style could very possibly possess more senility than sublimity.[36]

In an *early* review Kinsella would appear to see the poems Wallace Stevens grouped as *The Rock* at the end of his *Collected Poems* as an example of what Said calls late "harmony and resolution," their "serene beauty" informed by "age, the ending of life, and the anticipation of death" (PO, 164). In contrast, Kinsella's later commentary on Yeats's "The Tower," in *Readings in Poetry*, perceives in this poem of old age and imagined death a recalcitrance that is as much formal as it is declared: troubling the poem's concluding stream and its swansong is the sheer "risk[iness]" of the work—the "bathos" willfully courted in Yeats's fly-fishing imagery, and the perhaps questionable "success" of the "technical extremity" of the poem's slant rhymes, "Grattan"/"spat on," "barrel"/"star, all" (RP, 36, 37).[37] Neither Kinsella's account of Stevens nor his reading of "The Tower" seem applicable to the style of *Late Poems*, the style of which is very much part of the evolution of Kinsella's work since the late 1960s. And, besides, as I said at the beginning of this chapter, these are late *not* last poems.

Notes

[1] *More Poems* (1936) and *Additional Poems* (1937) would indeed appear after Housman's death.

[2] Thomas Kinsella, *Prose Occasions 1951–2006*, ed. Andrew Fitzsimons (Manchester: Carcanet Press, 2009), (cited in text as PO). Clarke's *Collected Poems* had appeared in 1936.

[3] Andrew Fitzsimons, "Peace and Nothingness," review of *Late Poems*, by Thomas Kinsella, *Poetry Ireland Review* 115 (April 2015), 103. Incidentally, Fitzsimons claims that *Late Poems* "nods towards Yeats in its title" (105); if so, it is a nod that averts its gaze: again, these are not *Last Poems*—a title that was almost certainly not Yeats's choice; see Richard J. Finneran, *Editing Yeats's Poems: A Reconsideration* (Basingstoke: Macmillan, 1990), 82–83.

[4] Thomas Kinsella, *Late Poems* (Manchester: Carcanet Press, 2013), cited in text as LP.

[5] Thomas Kinsella, *New Poems 1973* (Dublin: Dolmen, 1973), 18; repr. as a stand-alone poem in Thomas Kinsella, *Collected Poems 1956–2001* (Winston-Salem: Wake Forest UP, 2006), 100 (hereafter cited in text as CP).

[6] Maurice Harmon, *Thomas Kinsella: Designing for the Exact Needs* (Dublin: Irish Academic Press, 2008), 218.

[7] Catriona Clutterbuck, "Scepticism, Faith and the Recognition of the 'Patriarch-Mother' in the Poetry of Thomas Kinsella," in "Kinsella at Eighty," ed. Derval Tubridy, Thomas Kinsella special issue, *Irish Studies Review* 16, no. 3 (2008), 259, 260.

[8] *The English Poems of George Herbert*, ed. C. A. Patrides (London: Dent, 1974), 117.

[9] "Grace," in *English Poems of George Herbert*, 79.

[10] See Derval Tubridy, *The Peppercanister Poems* (Dublin: University College Dublin Press, 2001), 225.

[11] See William Shakespeare, *The Complete Sonnets and Poems*, ed. Colin Burrow (Oxford: Oxford UP, 2002), 438.

[12] Thomas Kinsella, *Readings in Poetry*, Peppercanister 25 (Dublin: Dedalus; Manchester: Carcanet Press, 2006), (cited in text as RP). "[D]isgrace" is glossed as "lacking grace or favour" in the commentary to *Shakespeare's Sonnets*, ed. Katherine Duncan-Jones, rev. ed. (London: Bloomsbury, 2010), 169.

[13] Donatella Badin, "'Making Sense or No Sense of Existence': The 'Plot' of Thomas Kinsella's *Late Poems* in the Light of Norberto Bobbio's *De senectute*" in *Imagining Ageing: Representations of Age and Ageing in Anglophone Literatures*, ed. Carmen Concilio (Bielefeld: transcript, 2018), 81.

[14] Harry Clifton, "A True Note on a Dead Slack String," review of *Fat Master* and *Love Joy Peace*, by Thomas Kinsella, *Irish Times*, February 18, 2012, https://www.irishtimes.com/culture/books/a-true-note-on-a-dead-slack-string-1.466027.

[15] Ben Jonson, "To the Memory of My Beloved, the Author Mr William Shakespeare: And What He Hath Left Us," in *The Complete Poems*, ed. George Parfitt, rev. ed. (Harmondsworth: Penguin, 1988), 265.

[16] Murray Krieger, *Ekphrasis: The Illusion of the Natural Sign* (Baltimore: Johns Hopkins UP, 1992), 10.

[17] Peter Denman, "Songs of Understanding," review of *Marginal Economy* and *Readings in Poetry*, by Thomas Kinsella, and *The Doll with Two Backs and Other Poems*, by Maurice Harmon, *Poetry Ireland Review* 87 (August 2006), 107.

[18] In contrast to Fish's claim, in *Is There a Text in This Class?* (1980), that the meaning ascribed to a work is limited solely by contextual factors, Iser's *The Implied Reader* (1974) and *The Act of Reading* (1978) argue that the reader responds to and realizes a text through the imaginative completion of its "gaps." Richards's explorations of reader-response in *Principles of Literary Criticism* (1924) and *Practical Criticism* (1929) led to his revisionary reading of *Coleridge on Imagination* (1934). Kinsella's readings in this Peppercanister volume are, unfortunately, too brief to substantiate fully a parallel with Richard's influential interpretation of Coleridge.

[19] W. J. McCormack, "Politics or Community: The Crux of Thomas Kinsella's Aesthetic Development," Thomas Kinsella Special Issue, *Tracks* 7 (1987): 63. McCormack's hyperbole is a minor misprision in that, as Fitzsimons correctly argues, the critical commonplace that *Nightwalker* marks a decisive and absolute shift in Kinsella's poetic from "traditional" to more "open" modes is problematized, though not thereby nullified, not least by subsequent works that resort to rhyme and meter, e.g., *Open Court*: "Rather than total abandonment of traditional procedures what in fact takes place is an addition to existing means." Andrew Fitzsimons, *The Sea of Disappointment: Thomas Kinsella's Pursuit of the Real* (Dublin: University College Dublin Press, 2008), 77.

[20] Fitzsimons, "Peace and Nothingness," 105.

[21] See Burrows's commentary in Shakespeare, *Complete Sonnets and Poems*, 440. For the biographical context to "The Affair," see Harmon, *Thomas Kinsella*, 204–6.

[22] See Tubridy, *Peppercanister Poems*, 172–73.

[23] Thomas Kinsella, *Marginal Economy*, Peppercanister 24 (Dublin: Dedalus; Manchester: Carcanet Press, 2006), 15.

[24] Conor Cruise O'Brien, "Micks and Prods," review of *The New Oxford Book of Irish Verse*, ed. Thomas Kinsella, *Observer*, 8 June 1986, 25.

[25] With Robert Greacen, Iremonger edited Faber and Faber's *Contemporary Irish Poetry* (1949).

[26] *The Complete Prose Works of Matthew Arnold*, ed. R. H. Super, vol. 3, *Lectures and Essays in Criticism* (Ann Arbor: University of Michigan Press, 1962), 140

[27] Fitzsimons, *Sea of Disappointment*, x.

[28] Harmon, *Thomas Kinsella*, 212.

[29] Theodor W. Adorno, *Negative Dialectics*, trans. E. B. Ashton (London: Routledge & Kegan Paul, 1973), 320.

[30] Harmon, *Thomas Kinsella*, 215; Fitzsimons, "Peace and Nothingness," 105.

[31] John Haffenden, "Thomas Kinsella," in *Viewpoints: Poets in Conversation with John Haffenden* (London: Faber and Faber, 1981), 106.

[32] This is Harmon's understanding of the last two Peppercanisters: see Maurice Harmon, "'The Rhythms of the Real,'" review of *Fat Master* and *Love Joy Peace*, by Thomas Kinsella, *Poetry Ireland Review* 106 (April 2012): 14–18.

[33] Eve Kosofsky Sedgwick, *Touching Feeling: Affect, Pedagogy, Performativity* (Durham: Duke UP, 2003), 24.

[34] Edward Said, *On Late Style: Music and Literature Against the Grain* (London: Bloomsbury, 2006), 7, 6. Said is dependent on a *locus classicus* of the discussion around late style: Adorno's "Spätstil Beethovens" (1937); see Theodor W. Adorno, "Late Style in Beethoven", in *Essays on Music*, ed. Richard Leppert, trans. Susan H. Gillespie (Berkeley: University of California Press, 2002), 564–68.

[35] Gordon McMullan and Sam Smiles, "Introduction: Late Style and its Discontents," in *Late Style and its Discontents: Essays in Art, Literature, and Music*, ed. Gordon McMullan and Sam Smiles (Oxford: Oxford UP, 2016), 3.

[36] As in Antony's recognition: "I am so lated in the world that I / Have lost my way for ever" (*Antony and Cleopatra*, 3.11.3–4). Shakespeare's own purported late style

(the product of his middle age and including collaborations) is skeptically interrogated in Gordon McMullan, *Shakespeare and the Idea of Late Writing: Authorship in the Proximity of Death* (Cambridge: Cambridge UP, 2007).

[37] Kinsella's third exemplum in *Readings of Poetry*, "The Love Song of J. Alfred Prufrock," is an interesting case study in this context: a poem in which Eliot ventriloquizes a man of indeterminate age who yet declares "I grow old . . . I grow old . . . / I shall wear the bottoms of my trousers rolled," and written by a man barely in his twenties. *The Complete Poems and Plays of T. S. Eliot* (London: Faber and Faber, 1969), 16.

CHAPTER 11

"Imaginative Reality"

THOMAS KINSELLA AND VISUAL ART

DERVAL TUBRIDY

This chapter will examine the importance of art for the development of Kinsella's writing career. It will trace the poet's early engagement with the image through his association with Liam Miller's Dolmen Press in books published between 1952 and 1972 and will explore the diverse iconography that underpins Kinsella's Peppercanister poems from 1972 to 2011, arguing that these images are integral and necessary for a full reading of Kinsella's mature work.[1] Kinsella's relationship with art is fundamental to his aim of eliciting a "web of order" from lived experience. His collaboration with artists on the illustrations of his poems and translations, and the integration of archival images into his Peppercanister series, serve to deepen the poet's exploration of contemporary history and his inquiry into the psyche.

Kinsella's association with Miller's Dolmen Press played a significant role in how the young poet developed his engagement with art, as it introduced him to a circle of Dolmen artists and gave him a broad understanding of the art of bookmaking and of fine art printing. His first collection, *The*

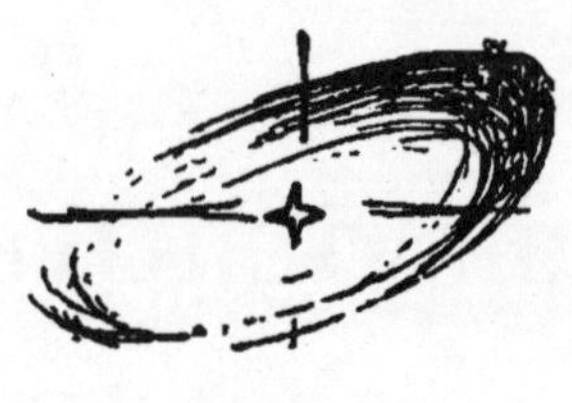

Figure 1. Two images by Liam Miller for *The Starlit Eye*, page 7.

Starlit Eye (1952), was illustrated by Miller himself in an edition of 175 copies, 25 of which were a special edition signed by the poet. Six line drawings in black explore the limen between the landscape and the sky and evoke the way Kinsella's lines conflate affective experience of space with the exigencies of love: "The breathing sea in Dublin Bay / is broad and dark this end of day. / Under a chill and constant wind / she pours her tenuous waters in." The insistent rhythms of the poetry are leavened by Miller's deft lines as they retrace the form of the oval to convey a sense of space and movement, intersected by the horizon and, in the fourth and fifth image, the figures of the lovers. Below the colophon a final image features the silhouette of a Dolmen megalithic tomb: a fitting reference to the press itself.

Two years later Kinsella's translation of the legend of Deirdre of the Sorrows taken from the book of Leinster, *Longes Mac nUsnig: Being the Exile and Death of the Sons of Usnech*, came out in an edition of 225, 25 of which were signed special editions, and all were illustrated by Mia Cranwill (1880–1972). Cranwill's ten images emulate the interconnected semi-abstract style of Old Irish illuminated manuscripts, interwoven with figural representations to further support the narrative of Kinsella's rendition of the Deirdre saga. The volume opens with a visual reference to Dolmen, the tomb's three upright stones and single horizontal one forming the image on the frontispiece. The type is in black, with striking red capitals. Cranwill's images make effective use of repetition and of parallel lines to convey dynamism. Even at this early stage of his career, Kinsella's work on translation informed his writing. *Death of a Queen*, a poem inspired by the story of Deirdre, was published as a Dolmen chapbook in 1956 with an image of Deirdre and her lover Naoise rendered by Bridget Swinton in flowing green lines, the lovers' heads superimposed by five vertical lines to represent both their love and their exile. Dolmen returned to this legend in 1960 with revised edition of the tale titled *Lognes Mac Usnig: The Exile of the Sons of Usnech & the Exile of Fergus & The Death of the Sons of Usnech & Deirdre* with a single illustration by Swinton of Naoise: a delicate line drawing in gold on the red cover and in green on the title page of the volume.

Kinsella's translation of the eighth-century Irish prayer *Faeth Fiadha* or *The Breastplate of Saint Patrick* was a popular volume that was published in a number of illustrated editions that reflect contemporary interpretations of Celtic motifs and references to older ecclesiastical traditions.[2] The first edition of 275 copies was published in February 1954 with images by Henry Neville Roberts (1882–1966) including a trifold knot within a triangular motif and an open hand framed by a circular mandala. It was through his friendship with Roberts that Kinsella met Miller and became involved with the Dolmen Press. That same year, a private edition of 200 copies was printed by Dolmen for John McGuire with a cover design by Louis le Brocquy (1916–2012). Le Brocquy's brown with green hand coloring depicts the Neolithic triskelion, or three spiral motif, found, for example, carved in stone near the entrance to Newgrange passage tomb. This first collaboration would pave the way for the Kinsella's ground-breaking translation *The Tain*

(1969) with extensive illustrations by le Brocquy: a *livre d'artiste* of the highest order.[3] The 1957 edition of *The Breastplate of Saint Patrick* featured woodcuts by Gerrit van Gelderen, Dutch naturalist, illustrator, and filmmaker (1926–1994).

Kinsella's translations of Old Irish verse continued with the publication of *33 Triads* (1955), a bold and epigrammatic rendering of Old Irish sayings or judgements from the ninth century which can be found in manuscripts from late Medieval times, particularly the fifteenth-century *Book of Lecan*. 275 copies of this edition were published, which included 75 signed and numbered special editions. The blunt wisdom of these triads is complemented by ten illustrations from Pauline Bewick, her powerful and sinuous lines drawing for their inspiration on the dynamics of Pablo Picasso's cubist iconography. Bold shapes connect semi-abstract figures in profile and full-face within a square format of the nine small images that are interspersed throughout the volume, similar in size to the illustrations in *The Starlit Eye*. For the larger title image Bewick places woman center stage. The face of a woman deep in thought, her jaw resting on her right hand, is framed by long hair that covers half her face and scrolls down to the elbow, skirting an exposed breast. This striking image resonates with the way in which Kinsella's translations of Irish legends celebrate the strength and sexuality expressed by Old Irish verse.

1970 saw the publication of Kinsella's poem "Nuchal"—which was later incorporated in *New Poems* (1973)—as part of a fine art portfolio of four prints by Patrick Hickey, John Kelly, Leslie MacWeeney, and Anne Yeats. "Nuchal" (described later as "a fragment") gives us a glimpse of a woman resting at the edge of the waters of "four great rivers" that issue from her trailing fingers and travel in the four cardinal directions across land to sea: "Four rivers reaching toward th'encircling sea." This image of origins draws on elemental beginnings, the "fish-spirits" of water and the "snake-spirits" of land, and takes us back to the title, "Nuchal," the nape of the neck, from the medieval Latin *medulla oblongata*, and the Arabic *nuka*: spinal marrow. Animating these is *Danu*, perhaps, mother goddess of the Tuatha Dé Dannan, the people of Danu. The four prints visualize the scene set by Kinsella. In tones of blue, Yeats's image gives us the figure of the goddess resting with arm outstretched, surrounded by reeds and water; the slope of her shoulder blades echoes the rise of the hills behind as a full moon rises above them. In dark earth tones, MacWeeney gives us a close focus of a somnolent moon resting above the flowing waters. Both Hickey and Kelly emphasize the earth. Kelly's print, in darkest green and grey, traces the lines of the riverbed across a wide horizon. Hickey gives us a cross-section of earth and water, with moon above, his tones of brown and red picking up on Kinsella's description of the third river: "A third runs Westward in its deeper bed, / tigrish, through narrow gorges, winy red."

In the early years, Kinsella's work of translation informed his poetic development and consolidated a practice of counterpointing the visual image with the printed word in publications that valued excellence in all aspects of bookmaking. His 1956 volume *Poems* includes a title image of a cockerel and an egg in brown ink by Elizabeth Rivers (1903–1964), an indication of the poet's growing interest in Jungian themes that would find form in *Notes from the Land of the Dead* (1973) and *One* (1974). Even without illustration, the graphic design of Dolmen books was given careful consideration. The title lettering of *Another September* (1958) was designed by Michael Biggs (1928–1993), and the titles of later volumes *Wormwood* (1966) and *Nightwalker* (1967) were designed by Ruth Brandt (1936–1989). In 1972, Miller and archaeologist Hugh Kearns collaborated on the design of artwork for Kinsella's poem *Finistère*, published that year by Dolmen and incorporated two years later into the "Finistère" section of *One*. Miller and Kearns drew on images from the Neolithic sites at Newgrange and Knowth in County Meath, and the Donagh or St. Patrick's cross in Cardonagh, County Donegal to create four illustrations that hark back to a primal past as the poet dives deep into the psyche: "I / One . . . I smelt the weird Atlantic. / Finistère . . . / Finisterre . . . / The sea surface darkened. The land behind me, / and all its cells and cysts, dark." Opposite these opening lines is a circular image composed of abstract symbols drawn from the Neolithic art found on the kerbstones of Knowth and the entrance stone of Newgrange. Spirals, wave forms, concentric half circles, and a dotted square are joined by a scattering of minute dots to form an image of those "cells and cysts" about which Kinsella writes as he delves into the primordial substance of the self. The second image of the book also takes a circular form in which is nestled a triskelion overlain by dense dots, the flowing lines of the three interconnected spirals recalling "all the currents of the ocean" about which Kinsella writes in the lines underneath the image, and the "poolspirals opening on / closing spiralpools / and dances drilled in the rock / in coil zigzag angle and curl." The last two images of the book are drawn from the figure carved on a small pillar that is situated on the left side of the west face of the Donagh Cross. Depicting a pilgrim or traveler (satchel in hand), the figure faces us with arms crossed below his or her waist. The fourth image is a small section of this figure, a horizontal rectangle revealing a glimpse of its eyes, nose, and mouth in a print that emphasizes the texture of the red sandstone out of which the figure is carved. Kinsella's interrogatory lines—"Who / is the word that spoken / the spear springs / and pours out terror"—seem, at this point, to issue from the ancient face. A full image of this pilgrim figure is featured at the end of the volume, before the colophon, standing alone like a herm: a milestone or boundary mark to guide the poet as he begins a new phase of poetic inquiry.

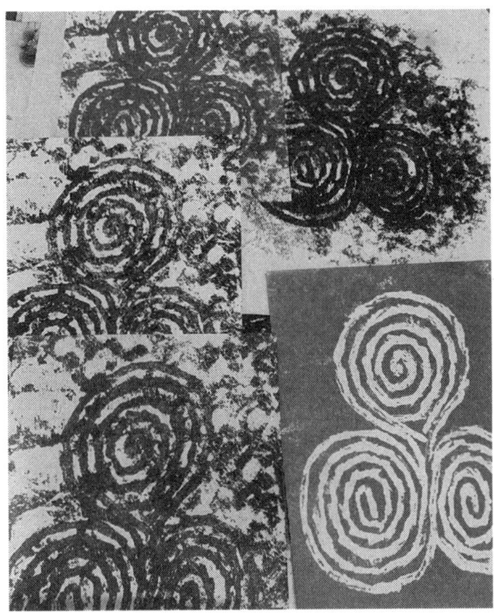

Figure 2. Test prints of Newgrange triskelion for *Finistère*.

1972 marked a transition for Kinsella in how his work was published. That year, Kinsella founded the Peppercanister Press, which became the imprint of all his future poetry, gathered subsequently in collections by Oxford University Press, Carcanet Press, and Wake Forest University Press. Kinsella took with him what he had learned at Dolmen about the integration of word and image and the attention to fine printing methods to produce a distinctive, if varied, series of poetry editions in which the image contributes to the reader's understanding of the poetry.[4] This practical experience informed the aesthetic of the Peppercanister Press which he developed in collaboration with Miller's Dolmen Press until the early 1980s when Peppercanister volumes benefited from the expertise of John F.

Deane's Dedalus Press. The diverse iconography that Kinsella chose for the covers of the Peppercanister editions reveals the depth of scholarship that the poet undertook as he wrote. Acting as both a supplement to the poetry, and a framing device for our interpretation, these images reflect Kinsella's sustained interest in Celtic history and mythology and his examination of how this history has influenced the development of a twentieth-century and contemporary Irish identity. Following the example of the medieval Irish scribes, Kinsella also looks to European imagery to contextualize his examination of political histories, drawing on Denis Diderot (1713–1784) and Albrecht Dürer (1471–1528), amongst others, to situate his concerns within a broader frame, while retaining a central interest in Irish history.

The images used in the first four Peppercanister editions have socio-historical relevance and allude directly to the subject matter of the poems. The 1972 shooting of 26 civil rights demonstrators in Derry galvanized the introspective poet and led to the publication of *Butcher's Dozen* (1972), a swift and urgent ballad excoriating political injustice. Its cover is blunt: the image of a coffin in black on which is the number thirteen, a device taken from the badge used at a civil rights protest march in Newry which the poet attended. *A Selected Life* (1972), designed by Miller, and *Vertical Man* (1973) celebrate the life and work of Kinsella's friend, composer Seán Ó Riada (1931–1971). Both books feature an image of Ó Riada which was derived from a medallion by the sculptor Seamus Murphy (1907–1975) based on the death mask of the composer. *A Selected Life* places the mask on the cover; *Vertical Man* places it under the epigraph, "... Master, your health" (taken from the last line of *A Selected Life*), at the opening of the poem where the speaker raises a glass to his dead friend one evening in "Philadelphia: 3 October 1972"—"Over the gramophone your death-mask / was suddenly awake / and I felt something of you"—in a meditation that recalls Kinsella's earlier poem "Baggot Street Deserta." *The Good Fight* (1973) addresses the cultural and political shock that resulted from the assassination of John F. Kennedy, President of the United States, where Kinsella now made his home. Four images of the head of ancient Greek philosopher Plato preface each section. These are taken from sculptures in museums in Athens, Cambridge, Aix en Provence, and Syracuse, respectively, and sourced by Kinsella from *The Portrait of the Greeks* by Gisela Richter.[5] The influence of Miller's and Kearns's illustrations for *Finistère* is evident in *The Good Fight*: the textured stone of the last two images of that volume is also evident in the rough surface of Plato's heads. Kinsella arranges the heads so that the images portray progressive degeneration: the imperious frontal portrait of Plato on the cover shifts to four heads in profile, each in relative stages of erosion. These images provide an iconographic structure through which the poet draws a parallel between the Kennedy era and Plato's ideal Republic (with the President in the role of the philosopher-king). The gradual erosion of Plato's visage provides a visual counterpoint to the loss of idealism experienced after the assassination when, as Kinsella's speaker explains, "it is appropriate for us / to proceed now and make our attempts / in private, to shuffle off and disappoint / Plato." Further disappointment is evident many decades later in Kinsella's poem "Street Game for the Over 15s." The voice that harried the local politics of Ireland in "Nightwalker" and "Open Court" turns its attentions to Kinsella's adopted land with a swift and severe sketch of statecraft that portrays a presidential figure as "Bluntsubnormal" and politics as an endgame: "Form a circle, Throw the hatchet. / Run for cover / If he catch it. // Hide and seek."[6]

The next four Peppercanisters—*One*, *A Technical Supplement*, *Song of the Night and Other Poems*, and *The Messenger*—are possibly the most visually complex editions of the series, displaying Kinsella's collaboration with contem-

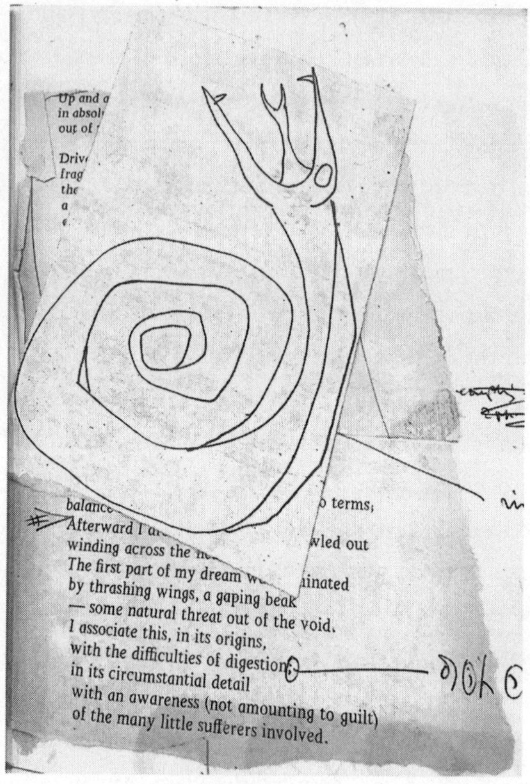

Figure 3. Manuscript pages of *One* with a mock-up of Anne Yeats's coiled snake illustration.

porary Irish artists, his facility with archival research to source images, his own artistic expression, and his adept analysis of popular iconography. In *One* (1974), Kinsella returns to the concerns of *Finistère* which is included in this volume. Kinsella collaborated with Irish artist Anne Butler Yeats (1919–2001), daughter of W. B. Yeats, with whom he worked when both were directors of the revived Cuala Press. Yeats contributed seven drawings to the volume, each characterized by her distinctive loose and lyrical line. She draws on mythical and psychological themes from the poems with images that evoke primal, mythical, and Jungian ideas of origin. The head of a snake features on the cover and is repeated at the end of the Prologue, reflecting the snake's connection with transformation or rebirth through the shedding of skin: "in a final spasm, leaving my decrepit skin." The frontispiece features the image of a snake coiled around a tree, alluding to the mythical chthonic serpent that is often depicted coiled around the tree of life: a symbol of the tension between good and evil. A coiled snake with outstretched tongue faces the opening of the Preface, the energy of Yeats's line echoing the urgency of Kinsella's lines: "Up and awake. Up straight / in absolute hunger / out of this black lair, and eat!" Yeats's snake is a symbol of fertility, and of the awakening of the chthonic snake from its underground lair. Its coiled form evokes by association the ouroboros: a coiled snake that takes its tail in its mouth and is considered a symbol of the eternal cycles of life, death, and rebirth. The scene shifts to a seascape in "Finisterre," a tale of a sea journey or *immram*: a tale about the hero's journey to the otherworld. Such journeys figure in Kinsella's poetry as a journey into the self as body, "all its cells and cysts," and as psyche, "a dreamy power loosened at the base of my spine." Yeats's drawing features a heaving sea with crescent moon and clouds above depicting the poem's speaker as he "hesitated before that wider sea [. . .] grey upheaving slopes of water / sliding under us, collapsing, / crawling onward, mountainous." At the center of the image in the next poem, "The Oldest Place," is a cloaked figure—the "I" or "One" of "Finistère"—or the "ghost" of the speaker's dream: "A draped black shaft under the starlight." The rough and frenzied lines that make up this image evoke the broken ground on which she stands: "bars and blocks and coils of restless metal / piled about it." The crescent moon, clouds, and stars that surround the figure are rendered in Kinsella's verse as "a complex emptiness shimmered in front of the stars." In the final three poems, "38 Phoenix Street," "Minstrel," and "His Father's Hands," Kinsella's concerns turn closer to his own family. Yeats has rendered these inquiries in abstract form as elemental chromosomatic marks, the "little directionless instincts / uncoiled from the wet mud-cracks" that signal the continuation of life. Yeats's final image draws together the mythic, psychic, and familial explorations of these poems in a spiral ovoid image that evokes the "O" of "One," the "cells" that "are alive with bits and pieces" and lines from the Epilogue in which "The great cell of nightmare rose in pallor / and shed its glare down on the calm gulf."

With *A Technical Supplement* (1976), Kinsella turns to questions of epistemology and the possibilities of poetry. Written in twenty-four sections to mark the hours of a day, Kinsella negotiates psychic and somatic meditations in which the visceral energies of the body, both animal and human, are central. Situating his inquiry within the scope of the European Enlightenment, Kinsella counterpoints his verse with six images by Robert Bénard (1734–1777) that accompany Diderot's *Encyclopédie* to create a complex and nuanced interplay between text and image in which the visual supports and deepens our reading of the poetry. The cover of *A Technical Supplement* features the image of an upright penknife, and the frontispiece is a diagram of the correct manner in which to write: a shirted hand delicately holds a quill while the numerals one to nine indicate further explication of the art of handwriting that is to be found in the text of the *Encyclopédie*. The third image is an engraving of the ancient Greek figure of Laocoön taken from the statue of Laocoön and his sons excavated in Rome in 1506 and now housed in the Vatican museum. The figure of Laocoön is glossed like a diagram, with lines and figures explaining the correct proportions of the human body. The agony of Laocoön's strangulation contrasts starkly with the idealization of his physical proportions, and the adjacent verse which interweaves a visceral apprehension of the body—"there is no containing skin / as we understand it, but 'contained' muscles"—with the sense of the body as a phenomenological whole—"the solid posture / grew graceful. / A light architecture. / No-stress against no-stress." Kinsella is particularly attentive to the political implications of knowledge and frames his visual engagement with Diderot's *Encyclopédie* with a petition to "Blessed William Skullbullet," the seventeenth-century cartographer, Sir William Petty, who was charged with surveying and mapping the island of Ireland (the Down Survey of Ireland 1656–1658) to identify profitable land to be forfeited from the Catholic Irish and given to Cromwell's soldiers, a subject to which Kinsella returns in the 2000 volume *Littlebody*.

The fourth image is an oblique view of a dissected human head: the neck and ear are stripped away to reveal veins, arteries, and nerves, the rear cranial plates of the skull a vital contrast to the facial features in repose. This image is placed opposite section nine, which deals with the speaker's visit to an aquarium, "Gross anemones flowered open / flesh-brilliant on slopes of rock," but speaks more clearly to section two in which the act of dissection is detailed, and the abattoir of sections six and seven. The final two images illustrate surgical procedures, and they contextualize Kinsella's dissection of politics, poetry, and presence. The fifth illustration shows a man's right hand holding a surgical probe which pierces the eye of another as it is being restrained by the man's left hand. Kinsella's focus on creophagus practices of the "grove of beasts" in previous sections—Swift's slaughterhouse, the Lizard ingesting its prey—takes a constructive turn with the fifth illustration, which illustrates a new eighteenth-century technique of cataract surgery developed by Jacques Daviel in France. The knife is a tool

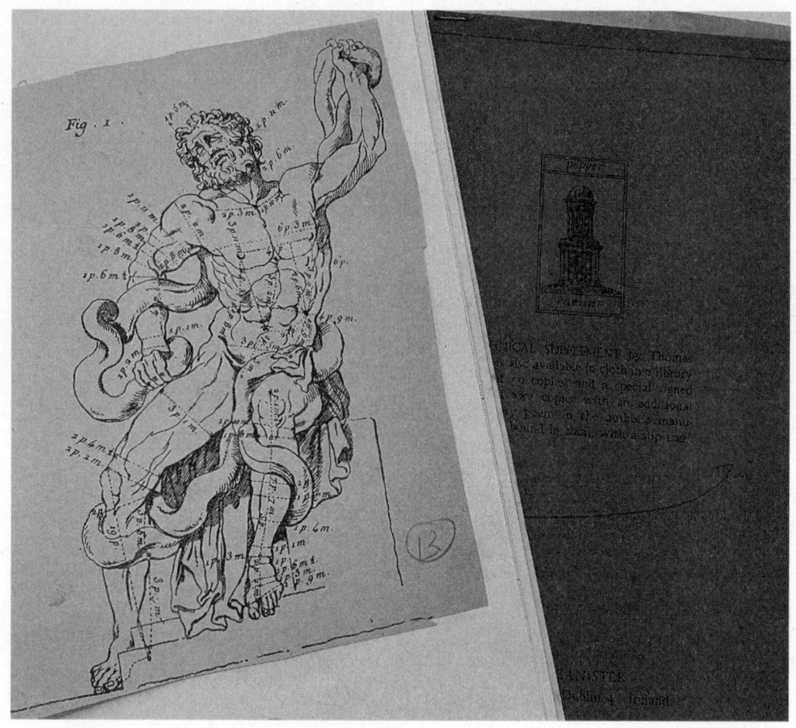

Figure 4. Mock-ups for *A Technical Supplement*, featuring an image of Laocoön and the back cover.

of construction as well as destruction (sections four and five contrast the cut that leads to new life with the cut that kills). Here the surgeon will remove the occluded surface to enable clear vision, as Kinsella alludes to in section three: "—lenses, letting the light pass easily in either direction." Yet this knife is also the "private blade" with which the poet dissects his sense of self and the histories out of which it is constructed. The self's isolation—"Where is everybody?"—opens section twenty-two, and the poet watches his reflection diverge, "his head opening like a rubbery fan." Kinsella's account of a psychic break is in stark contrast with the facing illustration: an image of the surgical procedure of *trepannage*, which involves boring a hole into the skull of a living person to alleviate cranial concussion or contusion. Bénard's engraving shows a surgeon delicately boring a hole into the right temple of a patient's head using a trepanning brace. As with previous illustrations, the human figures are outfitted as gentlemen and the patient is serene. The ordered ritual of the eighteenth-century surgical procedure is in marked contrast to the poet's contemporary disarray—"I might have driven my fist at the mirror / and abolished everything"—and alludes both to the modern practice of lobotomy to alleviate mental illness, and the poet's experience of "the split id." Section fifteen expresses the speaker's joy in his craft: "The pen writhed. It moved / under my thumb!" yet the muse remains an ambivalent presence, a "sad prowler on our landing again." As the volume ends, the images of anatomy, surgery, and dissection meld with those of penknife and writing to announce the continued "fall" of the speaker as the "divider waits, shaped / razor sharp to my dream print."

Kinsella's own ink drawings provide the illustrations for *Song of the Night and Other Poems* (1978). The "dark waters" of Kinsella's inward turn are reflected in the black ink of a winged creature that adorns the cover, title page, and the last page of the edition. Kinsella's drafts of the poems in this edition contain drawings of herons and bats that he observed when exploring the banks of the river about which he writes in "Tao and Unfitness at Inistogue on the River Nore." Continuing the themes of introspection and self-analysis of previous volumes, Kinsella considers the nature of love as he recalls key anniversaries in his life and the locations, both in Ireland and the United States, where his life took a decisive turn. These sketches of bats and herons are transformed by the strong lines of Kinsella's pen

SONG
OF THE NIGHT
AND OTHER POEMS

Figure 5. Comparison of Kinsella's two illustrations for *Song of the Night* featured in the title page and the final page of the book.

into vibrant and dynamic images of creatures in flight, emblematic, perhaps, of the moment of release signaled at the end of the volume in "Carraroe": "A part of the mass / grated and tore, cranking harshly, / and detached and struggled upward / and beat past us along the rocks, / bat-black, heron-slow."

If *A Technical Supplement* is one of Kinsella's most visually complex and rewarding editions, then *The Messenger* (1978) is remarkable for the complex iconography of its cover that both frames and contextualizes Kinsella's verse. Designed by Jarlath Hayes (1924–2001), the cover of this eighth Peppercanister is a reworking of the widely disseminated Catholic magazine *The Messenger*. The address of the Irish Messenger Office—5 Great Denmark Street, Dublin—that is printed at the base of the cover is replaced by that of Kinsella's own imprint: "Peppercanister / 47 Percy Lane, Dublin 4." Kinsella retains the vivid red of the original cover, but Hayes's design reworks the details of the intricate design to challenge cultural and religious assumptions of the time while also alluding to key themes in Kinsella's poetry. The source image features an image of a Christ as the sacred heart (his heart, crowned and illuminated, glows from his chest) standing on a sphere or globe, arms outstretched, head encircled by a halo. The image is framed by interlocking Celtic knots and flanked by two stylized serpent or dragon heads, recalling the Celtic ouroboros images of *One*. The title lettering of the religious publication also draws on Celtic iconography, utilizing Gaelic lettering rather than Roman. Two images on either side of Christ conjoin an Irish identity with that of Roman Catholicism: on the left we see a crown and two crossed keys, the fourteenth-century coats of arms of the Holy See and Vatican, on the right Ireland's heraldic emblem, the harp. Hayes reworks this iconography to reflect the values of Kinsella's father John Paul Kinsella, about whom the poet writes with such acuity in *The Messenger* and to whom the volume is dedicated: the Vatican heraldic symbol gives way to a label for Guinness's Extra Stout, alluding to John's place of work (recalled again in *The Pen Shop*), and the Irish harp is replaced by the plow and the stars, emblem of the Irish labor movement to which Kinsella's father devoted considerable energy (referenced also by playwright Seán O'Casey as the title of his 1926 play *The Plough and the Stars*). These substitutions alert the reader to key concerns of the emerging Ireland: the Church's extensive control of political, medical, and cultural aspects of Irish society and the tension between political aspirations for national identity and for social equality.

Hayes's redesign of *The Messenger* replaces Christ's outstretched figure with that of the Roman god Mercury, also known as the Greek god Hermes and associated with the Celtic god Lugus. Known as a messenger of the gods, Mercury oversees matters of commerce, communication, eloquence, travelers, and boundaries, and encapsulates, for Kinsella, the attributes and values of his father who, coming from a family of shopkeepers, began his working life as a messenger boy: "A new messenger boy / stands there in uniform, with shining belt!" Hayes's image of Mercury is taken from the 1580 statue of the god by Italian sculptor, Giovanni Bologna (1524–1608), now housed in the Bargello Museum, Florence. Christian iconography is replaced by Pagan concerns, and the outstretched pose of Christ in the religious magazine is refigured in Kinsella's writing as that of socialist revolutionary James Larkin.[7] Writing through the eyes of a child, Kinsella recalls his father's rejection of Church control as his father walks him out of Mass in protest at Father Collier's rejection of socialism, "a black mouth shouting / Godless Russia after us." Remembering condolences at his father's funeral, the speaker articulates John Kinsella's actions for justice in his workplace at Guinness as he "formed their first Union; and entered their lists. / Mason and Knight gave ground in twostep, / manager and priest disappeared." Yet ultimately his actions prove futile as these powerful figures simply "reappeared under each other's hats; / in jigtime, to the ever popular / *Faith Of Our Fathers*, he was high and dry." In his redesign of the religious publication, Hayes retains the framing device that features the ouroboros dragon or snake, extracting an element of it to feature opposite the opening lines of Kinsella's poem, contextualizing the speaker's grief at the loss of his father: "*A moist movement within. / A worm winds on its hoard.*" The Gaelic typography of the Catholic *Messenger* is also retained and is used in lower case for the title of Kinsella's *Messenger*.

The Messenger was the last Peppercanister to be printed by Dolmen, and in 1986 Kinsella resigned his directorship of Dolmen Press.[8] Thereafter, the subsequent Peppercanister editions were more simply illustrated, with the primary visual focus being the cover, and they increasingly feature archival sources for imagery rather than collaborations with contemporary artists.

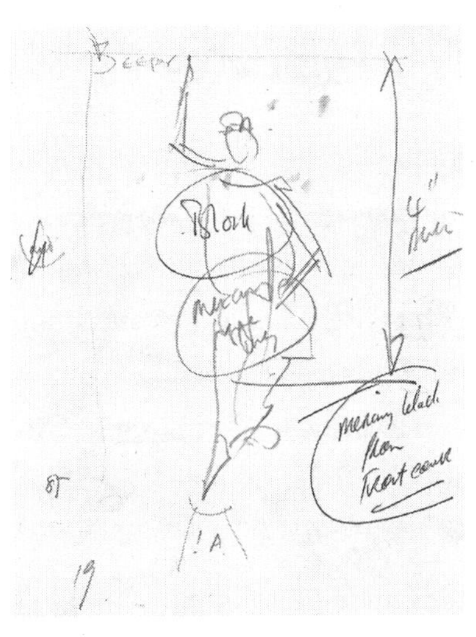

Figure 6. Sketch for *The Messenger* compared to a later mock-up.

As an example, the next three Peppercanisters, *Songs of the Psyche* (1985), *Her Vertical Smile* (1985), and *Out of Ireland* (1987) feature images taken from Patrick Weston Joyce's *A Smaller Social History of Ireland*. A circular image of a glass enamel ornament with petal-like curves of blue and white lines is printed in black and white on the cover of *Songs of the Psyche*, described in Joyce's book as "a flat circular disk, half-inch thick, the body of dark blue glass, with a wavy pattern of white enamel, like an open flower."[9] The image is repeated at the outset of the thirteen-poem sequence "Songs of the Psyche" that forms the central work of the volume, and evokes an outward movement that instigates a return to introspection characteristic of Kinsella's poetry at this time. *Her Vertical Smile* returns to the concerns of the earlier *Vertical Man* where music and composition frame a consideration of artistic practice within historical exigencies. Kinsella's epigraph to *Her Vertical Smile* references both Ó Riada and Gustav Mahler, and the cover image situates both within the music of the spheres. Drawn from an astronomical image from 1400 held in the Royal Irish Academy, the cover image depicts a pre-Copernican view of the sun orbiting around the earth, with explanatory text in Old Irish lettering. *Out of Ireland* also evokes Ó Riada, as the setting of the poem is a memorial service for the composer, and Yeats, from whose poem "Remorse for Intemperate Speech" the title comes. Here, Kinsella considers the legacies of history and the bifurcation of language that is his inheritance. The cover of *Out of Ireland* features a portrait of the ninth century philosopher Johannes Scotus Eriugena drawn by George Petrie (1790–1866)—artist, antiquarian, and scholar of ancient Irish music—from a statue over the entrance to Brasenose College Hall, Oxford.

With *St Catherine's Clock* (1987) Kinsella again collaborates with Hayes. Drawing directly on the history of Robert Emmet (1778–1803), who was executed outside St. Catherine's Church, Thomas Street, Dublin on the afternoon of September 20, Hayes presents the ornate hands of a clock, referencing the opening poem of the volume: "The clock / on the squat front of St Catherine's / settled a gilded point / up soundless into place." The clock of Hayes's cover marks three o'clock, the "third hour" mentioned in the last poem of the volume.[10] A single drop of blood, printed in red, hangs below the clock, directly in line with the long hand pointing to twelve. Hayes's image is repeated in monochrome on the title page of the volume. Kinsella's interest in the visual image is notable in this volume not because of his use of imagery as a structural and interlocutory device as we see in *A Technical Supplement*, but by how he uses contemporary representations of historical events as a means through which to frame and interpret both national and personal histories. Kinsella's ekphrastic response to three prints reproduced in *Robert Emmet: The Insurrection of 1803*[11] interrogates the narratives and representations of history, as they provide the foundation for both national and personal identities. The first two prints are referenced in the poem titled "1803," the year of Emmet's death. The first of these, described by Kinsella as "*After the engraving by George* Cruikshank"[12] depicts the killing of Arthur Wolfe, First Viscount Kilwarden and Chief Justice of the King's Bench (1739–1803), and his nephew Rev. Richard Wolfe, in Thomas Street as they sought refuge in Dublin Castle from the United Irishmen who had marched on Dublin to seek parliamentary reform. Kinsella is attentive to the politics of representation as his speaker's eye is drawn to how Kilwarden's coachmen are depicted with refined features, "picked, like his horses, from a finer breed," while the attackers are depicted in a grotesque manner as a "pack of hatted simians." The second print depicts the execution of Robert Emmet, which involved his hanging and subsequent beheading. The title that Kinsella gives the print, "*From a non-contemporary nationalist artist's impression*," is that used in the source material. Kinsella's lines amplify the political perspectives underscored by the image: Kilwarden's killing is deemed an "outrage," yet the public witnessing Emmet's execution are "horrified." The poet incorporates phrases and attitudes from different versions of Emmet's speech from the dock to generate a sense of noble endeavor, describing him as "sacrificed on the altar of truth and liberty." This sensibility is brutally undercut by bathetic lines describing the beheading of Emmet's dead body, as his "pasty head is separated and brandished aloft." The third image Kinsella references in the poem titled "1792" is a work in watercolor and ink on paper titled "Saint Catherine's, Thomas Street, Dublin" by the artist and draftsman James Malton (1761–1803).[13] Kinsella quotes the signature that Malton used: "*Jas. Malton, del*," in

Figure 7. Timothy Engelland's woodblocks for the limited Dolmen edition of *One Fond Embrace* compared to the cover of the Dedalus edition.

telling counterpoint to the anonymity of the earlier "non-contemporary nationalist artist," drawing our thoughts to questions of authorship, history, and narrative. Through his use of imagery, Kinsella frames his negotiations of history visually as he traces the familial and the social across shared places in a personal *dinnseanchas* that articulates the complexities of Irish identities.

Kinsella's excoriation of contemporary social politics in 1980s Ireland detailed in *One Fond Embrace* leans on Jonathan Swift's "A Modest Proposal" to lambast church and state alike. The poem was initially published in 1981 as a limited edition of 300 copies with illustrations by Timothy Engelland

(1950–2012). Engelland's hand-colored woodcuts focus on the figure of the writer, and of his material. Two strong woodcuts bordered in black are placed at the beginning and end of the volume. The first depicts a male figure in silhouette seated in an armchair, head on hands, deep in thought. In the foreground is a glass bottle of ink, open, with its dropper placed in front: the "organic pot" that Kinsella refers to at the opening and the close of the poem, which is both the ink and the imaginative material of the poet's writing. The second image is of the figure's hand, writing lines across the page of a notebook, in reference to the speaker's sense of the impotence of his excoriation of Dublin planners and developers, and the frustration generated by the failed protests against the development of the Viking Settlements at Wood Quay in which Kinsella was deeply involved. Here Kinsella invokes Diderot from *A Technical Supplement*, in particular the letter that Diderot wrote to Voltaire that is quoted in that sequence: "The pen writhed // and moved under my thumb / and dipped again / in its organic pot." Kinsella chose to develop and republish *One Fond Embrace* in 1988 under his Peppercanister imprint in conjunction with Dedalus Press, who would henceforth support the publication of the Peppercanisters and manage their production in a relationship similar to that which Kinsella had with Miller's Dolmen Press. Brendan Foreman designed the cover of this edition, drawing on the motif of the last supper that Kinsella exploits in his sequence: "Take your places around my table // one last time together." Foreman's cover adapts an etching by Dürer titled "The Last Supper" by removing the central figures of Jesus and John, leaving twelve apostles seated around the table, six to the right and six to the left. Foreman's design shifts the visual emphasis of the poem away from the figure of the poet foregrounded by Engelland in the 1981 edition to focus on how Kinsella perverts the ideas of sacrifice and redemption—"Take one another / and eat"—in a manner that emulates Swift's deliberately provocative suggestion in "A Modest Proposal," that the answer to Irish poverty was to sell the children of the poor for food, taking care to "render them plump and fat for a good Table."

Kinsella turns again to Dürer for images to integrate the concerns of *Madonna and Other Poems* (1991) and *Open Court* (1991). Kinsella described the former as "a set of 6 poems on the subject of the woman companion,"[14] and the powerful female image on the cover underscores this theme. Kinsella chooses Dürer's woodcut "Nude Woman with the Zodiac," which features a woman holding the heavenly spheres marked by the signs of the zodiac. For *Open Court* Kinsella looks to Dürer's woodcut "Head for the purpose of the study of Phrenology." The woodcut depicts the head of a man whose forehead is traced with the letters of the alphabet. These phrenological marks served to indicate how the measurement of the skull can predict mental traits, a discredited science developed by Franz Joseph Gall in 1796 and popular in the nineteenth century. Kinsella takes this motif to mock the world of letters, which is a central theme of the poem, and also the disparity between appearance and the reality that Kinsella's poetic speaker discerns.

The cover of *The Pen Shop* (1997) features a photograph of Oliver Sheppard's statue of the fallen mythical hero Cúchulainn with a crow, symbol of Mórrígan, goddess of war, perched on his shoulder. Through Sheppard's statue—situated in the General Post Office on O'Connell Street, Dublin, which was a central location for the 1916 Rising—Kinsella again weaves his analysis of familial history into the fabric of the narratives of national culture. *The Familiar* (1999), sees Kinsella return to his early interest in medieval illuminated manuscripts with two images that echo those of *Faeth Fiadha*: the first is of two animals, a fox and a hare perhaps, inspired by the ornamentation of the *Book of Kells*. The second image of *The Familiar* is the figure of Christ with hands outstretched that marks the end of Kinsella's seven-part meditation on love. The title poem, "The Familiar," ends with a rewriting of the Calypso episode of Joyce's *Ulysses* in which Bloom carefully attends to making breakfast for his wife. Kinsella's closing lines frame the image of Christ, and of the poet, with a wry humor: "I stood in my dressing gown / with arms extended / over the sweetness of the sacrifice." In *Godhead* (1999), Kinsella explores the triumvirate nature of the Christian deity. Kinsella's choice of cover image—a bearded male face surrounded by hair and the feathers of wings held within a circular pattern—is taken from Klaus Holitzka's coloring book for adults *Mandalas of the Celts* (1996), serving to frame the poet's concerns through the perspective of the mandala, a visual tool to focus meditation that widens the poet's reach beyond the Christian and the European to include an understanding of Eastern spiritualities.

Kinsella looks again to archeological imagery for the cover of *Littlebody* (2000). The lithe figure of a *luchorpán* features on the cover, a soft cap on his head and a set of pipes under his armpit. This is the dancing *daimon* or "Demon dwarf" that the poet speaker meets on the "fragrant slope" of the Wicklow mountains in section six of "*Glenmacnass*." Kinsella notes in the colophon that the image comes "from a rubbing of a 15/16th century carving of a piper on a stone formerly at Woodstock Castle," a thirteenth-century Norman Keep.[15] The carving depicts a medieval figure playing the Irish warpipes or *píob mór*, a fitting reference to the castle's important role as a fortification. Kinsella redeploys the image, transforming it into the ancient *luchorpán* or leprechaun figure who originated as a water sprite, thus connecting *Littlebody* with *Citizen of the World* through the figure of the water nymph in "Undine." Kinsella's poet speaker surprises the pipe playing Littlebody and claims his due, a "fat purse," only to be reprimanded by the sprite for his own acquisitive attitude: "showing your skills / with your eye on your income." Several years later, in *Marginal Economy* (2006), Kinsella comments directly on the cover of the Peppercanisters and the role they have to play in the reception of his work. "The Affair" traces the poet speaker's animosity towards one who shared the poet's own dual role as poet and civil servant—"in the same section, in the same Department"—and whose critical misreading of the poet's work is based on the misinterpretation of a cover image. The poet decries "a murderous review: / a flow of acid colloquialisms / dismissing the main thesis / based on a misreading of the images off the cover. . . ." The cover is a graphic representation of a sunset over water, the half-obscured sun rendered with geometric accuracy in a single monochrome line, separated from its reflection by a strong horizontal line, bringing to the fore the sense of acceptance and ease that marks "*Rhetoric of Natural Beauty*," the final poem of the volume, as the poet contemplates a "crimson ocean sunset / halved on a calm horizon."

The impulses and ideologies that inform conflict are the predominant themes in *Man of War* (2007) and *Belief and Unbelief* (2007). The covers of both connect the concerns of the volumes by integrating historical detail into the poet's exploration of how primal instincts to survive are mediated through complex social systems informed by religion and imperialism to create the discord and chaos that the poet speaker seeks to understand. The cover of *Man of War* depicts a moment of bloodshed during the Christian crusades against Islam, the helmeted Europeans spearing the warriors of the Levant. Kinsella takes his image from Elizabeth Hallam's *Chronicles of the Crusades*.[16] As an addendum, in "Notes," Kinsella weaves his exploration through an intertextual engagement with a hymn from the Dead Sea Scrolls and verses from the *Book of Job* and *The Iliad*. The third of these "Notes" titled "A sleeping cancer" describes the horrors of the First Crusade (1096–1099),

Figure 8. Peppercanister covers for *The Familiar* and *Marginal Economy*.

including the massacre of Jews in Germany in 1096 known also in Hebrew as the Edicts of 4856. Kinsella is excoriating in his analysis of the "cause of no account" behind which "the human creature / assembles together": "Drunk on Jewish blood, / they wiped their swords, and crossed the Rhine, renewed, / raping onward toward Jerusalem." The cover image of *Belief and Unbelief* acts as a counterpoint to that of *Man of War*, as Kinsella chooses a moment of animal violence that is primal and necessary in contrast to the human warfare that he objurgates. The image is that of a mosaic from the fourth century held by the Capitolini Museums of Rome depicting a female tiger attacking a calf. In the poem "Art Object" Kinsella meditates on the moment of the kill—"Her face buried in the live neck / her top lip pulled back"—situating the killing in an equilibrium between the predator and the prey who "accepts it / with panic and protest, but understanding. Another's needs fulfilled."

Fat Master (2011) and *Love Joy Peace* (2011) complete the Peppercanister series to date.[17] A sense of fulfilment pervades both volumes, as the speaker comments when contemplating his Other in "Tenants in Common": "I have decided, therefore, / to make as much of things as I can." Music connects both of these books: the agile fingers of the "Fat Master" on the keys of the organ that graces the cover of that volume, and the contralto's jazz emanating from the basement in the opening poem, "Reserved Table," of *Love Joy Peace*: "she murmured above our heads about love and blood / as we settled in our places at her feet." A photograph of the pipes of a church organ on the cover of *Fat Master*, "the choir of pipes erect, multiplex," situates the poem of that name as a nodal point for our reading, their "bass lungs" delivering the "prime theme" of Kinsella's poetry. Love, joy, and peace lie at the heart of Kinsella's matter. In the poem of that title, Kinsella's poet speaker recalls how those words formed a tag graffitied across his "first neighbourhood": "there was an unknown that no one ever saw / who left his mark everywhere / Love Joy / Peace / white inside the white sign of a heart." In a nod to concrete poetry, Kinsella typesets the words "love," "joy," and "peace" in capitals to form the shape of a heart, the final word "peace" underscoring the link between "love" and "joy." The cover image of a red brick wall with these words spray-painted in white, encircled by the white outline of a heart (which is replicated in monochrome before the colophon), describes the early graffiti that inspires Kinsella's meditation on the impulses of sacrifice, the iniquities of religious values, and—at the heart of all—the true value of steady and constant work, of "earthly genius, / the day labourer."

Kinsella's poetry involves a careful articulation of intertwining narratives drawn from the intimacies of love, family histories, contemporary ideologies, and his extensive work in the translation of literature and mythology written in the Irish language. His is a scholarly poetry that builds its resonances through an intertextuality that gives grace to polyphony. The visual image sounds clearly through this polyphony while never taking a dominant line. Kinsella's close working relationship with Miller and his early involvement with the artists associated with the Dolmen Press honed the poet's eye for the visual and ensured that the image played a central part in the early Peppercanister editions. While Kinsella admits that the special editions of Peppercanister titles owed much to Miller's "commitment to quality in materials and design," it is clear that the balance between word and image evident in Dolmen titles formed an important element of books such as *One*, *A Technical Supplement*, and *The Messenger*. Yet as Kinsella became distanced from Dolmen, and found his professional obligations taking him away from the literary and artistic milieu that had nourished his early engagement with illustration, the position of the visual image in the Peppercanister editions became confined primarily to the cover. Rather than the multifractal coherence of word and image that defines many of the editions of the 1970s to the mid-1980s, the later Peppercanisters use the visual image to articulate a nodal point within the sequence of poems, orientating our reading and framing our response. Kinsella's late poem "Into Thy hands" suggests a consolidation of his practice with the clarity of experience and self-knowledge: "The parts self-selected, / tried along the senses, / founded on hard practice. / The whole shaped and corrected / to stand unsupported." The prints that accompany Kinsella's early poems and translations, the commissioned designs and devices that frame his work, and the appropriated and adapted images that enter into dialogue with the poet's laconic line, are each part of the "given substance" of his poetry, forming an integral and necessary part of our reading.

Notes

[1] Due to space considerations, not every Peppercanister publication is discussed in this chapter. For further analysis of art in Kinsella's mature work see Derval Tubridy, *Thomas Kinsella: The Peppercanister Poems* (Dublin: University College Dublin Press, 2001).

[2] Kinsella based his translation on the eleventh-century manuscript, *Liber Hymnorum* or *Book of Hymns*, found in the library of Trinity College Dublin (TCD MS 1441). The hymn is a pagan spell of concealment (the *féth fíada* used by the Tuatha Dé Dannan) and was recited by Saint Patrick as a *lorica* or prayer of protection.

[3] Kinsella's collaboration with le Brocquy and Miller on the *Tain* is discussed in Chapter 6, "Making the Great *Tain*," by Thomas Dillon Redshaw.

[4] In an interview with Denis O'Driscoll, Kinsella described setting some of his early poems on Miller's Adana printing press: "I would play my part, holding the print and inserting the pieces upside down." Denis O' Driscoll, "An Interview with Thomas Kinsella" in *Poetry Ireland Review* 25 (Spring 1989): 59.

[5] Gisela Richter, *The Portraits of the Greeks*, vol.2 (London: Phaidon, 1965). The cover image and that facing part III come from a head in the National Museum, Athens (plate 21, figs. 957–8). The frontispiece image is held in the Fitzwilliam Museum, Cambridge (plate 16, fig. 946). The image facing part II comes from the Musée Granet, Aix en Provence (plate 14, fig. 939). The final image, facing the last page of the poem, is from the National Museum, Syracuse (plate 9, fig. 921).

[6] Kinsella, "Street Games for the Over 15s," *The Irish Times*, August 1, 2020.

[7] James Larkin (1874–1947), head of the Irish Transport and General Workers Union, and chief organizer of the 1913 Dublin strike and lock-out.

[8] Kinsella explains his changing relationship with Dolmen in "The Dolmen Press," *Prose Occasions 1951–2006*, ed. Andrew Fitzsimons (Manchester: Carcanet Press, 2009).

[9] P. W. Joyce, *A Smaller Social History of Ancient Ireland*, 2nd ed. (London: Longman, Green; Dublin: M. H. Gill, 1908), 294.

[10] In his revision for the Wake Forest edition of *Collected Poems* Kinsella omits the first two lines of the last poem of *St Catherine's Clock* "1740." In the Peppercanister edition, the poem opens thus: "About the third hour. // Ahead, at the other end / of the darkened market place."

[11] Geraldine Hume and Anthony Malcomson, *Education Facsimiles 181–200: Robert Emmet—The Insurrection of July 1803* (Belfast: Public Records Office of Northern Ireland, 1976).

[12] W. H. Maxwell, *History of the Irish Rebellion in 1798 with Memories of the Union and Emmet's Insurrection in 1803*, illustrated by George Cruikshank (London: Baily Brothers Cornhill, 1845).

[13] Malton's explorations of Dublin buildings and streetscapes were republished by the Dolmen Press in *Georgian Dublin: Twenty-five Aquatint View in Colour*. Introduction and notes by Maurice Craig (Dublin: Dolmen Press, 1984).

[14] Kinsella's notes for a program for Radio Telefís Éireann on December 3, 1991. Thomas Kinsella Papers, Woodruff Library, Emory University, box 29, folder 10.

[15] The carving was later moved to Kilkea Castle, Castledermot in County Kildare and is now believed to be lost.

[16] See also Jean Joinville and Geoffroi de Villehardouin, *Chronicles of the Crusades*, translated with an introduction by M. R. B. Shaw (London: Penguin Books, 1969).

[17] Subsequently collected in *Late Poems* (Manchester: Carcanet Press, 2013).

CHAPTER 12

"Fair Elinor. O Christ thee save"

ELEANOR KINSELLA'S SUBLIME PRESENCE IN THE POETRY OF THOMAS KINSELLA

ADRIENNE LEAVY

In the poem, "Artists' Letters" from *Song of the Night and Other Poems* (1978), Thomas Kinsella describes the experience of happening upon a box of old love letters written to his wife Eleanor Kinsella when they were in the initial stages of their courtship. From the vantage point of two decades later he recalls his youthful philosophy: "There is one throw, no more. One / offering: make it." These letters also reveal the poet's intense engagement with this key relationship in his life: "My apologies, but you are my beloved / and I will not be put off."[1] With these two statements Kinsella not only declared the primacy of his love for Eleanor, which was to continue throughout their life together, but also his early realization that once the choice was made, their lives and his artistic fate would be irrevocably entwined. In an early interview, Kinsella confirmed as much: "I think it was meeting the particular woman whom I eventually married that got me seriously writing love poetry, which was the first poetry I now regard as valid."[2] This chapter will examine the evolving aesthetic representation of Kinsella's relationship with Eleanor and argue that the poet's developing view of life as an ordeal is teased out in his love poetry, and that this poetry ultimately reaffirms his belief in the redemptive power of their union.

Since the beginning of Kinsella's career in the mid-1950s, Eleanor, who is often referred to as the "Beloved," has been aesthetically associated with his poetry.[3] His first full-length collection *Poems*, published in 1956, was presented as a wedding present to her and includes the poem "Echoes," wherein the poet sets forth the aesthetic manifesto for his love poems: "Love, I consider a difficult, scrupulous art." When Kinsella first met Eleanor Walsh in 1951 she was a radiology student at University College Dublin; however, she was forced to abandon her studies when she developed tuberculosis, which at that time was still a life-threatening disease in Ireland. She was subsequently hospitalized for two years (1952–54) in St. Mary's Hospital in Phoenix Park, and the couple's early courtship occurred during this period. Kinsella's experience of watching Eleanor battle this disease informed his burgeoning poetic sensibility, and much of his early work is infused with a realization of the fragility and the precariousness of both life and romantic love. This view was confirmed some years into their marriage when Eleanor became seriously ill with a rare debilitating condition, myasthenia gravis, which required treatment in the US as none was available in Ireland.

"A Lady of Quality," which describes the poet's visit to his Beloved at St. Mary's while she was convalescing, is typical of Kinsella's initial lyric style, which owed much to the example of Auden.[4] The formal elegance of the poem creates a measured, detached tone, which serves to temper the intimacy of this love poem. The specter of mortality is ever present, even though the lovers try to talk around it with "pillow-chat," hoping to "bless the room from present dread / Just for a brittle while." In her reading, Lucy Collins points out that "the woman, though real and cherished, becomes strangely metonymic, losing her specific identity to gain a timeless universal role."[5] Yet the poet's representation of the Beloved in this manner can also be read as a creative strategy to counter the fear of mortality as the very real threat of death is purposely transformed into an artistic abstraction. In the latter part of "A Lady of Quality," the poet shifts his perspective from Eleanor to himself as he attempts to maintain some sense of aesthetic order in the face of personal turmoil: "While I communicate again / Recovered order to my pen." Kinsella questions whether he can do creative justice to their relationship, and, not for the last time, he confronts the challenges their relationship will pose to his work as a poet: "It will be hard, it seems, and I / Would wish my heart to justify / What qualities remain."

One of Kinsella's most anthologized poems, "Another September," from his second collection of the same name, published in 1958, focuses again on Eleanor.[6] The poem captures the poet in a detached and reflective mood as he watches his sleeping wife in the bedroom of her childhood home: "that unspeaking daughter, growing less / Familiar where we fell asleep together." Eleanor is welcomed back into the house by "Domestic Autumn," but the poet, who describes himself as "this half-tolerated consciousness," is not. The poet's mode of address is deliberately indirect and self-aware, and the poem is a clear example of Kinsella's early classical aesthetic. Arguably, the poem leaves itself open to criticism, as the woman is silenced by virtue of sleep and therefore relegated to the margins of the poem in contrast to the poetic speaker, whose virile consciousness "plants its grammar in her yielding weather." However, Eavan Boland, who consistently challenged the Irish poetic tradition for its history of excluding women by silencing them, has written approvingly about "Another September." For Boland, the poem offered an example to her as a young poet of how a domestic environment could be a credible setting for poetry. She observed that Kinsella's achievement lay in his ability to write beyond traditional "pastoral elegies" and what she terms "Yeatsian rhetoric" and craft a domestic poem that was engaged in a "tense combative conversation with poetic convention."[7] Boland reads this poem as one in which the poet uses the tropes associated with nature as a means to enter an interior domestic scene, "a country bedroom," thereby privileging the domestic space as a subject fit for a poem. And as Boland reflected, this is a poem involving real people, in an identifiable environment which she notes was "located in the new Ireland, where downright working lives were lived."[8]

The foundation upon which a great deal of Kinsella's poetry is constructed is a strongly held belief that life is a series of ordeals through which one must preserve in order to mature, both as an individual and as an artist. The first of Kinsella's marriage sequences, the aptly titled *Wormwood* (1966), builds on his themes of endurance and renewal, arguing that the sustaining force of the couple's love and their continuing growth together is a bulwark against inevitable loss and disappointment. As in his later marriage sequences, the poet speaks as both husband and artist, and the Beloved is imagined as both wife and muse, with the internal dynamics of the relationship analyzed from these varying perspectives. The prose prologue and seven short poems in *Wormwood* represent an attempt to transmute the bitterness and impermanence of life into an aesthetic creed of endurance. With unflinching honesty, the poet confronts the ordeal of marital strife and offers an unsparing assessment of the complex nature of the couple's relationship.

The title *Wormwood* comes from the Apocalypse of John, and Kinsella incorporates the relevant section as an epigraph that serves to explain the sequence title and also set the tone for these poems:

> *and a great star fell from heaven, burning as it were a torch; and it fell on the third part of the rivers and upon the fountains of waters; and the name of the star is called Wormwood; and the third part of the waters became wormwood; and many men died of the waters, because they were made bitter.*
>
> —Apocalypse: Ch.8, vv.10 and 11[9]

Despite this ostensibly grim introduction, the epigraph includes the possibility of a positive reading, as only a third of the waters were afflicted by the blighted star. Kinsella has maintained that *Wormwood* is an affirmative response to a period of marital discord and has characterized these poems as "love poems."[10] Notwithstanding the biblical gloss included at the onset of *Wormwood*, Kinsella's choice of title is doubly fascinating in its allusion to the words spoken by Shakespeare's Hamlet in Act III, Scene ii. In an aside during the play-within-a-play sequence, Hamlet utters the phrase "wormwood, wormwood." In the play, "wormwood" is a reference to the bitter extract of a plant, and Hamlet's words express the bitter moment for his family when his suspicions are confirmed that his mother has conspired in his father's murder by her new husband, Hamlet's uncle, King Claudius.

After the epigraph, the sequence begins with a direct address to the Beloved in the form of a prose prologue followed by six poems of various stanzaic lengths. While the poetic forms of the *Wormwood* poems are still traditional, these allegories of intense engagement with life signal the growing importance of Kinsella's impulse to aesthetically preserve and understand significant experience. The prologue opens with the poet offering his Beloved a "bitter cup," arguing that, "if we drink the bitterness and can transmute it and continue, we resume in candour and doubt the only individual joy – the restored necessity to learn." The poet then invites her to read the poems and see the speaker, who is "A waste, a nearly naked tree." The suffering speaker needs the love and support of the Beloved as he pursues his artistic calling, and he pleas for understanding—"open this and you will see." In the title poem, "Wormwood," the image of a tree reoccurs as the poet recalls a dream in which the couple's marriage is imagined as a tree "with a double trunk." The couple who comprise the union are pictured as two individual trees who have "grown into one," embarked on an "infinitesimal dance of growth." This growth through suffering is a fundamental aspect of the human condition, and Kinsella sees this "necessity to learn" from the experiences of life as "the only individual joy." The metaphor of intertwined trees, where the two tree trunks have left "a slowly twisted scar," underscores the idea that pain and love are both part of their union.

"Mask of Love," the poem which follows "Wormwood," continues chronicling the period of marital strife. Here, the lovers climb "the peaks of stress" from which vantage point they "wearily" confront each other "again and again." The poet cautions both himself and his wife to remember these stressful times and not to forget that their "very bodies lack peace." Again we see Kinsella's acknowledgment of ordeal as a necessary part of the continuing process of self-examination and the search for meaning. With "The Secret Garden" the *Wormwood* sequence shifts into a different, more hopeful mood. Images of destruction co-exist with images of beauty and nature, and the poet allows for the possibility of growth and regeneration in the form of their son, who will one day experience his own "sour encounter" with life and death. Amidst the inevitable erosion and ultimate decay of life, here symbolized by the withering garden where the poet "picks off one sick leaf," there is solace to be found in the person of his young son, who "smells of energy" and is "light as light" with incandescent "pearl flesh." In an early interview with John Haffenden, Kinsella asserted his belief that "the artistic act has to do with the eliciting of order from significant experience."[11] The *Wormwood* poems are an attempt to aesthetically scrutinize and arrange some semblance of order from this period of strife, which at times lends a documentary feel to the poems as in "First Light," where the "prone couple" is sleeping in the cold light of dawn after another argument: "where shrill / Lover and beloved have kept / Another vigil far / Into the night, and raved and wept."

In the final two poems, "Remembering Old Wars" and "Je t'adore," vignettes of suffering are tempered with images of steadfast support for one another. With each new dawn, "without hope of change or peace," the lovers recollect "their purpose" and "renew each other with a savage smile." And while the smile they direct at each other is "savage," which suggests an underlying hostility that their sleep does not erase, the couple is still depicted as renewing each other every morning. Recalling the earlier image of the intertwined trees, the couple are described as being "clamped together," suggesting a firm bond that cannot be broken. This optimism in the strength of their union is confirmed in the concluding poem, "Je t'adore," where the lovers are depicted as "Sighing in one another's / Iron arms, propped above nothing." There is nothing to sustain their precarious relationship except their faith in each other, and the poem concludes on a pragmatic note, with the couple praising "Love the limiter." Despite their differences, when all the other props are gone, love remains. By accepting the "bitter cup," the poet and his Beloved will find the strength to "grow towards the next ordeal." The *Wormwood* poems thus serve to confirm the strength of the couple's bond by celebrating their willingness to accept and embrace the cyclical aspect of the challenges their relationship will continue to encounter as they go through life together. As the sequence makes clear, love can be a panacea to the sorrow that is an inevitable part of the human experience.

Throughout this sequence, the elegant lyricism of Kinsella's early poetry is replaced with a new aesthetic toughness and linguistic rigor which attempts to replicate the actuality of domestic strife and ensuing loss of emotional control. Writing about the "cumbrousness" that begins to dominate Kinsella's work from *Nightwalker* forward, Seamus Deane's commentary on Kinsella's language is instructive with regard to the *Wormwood* poems:

> This loss of elegance seems to some readers to indicate a loss of control. But since the poet is trying to transmit to us the experience of lost control, his foregoing of elegance is not really an indication of failure. Instead, he chooses to demonstrate the process by which he arrives at his moment of balance. The poem is not a structure; it is an action in which structures appear and disappear as part of a complex process in which the poet, as well as the reader, is involved.[12]

Another noteworthy aspect of this suite of poems is that notwithstanding Kinsella's emphatic rejection of Catholicism, these poems of spiritual and emotional redemption through pain and suffering in many respects mirror the Catholic ethos of the poet's upbringing. In this regard, as in many other aspects of his work, Kinsella shares an affinity with James Joyce. In the present context, Kinsella's evocation of the feminine in his search for meaning arguably parallels Stephen Dedalus's search for the enabling feminine, a key aspect of Stephen's development in *A Portrait of the Artist as a Young Man*.[13]

Kinsella followed *Wormwood* with *Nightwalker and Other Poems* (1968), a seminal collection which includes his major love poem "Phoenix Park."[14]

Set on the eve of the couple's departure to the United States in 1965, this long poem is also an important example of the burgeoning formal and technical innovations that were to drive Kinsella's mature poetry. A journey poem, both typographically, in its representation of the Phoenix Park in Dublin, and emotionally, in its circuitous exploration of their life, the poem begins with the couple driving through the park and Eleanor, "quiet and watchful, this last visit." The poem celebrates among other things their shared decision to journey further together, with Kinsella leaving a secure career in the Irish Civil Service to take up a teaching position in the United States.[15] Many of the themes that have preoccupied Kinsella throughout his career surface in "Phoenix Park," and Eleanor is the aesthetic catalyst through which they are explored.

Divided into four distinct sections of varying lengths and written in blank verse, the poem opens near the entrance to St. Mary's Hospital, where the poet recalls how he found his way to Eleanor "by way of hesitation." Recalling her confinement in the hospital for tuberculosis and their initial courtship he writes: "Midsummer, and I had tasted your knowledge, / My flesh blazing in yours;" however, as always in Kinsella's work, the recognition of human fallibility is ever present: ". . . Autumn, I had learned / Giving without tearing is not possible." In response to Eleanor's complaint that he no longer writes any "love songs" for her, he offers her a dream and its preparation. After the couple leave the park "through the Knockmaroon Gate" and proceed "downhill to the Liffey road," past "the Strawberry Beds," to "sit drinking in a back bar in Lucan," the poet unfurls the dream to his wife, confident of her innate understanding of his offering: "Your body would know that it is positive / —Everything you know you know bodily." Donatella Abbate Badin, one of Kinsella's early commentators, has observed that in Kinsella's work "the dichotomy between man and nature, or between rationality and instinct, is often represented as a clash between male and female consciousness."[16] In emphasizing her female intuition, the poet risks the charge of gender stereotyping; however, this is only one of many qualities with which Eleanor is imbued. Later in the poem, Kinsella credits her strength and wisdom for facilitating his own intellectual development and intuitive knowledge, writing, "Laws of order I find I have discovered / Mainly at your hands." Acknowledging their mutual respect, the poet reaffirms their commitment to each other: ". . . so in love we persist; / That love is to clasp simply, question fiercely."

Anticipating the Jungian-inspired poems of Kinsella's psychic journey inwards that were to follow the *Nightwalker* collection, other-worldly figures also populate this poem. A ghostly child appears several times, first devouring mushrooms with "Death-pallor in their dry flesh, the taste of death." Later this child, who "plucks death and tastes it," is transformed at the close of the poem into "A child with eaten features eating something." In each instance, a "shadow" or a "shade" protects the child. As with the real woman in the poem whose knowledge is celebrated, the spectral females who appear in the poet's dream are also wise—"women-shapes pass / Unseeing, full of knowledge, through each other." The otherworldly aspect of the poem may seem incongruous in a love poem, but, for Kinsella, life and health are always provisional, with death and illness a constant in the human experience. Knowing this, the poet acknowledges the human frailty and ultimate mortality of his Beloved: "You wait a minute on the path, absently / – Against massed brown trees – tying a flimsy scarf / At your neck. Fair Elinor. O Christ thee save."[17]

In "Phoenix Park," the "bitter cup" of *Wormwood* becomes the "ordeal-cup" which the lovers must accept, and Kinsella exhorts his Beloved to accept this poisoned chalice as part of life: "The ordeal-cup, set at each turn, so far / We have welcomed, sour or sweet. What matter where / It waits for us next, if we will take and drink?" Echoing the last poem in the *Wormwood* sequence, in the final section of this poem the couple reaffirms their faith in each other as the poet writes: "Continue, so. We'll perish in each other." Returning again to the past, in the closing stanzas Kinsella recalls his early life in the flat in Baggot Street, the site where he began writing poetry, "that room," and reminds Eleanor that she rescued him from a life of solitude: "My past alive in you, a gift of tissue / Torn free from my life in an odour of books."

The poem closes with a series of primordial images, foreshadowing the psychic exploration of personal and historical origins which would henceforth dominate Kinsella's work:

> A snake out of the void moves in my mouth, sucks
> At triple darkness. A few ancient faces
> Detach and begin to circle. Deeper still,
> Delicate distinct tissues begin to form,[18]

The description of Eleanor's "delicate distinct flesh" at the beginning of the poem is rewritten in the final line, as the poet embraces the intuitive, sensory journey into the unconscious that he is about to embark on in *New Poems*. Just as Eleanor's knowledge is "bodily," the poet henceforth will use his senses to try and understand both his familial history and the origins of Ireland as set forth in *Lebor Gabála Érenn* (*The Book of Invasions*). By ending "Phoenix Park" with a comma instead of a period, Kinsella underscores his view that his individual poems are open-ended and therefore resistant to closure. This perspective continues in the subsequent collection, *New Poems*, where the first line begins in mid-sentence, picking up the aesthetic train of thought left off at the close of "Phoenix Park":

hesitate, cease to exist, glitter again,
dither in and out of a mother liquid
on the turn, welling up from God knows what hole.[19]

The themes of renewal and regeneration explored in *Wormwood* and "Phoenix Park" resurface via a different imaginative perspective in *Out Of Ireland* (1987), a series of seven stylistically sparse poems set in the graveyard of St. Gobnait's Church in Ballyvourney, County Cork on the occasion of a memorial service for Seán Ó Riada. Philosophically, the sequence is inspired by the work of John Scotus Eriugena (c. 800–c. 877), an Irish theologian, philosopher and poet of the early monastic period. In the most literal sense, both of these writers were writing *out* of their native country, as Eriugena spent most of his career on the continent and Kinsella was at the time living in Philadelphia. Kinsella imagines a poetic affinity with Eriugena's ideas, writing in "The Furnace," "Eriugena's notion matching / my half-baked bodily own." The "harmonious certainty" that Kinsella admires in Eriugena could arguably be applied to what John F. Deane terms the poet's own "clear-eyed and pitiless exploration of self and society down the decades."[20] One of Kinsella's early critics, Maurice Harmon, astutely recognized how the poet's response to lived experience dovetailed with this ninth-century Irish intellectual:

> "The Furnace" adopts and provisionally accepts Eriugena's mystical account of manifest union with God as an analogy for the poet's own faith, articulated in the *Wormwood* sequence, in "Phoenix Park," *Nightwalker* and elsewhere, his trust in love, persistence, and the understanding that may be gained.[21]

Throughout the sequence, Eriugena's theories of rebirth and renewal through reason are affirmed in the context of the poet's relationship with his wife. The third stanza of the first short poem, "Entrance," recalls the couple's commitment to each other by quoting a core belief at the heart of "Phoenix Park"—"*that love is to clasp simply, / question fiercely.*" Further allusions to "Phoenix Park" are made in "The Furnace," as the poet recalls that he has "*consigned my designing will / stonily to your flames.*" The sexual and spiritual union of the couple in a "radiant clasp" dissolves their differences "Until gender returned / and we were made two again." The final stanza of "The Furnace" recalls the couple's previous drive in the rain through the Phoenix Park, where the wet grass was redolent of "A smoke-soft odour of graves . . . our native damp," as the poet now plants a cerebral "dry kiss / in your rain-wet hair." This careful cross-referencing with his earlier poem underscores the accumulating unity of Kinsella's poetic project, and of the continuing aesthetic presence of Eleanor within this project.

Kinsella's second dedicated marriage sequence, *Madonna and Other Poems* (1991), was published nearly twenty-five years after *Wormwood.*[22] In the interim period, Kinsella's work underwent a radical shift in form and tone,[23] and his aesthetic focus was primarily preoccupied with a Jungian quest for self-knowledge and individuation, and with interrogating the role of the artist in society. In *Madonna,* he returns to the subject of the female companion, and the poems offer a multi-faceted portrait of the Beloved who is imagined in various guises as wife, companion, muse, and goddess. Comprising four poems written in free verse and an epigraph in the *Collected Poems,* the sequence opens with a familiar Kinsella theme, a meditation on the nature of strife within love; however, unlike the poems in *Wormwood,* the couple's "loving upset" is minimized. Derval Tubridy has noted that the first line of the epigraph, "*Better is an handful with quietness,*" is a direct quote from Ecclesiastes IV: 6. Tubridy further points out that Kinsella here is elaborating on the overall themes of chapter IV of Ecclesiastes, which places great importance on partnership: "Two *are* better than one; because they have a good reward for their labor. For if they fall, the one will lift up his fellow: but *woe* to him *that is* alone when he falleth; for *he hath* not another to help him up."[24] The *Madonna* poems once more reinforce the importance of their partnership and the mutual support they derive from each other. The poet realizes that if he succumbs to bitterness, if his "blind fingers" forsake her face, then understanding would be lost and he would be destroyed: "Yet worst is the fool that foldeth his hands / and eateth his own flesh."

The primacy of the feminine is signaled in the first stanza of the opening title poem, where the couple are pictured in a church kneeling before a bank of votive candles, under a statue of Jesus, "the Body with the woman feet." Later in the poem, the couple's sexual union is described as their "two awarenesses / narrowed into one point, / our piercing presences exchanged / in pleasantry and fright," which recalls the lines in "Phoenix Park" where two lives "Burn down around one love," and the heat of passion in "The Furnace," that "melted the union of our will / to ineffable zero." As always in a Kinsella poem, the specter of mortality is never far from the surface, and the poet acknowledges, "the tally of our remaining encounters" is now "reduced by one." In a role reversal of the closing scene in "Nightwalker," where the nocturnal rambler spies "the dear shadow" of his wife through the kitchen window, "slicing and buttering / A loaf of bread," the poet here is pictured making tea and cutting grapefruit for himself and the Beloved.

This ritual of preparing an offering for the Beloved is repeated again in *The Familiar* (1999), a late marriage sequence that reaffirms the strength of the lovers' bond and celebrates the balance struck between the competing demands of love and creativity.[25] Here, the poet casts a retrospective glance back over their lives together and subsumes these experiences into a more complete portrayal of the Beloved. Whereas in *Wormwood* the tone of the marriage poems was disconsolate and at times verging on shrill, in this sequence the mood is one of loving acceptance, with the tension between love and art disappearing. And while the domestic space of the *Wormwood* household was an "empty" unwelcoming place, filled with "silence" except for the "ugly wail" of a young child, the home in *The Familiar* is a comfortable environment, with a cat in the kitchen, "Folded on herself." The sequence opens with an epigraph in which "Love" with his "sinewy bow / against His knee," informs the poet, "*Husband, here is a friend / beseeming thee.*" Eleanor's wise council throughout their marriage is acknowledged with courtly formality in the lines describing her as "Comely Wisdom wearing / a scarf around Her throat." This scarf is more durable than the "flimsy scarf" she ties around her neck in "Phoenix Park," suggesting the poet's awareness of his wife's strength. By capitalizing the figures of Love, Husband, and Comely Wisdom, Kinsella envisions the couple as uniting in love to form an emotional trinity.

Following this epigraph, the title poem revisits specific private moments within the lengthy span of their relationship. Their early days together are recalled along with an acknowledgment of their disparate temperaments, which were "mismatched under the sign of sickness." The moment when Eleanor moved into the flat in Baggot Street is remembered by the poet as the end of his isolation: "My last thoughts alone." The gargoyles over the entrance to the flat, who had watched over the poet's "solitary shortcomings," "looked down upon" the couple entering the flat together with their "animal thoughts." Their early sexual life together is revisited in language that valorizes the female body and the poet remembers his Beloved as the "Muse on my mattress." Section V of the poem shifts to the present tense, and Eleanor is associated with "the three graces" in the painting that hangs in the bathroom of their house. The aging lovers have attained a closeness that transcends their differences, and the image of the couple's legs "locked in friendship" suggests contentment with the familiar domesticity of their marriage.

In section VI of *The Familiar*, Eleanor is represented allegorically as a nymph, "spurning the blades of grass with little tough feet; / picking the pale-stemmed blossoms in her path." By employing the imagery of a nymph, Kinsella provides a nodding reference to an earlier Jungian poem about his Beloved, specifically section 7 of *Songs of the Psyche*, in which a nymph approached the poet "by a little-haunted path / with modest run advancing / dancing in her flowers." This song of the psyche celebrates the moment when the couple joined together to form a third entity, prefiguring the trinity in *The Familiar*:

She offered me her hands.

I took them in mine
– averse
            but it was enough:
we were no longer two
but a third.[26]

The nymph in *The Familiar* beckons the poet, "whispering: *Come*," reinforcing the importance of this ongoing union to the poet personally and artistically. A routine domestic scene is recreated in the final section of the poem, where the poet performs what Tubridy has called "the breakfast ritual sacrifice." The role reversal initially described in *Madonna and Other Poems* is extended here as the poet prepares breakfast for the couple and presents his offering "with arms extended / over the sweetness of the sacrifice," which is met with approval by the Beloved who states, "'You are very good. You always made it nice.'" Ruth Ling interprets these two lines as the Beloved thanking the poet not merely for each individual act of love, symbolized by the act of making breakfast, but rather as thanking the poet for each "individual poem that has been 'made,'" and for "the poet's ongoing, cumulative creative gift of being 'good' at love and poetry."[27]

The continuity with the past and the resistance to closure that characterizes much of Kinsella's work continues in "St John's," which revisits the setting of an earlier poem, "In the Ringwood," from *Another September*. In that earlier poem, Kinsella explored the historical connections of the area to the United Irishmen Rebellion of 1798 and the horrors of that "ancient slaughter." Eleanor symbolizes the suffering of past generations, as the poet writes, "My love cried out and I beheld her / Change to Sorrow's daughter." In this more recent poem, the couple have returned to Wexford and are exploring the new developments that have sprung up in the Ringwood forest. Here, the Beloved is the guiding force through the forest, as she is the one "in front, finding the way / along the edge of the Ringwood." The short poem "Wedding Evening" also recalls the couple's lengthy family history as their eldest daughter is described on her wedding day as "Sara in certainty." This small detail reveals how long the couple have been together, as the same daughter is remembered in the much earlier poem "Phoenix Park," around six years old, "in her Communion finery, / Our first-born, Sara in innocence." Aside from being a sustained meditation on the couple's evolving relationship, the sequence is a further example of the intertextual and historical dimensions one finds throughout Kinsella's work.

In his mature poetry, Kinsella's aesthetic affirmation of his relationship with Eleanor becomes more pronounced, with the initial dissonant tone of *Wormwood* giving way to an acceptance of their differing temperaments in "Phoenix Park," leading to a full embrace and celebration of their union in *Madonna* and *The Familiar*. In these latter sequences, the poetic speaker is no longer preoccupied with issues of death or decay, or the tension between the demands of love and art. Nor is the distance that characterized some of the early work in evidence. On the contrary, by calling attention in the latter sequence so explicitly to the idea of *familiarity*, Kinsella reinforces the impression of intimacy that pervades these poems. The deliberately non-romanticized early work, with its focus on sickness, death, and marital strife, has given way to a poetry that affirms Eleanor as a dynamic enabling force whose presence is central to Kinsella's poetic project of personal and creative understanding. Harmon concurs, interpreting Eleanor's presence as an "indispensable source of strength"[28] who sustains the poet in his life and his art. She is the wise life partner, "Comely wisdom," who embodies the creed of love the poet articulates in the late poem "Entrance"—"*that love is to clasp simply, / question fiercely*." The importance of women to Kinsella's poetics has also been noted by Catriona Clutterbuck, who differentiates Kinsella from his contemporary John Montague and near contemporary Seamus Heaney because of the "consistency and openness with which he invokes the feminine as central to his larger dynamic of understanding."[29] Ultimately, Kinsella's aesthetic examination of his marriage and his repeated invocation of the Beloved in his poetry should be read as fundamental to his life-long analysis of the self and his efforts to reach an understanding of actual experience. Andrew Fitzsimons characterizes the aesthetic importance of love to Kinsella's poetry thus:

> For Kinsella art and love perform the same ordering, "composite" function. Love, like art, creates an implicit frame around the fragmentary, a temporary appeasing of a recurring sense of disintegration.[30]

It seems appropriate, in closing, to give Eleanor the last word. The penultimate Peppercanister publication (number 29 in the series) is the appropriately titled *Love Joy Peace* (2011), which is a reference to a heart-shaped piece of graffiti dotted throughout the Kinsellas' first neighborhood. These three simple words, which the title poem replicates in a heart-shaped pattern, were "painted everywhere," with lettering "white inside the white sign of the heart." In the poem "Tenants in Common," the poet's muse, his "old opposite," is visualized as a Jungian snake, who slithers "up out of the shallows" to address the poet. Kinsella's archetypical muse is sometimes conflated with the figure of the Beloved, and here, the figure who addresses the poet throughout the poem before "her thin leathery lips" approached his neck is arguably one such manifestation:

"I had been hoping for this.
To solve our joint requirements:
you, needing my nothingness
to quieten your fevers;
I needing the leap of life
for my inertia.
We were made for each other."[31]

With this late poem, Kinsella reminds his readers of his role as a *maker* of poems, and the importance of Eleanor to this creative act of *making*.

Notes

[1] "Artist's Letters," in *Thomas Kinsella: Collected Poems* (Winston-Salem: Wake Forest UP, 2006). Unless otherwise noted, all poetry quotations are taken from this edition of Kinsella's *Collected Poems*.

[2] Thomas Kinsella, in *The Poet Speaks: Interviews with Contemporary Poets*, ed. Peter Orr (London: Routledge and Kegan Paul, 1966), 105.

[3] In the Western poetic canon there is a rich history of idealistic representations of the Beloved. See for example, sonnets by Petrarch and Shakespeare. Arguably,

Kinsella could be challenging the conventional use of this poetic trope by presenting a more realistic depiction of his Beloved.

[4] CP, 6.

[5] Lucy Collins, "A Little of What We Have Found: Kinsella, Women and the Problem of Meaning," Special Issue: Thomas Kinsella, *Irish University Review* 31, no. 1 (Spring/Summer 2001): 135–152.

[6] CP, 19.

[7] Eavan Boland, *A Journey with Two Maps: Becoming a Woman Poet* (London, New York: W. W. Norton & Company, 2011), 112.

[8] Boland, *A Journey with Two Maps*, 110.

[9] CP, 62.

[10] "Thomas Kinsella in Conversation with Adrienne Leavy" in *Reading Ireland* No.11 (Winter 2019), 8.

[11] John Haffenden, "Thomas Kinsella," in *Viewpoints: Poets in Conversation with John Haffenden* (London: Faber and Faber, 1981), 113.

[12] Seamus Deane, *Celtic Revivals: Essays in Modern Irish Literature* (Winston-Salem, NC: Wake Forest UP, 1985), 142.

[13] Kinsella has written on this aspect of Joyce's *Portrait*. See Thomas Kinsella, "A Portrait of the Artist as a Young Man: 'The Enabling Feminine: A Documentary Essay'" in *Reading Ireland* 11 (Winter 2019): 15–26.

[14] CP, 87.

[15] In 1965 Kinsella moved to the United States to accept a position as writer-in-residence and Professor of English Literature at Southern Illinois University in Carbondale. The Kinsellas moved to Philadelphia in 1970 when Kinsella accepted a position as Professor of English at Temple University. Dividing his teaching time between teaching at Temple and organizing courses in Ireland on the Dual Tradition of Irish literature, Kinsella remained at Temple for twenty years until his retirement in 1990.

[16] Donatella Abbate Badin, *Thomas Kinsella* (New York: Twayne, 1996), 35.

[17] Here Kinsella quotes a line from an old English ballad, "Lord Thomas and Fair Ellinor," found in the *Reliques of Ancient English Poetry* by Thomas Percy. The various spellings for the woman in the poem are Ellinor, Elinor, and Eleanor.

[18] CP, 94.

[19] CP, 95.

[20] John F. Deane, "'The Rough Course': Celebrating Thomas Kinsella," *Poetry Ireland News* (July/August 2007).

[21] Maurice Harmon, "Nutrient Waters," review of *Out of Ireland* and *St Catherine's Clock*, by Thomas Kinsella, *Poetry Ireland Review* 21 (Spring 1988): 20.

[22] CP, 305.

[23] For a detailed discussion on Kinsella's evolving poetic form see Andrew Fitzsimons, *The Sea of Disappointment: Thomas Kinsella's Pursuit of the Real* (Dublin: University College Dublin Press, 2008).

[24] Derval Tubridy, *Thomas Kinsella: The Peppercanister Poems* (Dublin: University College Dublin Press, 2001), 197; Ecclesiastes IV: 9–10.

[25] CP, 329.

[26] CP, 228, 229.

[27] Ruth Ling, "Re-familiarizing *The Familiar*: From Effigy to Elegy in the Recent Marriage Poems of Thomas Kinsella," Special Issue: Thomas Kinsella, *Irish University Review* 31, no. 1 (Spring/Summer 2001): 155.

[28] Maurice Harmon, (xxii).

[29] Catriona Clutterbuck, "Scepticism, faith and the recognition of the 'Patriarch-Mother' in the poetry of Thomas Kinsella," *Irish Studies Review* 16, no. 3 (2008): 245–365.

[30] Fitzsimons, *The Sea of Disappointment*, 14.

[31] Thomas Kinsella, *Love Joy Peace* (Dublin: Peppercanister Press, 2011), 12; *Late Poems* (Manchester: Carcanet Press, 2013), 86.

Notes on Contributors

BRIAN G. CARAHER was Chair of English Literature at Queen's University Belfast from 1993 to 2016. Caraher served as Head of Graduate Teaching and Research and as Research Director in Poetry, Creative Writing, Irish Writing, and Modern Literary Studies in the School of English during its most extensive period of growth and international recognition. He helped establish and fund the Seamus Heaney Center at Queen's University during its foundational period, 2000–2004. He has published widely on topics in aesthetics, modern poetry and poetics, theories of literary reading, literary pragmatics, genre theory, and cultural politics. His books include *Wordsworth's "Slumber" and the Problematics of Reading*, *Intimate Conflict: Contradiction in Literary and Philosophical Discourse*, *Ireland and Transatlantic Poetics*, *Thomas Moore and Romantic Inspiration: Poetry, Music, Politics* (with Sarah McCleave), and an extensive series of studies of James Joyce. He co-edits The Palgrave Literary Dictionary Series for Palgrave Macmillan.

LUCY COLLINS is Associate Professor of Modern Poetry at University College Dublin. Books include *Poetry by Women in Ireland: A Critical Anthology* (2012), and a monograph, *Contemporary Irish Women Poets: Memory and Estrangement* (2015), both from Liverpool University Press. She has published widely on twentieth-century poets from Ireland, Britain, and America, and is co-founder of the Irish Poetry Reading Archive, a national digital repository.

ALEX DAVIS is Professor of English at University College Cork. He is the author of *A Broken Line: Denis Devlin and Irish Poetic Modernism* (2000), and co-author of four collections of essays on anglophone modernist poetry. He is currently writing a study of literary modernism and crime writing: *Murder Most Modernist*.

GERALD DAWE (1952–2024) was the author of nine books of poetry including, most recently, *Another Time: Poems 1978–2023* (2023) and several essay collections including *The Wrong Country* (2018) and, most recently, *A City Imagined: Belfast Soulscapes* (2021). He was Professor of English and Fellow Emeritus, Trinity College Dublin.

ANDREW FITZSIMONS was born in Ireland and teaches at Gakushuin University, Tokyo. He is the author of *The Sea of Disappointment: Thomas Kinsella's Pursuit of the Real* (University College Dublin Press, 2008) and editor of *Thomas Kinsella: Prose Occasions 1951–2996* (Carcanet Press, 2009). He has written on contemporary Irish and British poetry, translated from Italian poets, including Dante, Montale, and Ungaretti, and has also translated *The Complete Haiku of Bashō* (University of California Press, 2022). His poetry has appeared in Ireland, Italy, Britain, Japan, Canada, and the US, and three collections have been published by Isobar Press.

PAUL GOSLING is a professional archaeologist and a member of the Institute of Archaeologists of Ireland. He lectures on Built Heritage in the Department of Heritage and Tourism at Galway-Mayo Institute of Technology. He has authored several research papers on the route of the *Táin*, including *The Route of Táin Bó Cúailnge in County Louth* (*Archaeology Ireland Heritage Guide* No. 69, 2015), *The Route of Táin Bó Cúailnge in Counties Roscommon and Longford* (*Archaeology Ireland Heritage Guide* No. 75, 2016), and *The Route of Táin Bó Cúailnge in Counties Westmeath and Meath* (*Archaeology Ireland Heritage Guide* No. 86, 2019).

HUGH HAUGHTON is Emeritus Professor of Modern Literature at the University of York. He is the author of *The Poetry of Derek Mahon* (Oxford University Press, 2007) and the editor of *The Chatto Book of Nonsense Poetry* (1988), *The Letters of T. S. Eliot*, Vols 1 & 2 (2007), *Second World War Poems* (2005), and Freud's *The Uncanny* (2005). He has written numerous essays on twentieth-century British and Irish poetry, including recently on Yeats, Michael Longley, and Eiléan Ní Chuilleanáin.

ADRIENNE LEAVY was born in Ireland and lives in Phoenix, Arizona. She is the editor and publisher of *Reading Ireland*, a digital journal of Irish literature and culture which is published twice a year. She has written widely on Irish literature and poetry, most recently contributing a chapter, "Irish Modernist Poetry After Yeats: Local, Regional and Transatlantic " in *A History of Irish Modernism* edited by Gregory Castle and Patrick Bixby (Cambridge University Press, 2019). She is currently working on a biography of Thomas Kinsella.

MARY O'MALLEY is an award-winning poet born in Connemara. She lived in Lisbon for eight years, where she taught at the Universidade Nova. She served several years on the council of Poetry Ireland and taught in the MA programs for Writing and Education in the Arts at NUI Galway for ten years. In 2013 she held the Chair of Irish Studies at Villanova University. She lectures and teaches widely in the US and Europe, and has been active in environmental education for over twenty years. She has published nine books of poetry, including *Valpariso*, which was inspired by her environmental work and her Residency on the National Marine Research ship. O'Malley has also published poetry translations from Irish, Spanish, and Catalan. Her most recent collection is *Gaudent Angeli* (Carcanet Press, 2019). O'Malley is a member of Aosdána and was awarded an Honorary Doctorate Degree by NUI Galway in 2021.

THOMAS DILLON REDSHAW is the founding editor of *New Hibernia Review* and the former editor of *Éire-Ireland*. He served as the first director of the Center for Irish Studies at the University of St. Thomas in Minnesota. Compiler of *Well Dreams* (2004), a guide to the works of John Montague, he has published extensively on Montague's poetry and on Liam Miller's Dolmen Press, as well as on the poetry of John F. Deane, Thomas McCarthy, Brian Coffey, and George Reavey.

GERARD SMYTH is a poet, critic, and journalist whose collections include *A Song of Elsewhere* (Dedalus Press, 2015), *The Fullness of Time: New and Selected Poems* (Dedalus Press, 2010), and *The Yellow River* (with artwork by Seán McSweeney and published by Solstice Arts Centre, Navan, 2017). His poetry has appeared in journals in Ireland, Britain, and the US as well as in translation in several European languages. He was the 2012 recipient of the O'Shaughnessy Poetry Award from the University of St. Thomas in Minnesota and is the co-editor, with Pat Boran, of *If Ever You Go: A Map of Dublin in Poetry and Song* (Dedalus Press), which was Dublin's One City Book in 2013. He is a member of Aosdána and the Poetry Editor of the *Irish Times*. His most recent collection, *The Sundays of Eternity* (Dedalus Press), was published in 2020.

DERVAL TUBRIDY is Professor of Literature and Visual Culture at Goldsmiths, University of London. Author of *Thomas Kinsella: The Peppercanister Poems* (UCD Press, 2001), and *Samuel Beckett and the Language of Subjectivity* (Cambridge University Press, 2018), she has published extensively on Modernism and Irish Studies with a focus on the visual arts and performance. Her work has been funded by the Fulbright Commission, the British Council, and the Arts and Humanities Research Council. She is co-director of the London Beckett Seminar and vice-chair of the British Association for Irish Studies.

Bibliography

Works by Thomas Kinsella in Chronological Order

The Starlit Eye. Dublin: Dolmen Press, 1952.

Poems. Dublin: Dolmen Press, 1956.

Another September. Dublin: Dolmen Press, 1958.

Moralities. Dublin: Dolmen Press, 1960.

Poems and Translations. New York: Atheneum, 1961.

Downstream. Dublin: Dolmen Press; London: Oxford University Press, 1962.

The Dolmen Miscellany of Irish Writing. Edited by Thomas Kinsella and John Montague. Dublin: Dolmen Press, 1962.

Wormwood. Dublin: Dolmen Press, 1966.

Nightwalker and Other Poems. Dublin: Dolmen Press; London: Oxford University Press, 1967; New York: Knopf, 1968.

The Tain. Dublin: Dolmen Press, 1969; London: Oxford University Press, 1970.

Butcher's Dozen. Peppercanister 1. Dublin: Peppercanister Press, 1972.

A Selected Life. Peppercanister 2. Dublin: Peppercanister Press, 1972.

Finistère. Dublin: Dolmen Press, 1972.

Notes from the Land of the Dead. Dublin: Cuala Press, 1972.

Notes from the Land of the Dead and New Poems. Dublin: Dolmen Press, 1973; New York: Knopf, 1973.

Selected Poems: 1956–1968. Dublin: Dolmen Press; London: Oxford University Press, 1973.

Vertical Man. Peppercanister 3. Dublin: Peppercanister Press, 1973.

The Good Fight. Peppercanister 4. Dublin: Peppercanister Press, 1973.

One. Peppercanister 5. Dublin: Peppercanister Press, 1974.

A Technical Supplement. Peppercanister 6. Dublin: Peppercanister Press, 1976.

Song of the Night and Other Poems. Peppercanister 7. Dublin: Peppercanister Press, 1978.

The Messenger. Peppercanister 8. Dublin: Peppercanister Press, 1978.

Fifteen Dead. Peppercanister Pamphlets, 1–4. Dublin: Dolmen Press, 1978; London: Oxford University Press, 1980.

One and Other Poems. Peppercanister Pamphlets, 5–7. Dublin: Dolmen Press; London: Oxford University Press, 1979.

Poems 1956–1973. Dublin: Dolmen Press; Winston-Salem, NC: Wake Forest University Press, 1979.

Peppercanister Poems 1972–1978. Winston-Salem, NC: Wake Forest University Press, 1980.

An Duanaire. 1600–1900: Poems of the Dispossessed. Translated by Thomas Kinsella. Edited by Seán Ó Tuama. Dublin: Dolmen Press in association with Board na Gaeilge, 1981, reprinted 1985.

Songs of the Psyche. Peppercanister 9. Dublin: Peppercanister Press, 1985.

Her Vertical Smile. Peppercanister 10. Dublin: Peppercanister Press, 1985.

The New Oxford Book of Irish Verse. London: Oxford University Press, 1986.

Out of Ireland. Peppercanister 11. Dublin: Peppercanister Press, 1987.

St Catherine's Clock. Peppercanister 12. Dublin: Peppercanister Press, 1987.

One Fond Embrace. Peppercanister 13. Dublin: Peppercanister Press, 1988.

Blood and Family. Peppercanister Pamphlets, 8–12. London: Oxford University Press, 1988.

Personal Places. Peppercanister 14. Dublin: Peppercanister Press, 1990.

Poems from Centre City. Peppercanister 15. Dublin: Peppercanister Press, 1990.

Madonna and Other Poems. Peppercanister 16. Dublin: Peppercanister Press, 1991.

Open Court. Peppercanister 17. Dublin: Peppercanister Press, 1991.

From Centre City. Peppercanister Pamphlets, 13–17. Oxford: Oxford University Press, 1994.

The Dual Tradition: An Essay on Poetry and Politics in Ireland. Peppercanister 18. Manchester: Carcanet Press: 1995.

Collected Poems 1956–1994. Oxford: Oxford University Press, 1996.

The Pen Shop. Peppercanister 19. Dublin: Peppercanister Press, 1997.

The Familiar. Peppercanister 20. Dublin: Peppercanister Press, 1999.

Godhead. Peppercanister 21. Dublin: Peppercanister Press, 1999.

Citizen of the World. Peppercanister 22. Dublin: Peppercanister Press, 2000.

Littlebody. Peppercanister 23. Dublin: Peppercanister Press, 2000.

Collected Poems 1956–2001. Winston-Salem, NC: Wake Forest University Press, 2006; Manchester: Carcanet Press, 2001.

A Dublin Documentary. Dublin, O'Brien Press, 2006.

Marginal Economy. Peppercanister 24. Dublin: Peppercanister Press, 2006.

Readings in Poetry. Peppercanister 25. Dublin: The Dedalus Press, 2006; Manchester: Carcanet Press, 2006.

Man of War. Peppercanister 26. Dublin: Dedalus Press; Manchester: Carcanet Press, 2007.

Belief and Unbelief. Peppercanister 27. Dublin: Peppercanister Press, 2007.

Selected Poems. Manchester: Carcanet Press, 2007.

Prose Occasions: 1951–2006, ed. Andrew Fitzsimons. Manchester: Carcanet Press, 2009.

Selected Poems. Winston-Salem, NC: Wake Forest University Press, 2010.

Fat Master. Peppercanister 28. Dublin: Dedalus Press; Manchester: Carcanet Press, 2011.

Love Joy Peace. Peppercanister 29. Dublin: Dedalus Press; Manchester: Carcanet Press, 2011.

Late Poems. Manchester: Carcanet Press, 2013.

Butcher's Dozen: Bloody Sunday Anniversary Edition. Peppercannister 30. Manchester: Carcanet Press, 2022.

Last Poems. Manchester: Carcanet Press, 2023.

Secondary Sources

Adorno, Theodor W. *Negative Dialectics*. Translated by E. B. Ashton. London: Routledge & Kegan Paul, 1973.

Badin, Donatella Abbate. "From 'An interview with Thomas Kinsella.'" Special Issue: Thomas Kinsella, *Irish University Review* 31, no. 1 (Spring/Summer 2001): 113–15.

———, ed. *Thomas Kinsella*. New York: Twayne, 1996.

———. "'Making Sense or No Sense of Existence,' The 'Plot' of Thomas Kinsella's

Late Poems in the Light of Norberto Bobbio's De senectute." In *Imagining Ageing: Representations of Age and Ageing in Anglophone Literatures*, edited by Carmen Concilio, 61-84. London: Bloomsbury, 2010.

Barthes, Roland. *Roland Barthes by Roland Barthes*. London: Vintage, 2020.

Baumgarten, Rolf. "Etymological Aetiology in Irish Tradition." Ériu XLI (1990): 115–22.

Beckett, Samuel. *Disjecta: Miscellaneous Writings and a Dramatic Fragment*. Edited with a foreword by Ruby Cohen. London: Calder, 1983.

Beichman, Janine, ed. *101 Modern Japanese Poems*. Compiled by Makoto Ōoka and translated by Paul McCarthy. London: Thames River Press, 2012.

Boland, Eavan. *A Journey with Two Maps: Becoming a Woman Poet*. London, New York: W. W. Norton & Company, 2011.

Boran, Pat, ed. *Flowing, Still: Irish Poets on Irish Poetry*. Dublin: Dedalus Press, 2009.

Bownas, Geoffrey and Anthony Twaite, trans. *The Penguin Book of Japanese Verse*. New Edition. London: Penguin, 1988.

Bowker, Gordon. *James Joyce: A New Biography*. New York: Farrar, Straus and Giroux, 2012.

Brodsky, Joseph. *Less Than One: Selected Essays*. New York: Farrar, Straus and Giroux, 1987.

———. *On Grief and Reason: Essays*. New York: Farrar, Straus and Giroux, 1997.

Brown, Terence. "Dublin in Twentieth-Century Writing." *Irish University Review* 8, no. 1 (Spring 1978): 7–21.

———. *Ireland: A Social and Cultural History, 1922–2002*. London: Harper Collins, 2005.

Casey, Kevin and Andy O'Mahony. "Two Interviews with Liam Miller." In *The Dolmen Press: A Celebration*. Edited by Maurice Harmon. Dublin: Lilliput Press, 2001: 23–45.

Caraher, Brian G. "Genre Theory: A Sociolinguistic Approach to the Aesthetics of Literary Form." In *Inspiration and Technique: Ancient to Modern Views on Beauty and Art*. Edited by John Roe and Michele Stanco. Bern and Oxford: Peter Lang, 2007: 293–309.

———. "Genre Theory: Cultural and Historical Motives Engendering Literary Genre." In *Genre Matters: Essays in Theory and Criticism*. Edited by Garin Dowd, Lesley Stevenson, and Jeremy Strong. Bristol: Intellect Books, 2006: 29–40.

———. "When Thomas Moore Was the Headline Act." In *The Reputations of Thomas Moore: Poetry, Music, Politics*, edited by Sarah McCleave and Triona O'Hanlon. London and New York: Routledge, 2020: 79–94.

Carson, Ciaran. "A Note on the Translation." In *The Táin: A New Translation of Táin Bó Cúailnge*. London: Penguin Classics, 2007.

Celan, Paul. *Selected Poems and Prose of Paul Celan*. Translated by John Felstiner. New York: W. W. Norton & Company, 2001.

Clifton, Harry. "A true note on a dead slack string." *The Irish Times*, February 18, 2012.

———. "In Praise of That Elegant Wordsmith Thomas Kinsella." *The Irish Times*, May 5, 2018.

Clutterbuck, Catriona, ed. Special Issue: Thomas Kinsella, *Irish University Review* 31, no. 1 (Spring/Summer 2001).

———. "Scepticism, Faith and the Recognition of the 'Patriarch-Mother' in the Poetry of Thomas Kinsella." In *Kinsella at Eighty*. Special Issue, *Irish Studies Review* 16, no. 3 (2008): 245–65.

Collins, Lucy. "A Little of What We Have Found: Kinsella, Women, and the Problem of Meaning." Special Issue: Thomas Kinsella, *Irish University Review* 31, no. 1 (Spring/Summer 2001): 135–52.

Craig, Patricia. "Playing to Empty Pockets." *The New York Review of Books*, May 13, 1982.

Crotty, Patrick. "Stunning Places: Thomas Kinsella's Locations." *Poetry Ireland Review* 87 (August 2006): 35–48.

Colum, Padraic. Introduction to *Anna Livia Plurabelle* by James Joyce. New York: Crosby Gaige, 1928.

Dawe, Gerald. "Blood and Family: Thomas Kinsella." In *Against Piety: Essays on Irish Poetry*. Belfast: Lagan Press, 1995: 113–26.

———. "Poetry as Example: Kinsella's Peppercanister Poems." In *Poetry in Contemporary Irish Literature*. Edited by Michael Kenneally. Dublin: Colin Smythe, 1995.

Davie, Donald. *Czeslaw Milosz and the Insufficiency of Lyric*. Cambridge: Cambridge University Press, 1986.

Deane, John F. "A Conversation, Dublin, September 1986." Thomas Kinsella Special Issue, *Tracks* 7 (1987): 86–91.

———. "'The Rough Course': Celebrating Thomas Kinsella." *Poetry Ireland News*, July/August 2007.

Deane, Seamus. *Celtic Revivals: Essays in Modern Irish Literature.* Winston-Salem, NC: Wake Forest University Press, 1985.

———. "Thomas Kinsella: 'Nursed Out of Wreckage.'" In *Celtic Revivals: Essays in Modern Irish Literature.* Winston-Salem, NC: Wake Forest University Press, 1985: 135–45.

Denman, Peter. "Songs of Understanding." Review of *Marginal Economy* and *Readings in Poetry*, by Thomas Kinsella, and *The Doll with Two Backs and Other Poems*, by Maurice Harmon. *Poetry Ireland Review* 87 (August 2006): 105–08.

Donoghue, Denis. *We Irish: Essays on Irish Literature and Society.* Berkeley and London: University of California Press, 1986.

Dunn, Joseph, trans. *The Ancient Irish Epic Tale Táin Bó Cúalnge.* London: David Nutt, 1914.

Eliot, T. S. *The Complete Poems and Plays of T. S. Eliot.* London: Faber and Faber, 1969.

Feldman, Jennie. Introduction to *Jacques Reda, Treading Lightly: Selected Poems 1961–1975.* Translated by Jennie Feldman. Manchester: Carcanet Press, 2005.

Fiacc, Padraic. *Ruined Pages: New Selected Poems.* Edited by Gerald Dawe and Aodán Mac Póilin. Derry: Lagan Press, 2012.

Fish, Stanley. "Is there a text in this class?" In *Campus Wars.* Edited by John Arthur and Amy Shapiro. Oxfordshire: Routledge, 1995: 49–56.

Fitzsimons, Andrew. *The Sea of Disappointment: Thomas Kinsella's Pursuit of the Real.* Dublin: University College Press, 2008.

———. "Peace and Nothingness." Review of *Late Poems* by Thomas Kinsella. *Poetry Ireland Review* 115 (April 2015): 103–05.

———. "Thomas Kinsella." In *The Cambridge Companion to Irish Poets.* Edited by Gerald Dawe. Cambridge: Cambridge University Press, 2018.

Flanagan, Ian. "'Tissues of Order': Kinsella and the Enlightenment Ethos." Special Issue: Thomas Kinsella, *Irish University Review* 31, no. 1 (Spring/Summer 2001): 65–66.

———. "Thomas Kinsella: An Interview." *Metre* 2 (Spring 1997): 108–15.

Frazier, Adrian. *John Behan: The Bull from Sheriff Street.* Dublin: Lilliput Press, 2015.

Frost, Robert. *The Poetry of Robert Frost: The Collected Poems Complete and Unabridged.* Edited by Edward Connery Lathem. New York: Henry Holt, 1969.

Garratt, Robert F. *Modern Irish Poetry: Tradition and Continuity from Yeats to Heaney*. Berkeley: University of California Press, 1986.

Gosling, Paul. "The Route of *Táin Bó Cúailnge* in Counties Roscommon and Longford." *Archaeology Ireland*, Heritage Guide 86 (September 2019).

Gramsci, Antonio. *Selections from the Prison Notebooks*. Edited and translated by Quintin Hoare and Geoffrey Nowell Smith. London: Lawrence and Wishart, 1971.

Grazer, Brian, and Charles Fishman. *A Curious Mind: The Secret to a Bigger Life*. New York: Simon & Schuster, 2015.

Greening, John. "Jibes at the Jibers." *Times Literary Supplement*, 5188, September 6, 2002.

Grossman, Allen R. "My Caedmon: Thinking About Poetic Vocation." In *The Long Schoolroom: Lessons in the Bitter Logic of the Poetic Principle*. Ann Arbor: University of Michigan Press, 1997: 1–17.

Haffenden, John. *Viewpoints: Poets in Conversation*. London: Faber and Faber, 1981.

Haley, Gene. "Places in the Tain: the Topography of the Táin Bó Cúailnge mapped and globally positioned." 2012. https://genehaleytbc.wordpress.com.

Hanley, Mary and Liam Miller. *Thoor Ballylee: Home of William Butler Yeats*. Second edition, revised. Dublin: Dolmen Press, 1977.

Harmon, Maurice. *The Poetry of Thomas Kinsella: With Darkness for a Nest*. Dublin: Wolfhound Press, 1974.

———. *Thomas Kinsella: Designing for the Exact Needs*. Dublin: Irish Academic Press, 2008.

———. "Thomas Kinsella, *Out of Ireland* and *St Catherine's Clock*." *Poetry Ireland Review* 21 (Spring 1988): 20–24.

———. "'Move, if you move, like water': The Poetry of Thomas Kinsella 1972–88." In *Contemporary Irish Poetry: A Collection of Critical Essays*. Edited by Elmer Andrews. Basingstoke: Palgrave Macmillan, 1992: 194–213.

Heaney, Seamus. *Death of a Naturalist*. London: Faber and Faber, 1966.

———. *Finders Keepers: Selected Prose 1971–2001*. London: Faber and Faber, 2002.

———. "Meaning Business (1970–1979)." In *Flowing, Still: Irish Poets on Irish Poetry*. Edited by Pat Boran. Dublin: Dedalus Press, 2009: 57–62.

———. *Opened Ground: Selected Poems 1966–1996*. New York: Farrar, Straus and Giroux, 1998.

———. *Station Island*. London: Faber and Faber, 1984.

———. *The Place of Writing*. Atlanta: Scholars Press, 1989.

Iser, Wolfgang. *The Act of Reading: A Theory of Aesthetic Response*. Baltimore: Johns Hopkins University Press, 1978.

———. *The Implied Reader: Patterns of Communication in Prose Fiction from Bunyan to Beckett*. Baltimore: Johns Hopkins University Press, 1974.

Jackson, Robert Wyse. *A Memorial Sermon Preached at Drumcliffe on the Occasion of the Centenary of the Birth of W. B. Yeats*. Dublin: Dolmen Press, 1965.

Jackson, Thomas. *The Whole Matter: The Poetic Evolution of Thomas Kinsella*. Syracuse: Syracuse University Press, 1995.

John, Brian. *Reading the Ground: The Poetry of Thomas Kinsella*. Washington, DC: Catholic University of America Press, 1996.

Johnston, Dillon. *Irish Poetry after Joyce*. Syracuse: Syracuse University Press, 1997.

Johnston, Maria. "Walking Dublin: Contemporary Irish Poets in the City." In *The Oxford Handbook of Modern Irish Poetry*. Edited by Fran Bearton and Alan Gillis. Oxford: Oxford University Press, 2012: 492–509.

Jonson, Ben. *The Complete Poems*. Revised edition. Edited by George Parfitt. Harmondsworth: Penguin, 1988.

Joyce, P. W. *A Smaller Social History of Ancient Ireland*. Second edition. London: Longman; Dublin: M. H. Gill, 1908.

Kiberd, Declan. *After Ireland: Writing the Nation from Beckett to the Present*. London: Head of Zeus, 2017.

Kinsella, Thomas. "The Divided Mind." In *Irish Poets in English, The Thomas Davis Lectures on Anglo-Irish Poetry*. Edited by Seán Lucy. Dublin and Cork: Mercer Press, 1972: 208–218.

———. "The Dolmen Press." In *The Dolmen Press: A Celebration*. Edited by Maurice Harmon. Dublin: Lilliput Press, 2001: 133–55.

———. "The Irish Writer." In *Davis, Mangan, Ferguson?: Tradition and the Irish Writer*. Edited by Roger McHugh. Chester Springs, PA: Dufour Editions, 1970: 57–70.

———. "Poetry Since Yeats: An Exchange of Views. Stephen Spender, Patrick Kavanagh, Thomas Kinsella, W. D. Snodgrass." *Tri-Quarterly* 4 (1965): 100–11.

———. "A Portrait of the Artist as a Young Man: 'The Enabling Feminine: A Documentary Essay.'" *Reading Ireland* 11 (Winter 2019): 14–25.

———. "Street Games for the Over 15s." *The Irish Times*, August 1, 2020.

Krieger, Murray. *Ekphrasis: The Illusion of the Natural Sign*. Baltimore: Johns Hopkins University Press, 1988.

Ling, Ruth. "Re-familiarizing *The Familiar*: From Effigy to Elegy in the Recent Marriage Poems of Thomas Kinsella." Special Issue: Thomas Kinsella, *Irish University Review* 31, no. 1 (Spring/Summer 2001): 153–71.

Liddy, James. *On Irish Literature and Identities*. Edited by Eamonn Wall. Dublin: Arlen House, 2013.

Leavy, Adrienne. "'As Clear as It Needs to Be': A Conversation with Thomas Kinsella." *New Hibernia Review* 25, no. 1 (Spring 2021): 65–78.

———. "'The Continuity of the Tradition': An Interview with Thomas Kinsella." *New Hibernia Review* 15, no. 2 (Spring 2011): 136–48.

Lynch, David. *Confronting Shadows: An Introduction to the Poetry of Thomas Kinsella*. Dublin: New Island Books, 2015.

Long, Maebh, ed. *The Collected Letters of Flann O'Brien*. Dallas: Dalkey Archive Press, 2018.

Madden, Anne le Brocquy. *Seeing His Way: Louis le Brocquy, A Painter*. Dublin: Gill and Macmillan, 1994.

Maxwell, W. H. *History of the Irish Rebellion in 1798 with Memories of the Union and Emet's Insurrection in 1803*. Illustrated by George Cruikshank. London: Bailey Brothers Cornhill, 1845.

McCabe, James. "Thomas Kinsella: 'the most notable career performance since William Butler Yeats.'" *The Irish Times*, May 17, 2016.

McCarthy, Thomas. "Journals, 1974–2014." *New Hibernia Review* 23, no. 3 (Autumn 2019): 9–34.

McCormack, W. J. *The Battle of the Books: Two Decades of Irish Cultural Debate*. Mullingar: Lilliput Press, 1986.

———. "Politics or Community: The Crux of Thomas Kinsella's Aesthetic Development." Thomas Kinsella Special Issue, *Tracks* 7 (1987): 61–77.

McMullan, Gordon and Sam Smiles. "Introduction: Late Style and its Discontents." In *Late Style and Its Discontents: Essays in Art, Literature, and Music*. Edited by Gordon McMullan and Sam Smiles. Oxford: Oxford University Press, 2016.

Miller, Liam. *Dolmen XXV: An Illustrated Bibliography of the Dolmen Press 1951–1976*. Dolmen Editions 25. Dublin: Dolmen Press, 1976.

Mellors, Anthony. *Late Modernist Poetics from Pound to Prynne*. Manchester: Manchester University Press, 2005.

Montale, Eugenio. *Per Conoscere Montale: Antologia corredata di testi critici*. Edited by Marco Forti. Milano: Mondadori, 1986.

Morgan, Bill, ed. *I Greet You at the Beginning of a Great Career: The Selected Correspondence of Lawrence Ferlinghetti and Allen Ginsberg 1955–1997*. San Francisco: City Lights, 2015.

Neeson, Eoin. *The Imperishable Celtic Epic, An Tain*. Dublin: Prestige Books, 2004.

Ní Bhriain, Ailbhe: "'Le Livre d'Artiste': Louis Le Brocquy and 'The Tain' (1969)." *New Hibernia Review / Iris Éireannach Nua* 5, no. 1 (2001): 68–82.

Nobuo, Ayukawa. *Shishu (Collected Poems) 1945–1955*. Tokyo: Arechi Suppansha, 1955.

O'Brien, Conor Cruise. "Micks and Prods." Review of *The New Oxford Book of Irish Verse*, edited by Thomas Kinsella. *Observer*, June 8, 1986.

O'Driscoll, Dennis. "His Wit: Humour and Satire in Thomas Kinsella's Poetry." Special Issue: Thomas Kinsella, *Irish University Review* 31, no. 1 (Spring/Summer 2001): 1–18.

———. "Interview with Thomas Kinsella." *Poetry Ireland Review* 25 (Spring 1989): 57–65.

———. *Troubled Thoughts, Majestic Dreams; Selected Prose Writings*. Oldcastle: Gallery Press, 2001.

Orbert, Julia C. "Space and Trace: Thomas Kinsella's Postcolonial Placelore." *New Hibernia Review* 13, no. 4 (Winter 2009): 77–93.

Orr, Peter, ed. *The Poet Speaks: Interviews with Contemporary Poets*. London: Routledge and Kegan Paul, 1966.

Ramsey, Patrick, ed. *My Twentieth Century Life: A Padraic Fiacc Miscellany*. Belfast: Lagan Press, 2009.

Richards, I. A. *Practical Criticism: A Study of Literary Judgment*. With a new introduction by Richard Hoggart. Oxfordshire: Routledge, 2017.

———. *Principles of Literary Criticism*. First edition. Oxfordshire: Routledge, 2001.

Richter, Gisela. *The Portraits of the Greeks*. Volume two. London: Phaidon, 1965.

Said, Edward. *On Late Style: Music and Literature Against the Grain*. London: Bloomsbury, 2006.

Schaupt, Susan, trans. *Der Rinderraub: Alterisches Epos*. Berlin: Rütten und Loening, 1976.

Sedgwick, Eve Kosofsky. *Touching, Feeling: Affect, Pedagogy, Performativity*. Durham, NC: Duke University Press, 2003.

Shakespeare, William. *Complete Sonnets and Poems*. Edited by Colin Burrow. Oxford: Oxford University Press, 2008.

Smith, Michael. "Thomas Kinsella in Interview with Michael Smith." *Poetry Ireland Review* 75 (Winter 2002/2003): 108–119.

Smyth, Gerard. "Thomas Kinsella." *The Irish Times*, February 6, 2007.

Stevens, Wallace. *Collected Poetry and Prose*. New York: Library of America, 1997.

Stewart, Susan. *On Longing: Narratives of the Miniature, the Giant, the Souvenir and the Collection*. Durham, NC: Duke University Press, 1993.

Tubridy, Derval. "Difficult Migrations: the 'Dinnseanchas' of Thomas Kinsella's Later Poetry." Special Issue: Thomas Kinsella, *Irish University Review* 31, no. 1 (Spring/Summer, 2001): 172–86.

———, ed. *Kinsella at Eighty: Special Issue, Irish Studies Review* 16, no. 3 (2008).

———. *Thomas Kinsella: The Peppercanister Poems*. Dublin: University College Dublin Press, 2001.

Turpin, John. "Life Class: The Student Revolution at the National College of Art, Dublin, 1968–71." *Éire-Ireland* 27, no. 3 (Fall 1992): 18–43.

Tymoczko, Maria. *Translation in a Postcolonial Context: Early Irish Literature in English Translation*. Manchester: St. Jerome Publishing, 1999.

Van Hulle, Dirk. *Manuscript Genetics, Joyce's Know-How, Beckett's Nohow*. Gainesville, FL: University Press of Florida, 2008.

Van Mierlo, Wim. "Reflections on Textual Editing in the Time of the History of the Book." *Variants: The Journal of the European Society for Textual Scholarship* 10 (2013): 133–61.

Walshe, Eibhear. "Censorship, Law and Literature." In *Irish Literature in Transition 1940–1980*. Edited by Eve Patten. Cambridge: Cambridge University Press, 2020: 169–84.

Wheatley, David. "The dethroned god." *The Guardian*, July 7, 2007.

White, S. J., ed. *Irish Writing* 34 (Spring 1956).

Wordsworth, William. *The Prelude*. Edited by Jonathan Wordsworth, M. H. Abrams, and Stephen Gills. New York: Norton, 1947.

Yeats, W. B. *The Poems: A New Edition*. Edited by Richard J. Finneran. New York: Macmillan, 1983.

———. *The Trembling of the Veil*. London: Privately printed for subscribers only by T. Werner Laurie Ltd., 1922.

Index

Note: References in *italic* refer to figures. References followed by "n" refer to notes.